Gregor Strasser and the Rise of Nazism

By the Same Author:

NAZI YOUTH IN THE WEIMAR REPUBLIC

THE WEIMAR ERA AND HITLER 1918–1933: A CRITICAL BIBLIOGRAPHY

THE SHAPING OF THE NAZI STATE (editor)

THE GERMAN YOUTH MOVEMENT 1900–1945: AN INTERPRETATIVE AND DOCUMENTARY HISTORY

THE NAZI MACHTERGREIFUNG (editor)

Gregor Strasser and the Rise of Nazism

PETER D. STACHURA

University of Stirling

London
GEORGE ALLEN & UNWIN
Boston Sydney

**George Allen & Unwin (Publishers) Ltd,
40 Museum Street, London WC1A 1LU, UK**

George Allen & Unwin (Publishers) Ltd,
Park Lane, Hemel Hempstead, Herts HP2 4TE, UK

Allen & Unwin, Inc.,
9 Winchester Terrace, Winchester, Mass. 01890, USA

George Allen & Unwin Australia Pty Ltd,
8 Napier Street, North Sydney, NSW 2060, Australia

First published in 1983

British Library Cataloguing in Publication Data

Stachura, Peter D.
Gregor Strasser and the rise of Nazism.
1. Strasser, Gregor 2. Germany – Politics and government – 1918-1933 –Biography
I. Title
943.085 DD247.S/
ISBN 0-04-943027-0

Library of Congress Cataloging in Publication Data

Stachura, Peter D.
Gregor Strasser and the rise of Nazism.
Bibliography: p.
Includes index.
1. Strasser, Gregor, 1892-1934. 2. National socialism –Biography.
3. Germany – Politics and government –1918-1933. 4. Germany – Politics and government – 1933-1945. I. Title.
DD247.S78S73 1983 943.08'092'4 [B] 82-24327
ISBN 0-04-943027-0

Set in 10 on 11 point Plantin by Fotographics (Bedford) Ltd,
and printed in Great Britain
by Mackays of Chatham

For Gregory and Madeleine

Contents

Preface

Since commencing the research for this book in autumn 1974, I have accumulated many debts to a large number of persons and institutions at home and abroad for their invaluable assistance. The staffs of the archives and libraries where I worked could not have been more helpful and friendly in dealing with my inquiries about source material: the Bundesarchiv, Berlin Document Center, Institut für Zeitgeschichte, Bayerisches Hauptstaatsarchiv (Allgemeines Staatsarchiv, Kriegsarchiv, Geheimes Staatsarchiv, Staatsarchiv München), Hauptstaatsarchiv Düsseldorf, Hessisches Hauptstaatsarchiv, Staatsarchiv Koblenz, Hauptstaatsarchiv Stuttgart and the Institute of Contemporary History and Wiener Library.

The British Academy, the Carnegie Trust, and the Twenty-Seven Foundation generously provided funds which helped finance my numerous visits over the years to archives in West Germany.

I am most grateful to Frau Vera Hierl-Hartegg for granting me permission to consult the papers of her late husband, Konstantin Hierl, in the Bundesarchiv, and similarly to Herr Thomas Passarge for allowing me access to his father's *Nachlass* in the same archive. Dr Paul Alexander Schulz and Frau Renate Strasser kindly answered questions concerning Gregor Strasser and his associates which I put to them. Herr Christoph Cornelissen and his parents deserve my gratitude for transcribing several private letters written by Strasser whose illegibility had defeated me. Dr Winfried Mogge and Dr Jill Stephenson were very considerate in sending me a number of documents relating to Strasser's political activities.

Dr Stephenson read a portion of my manuscript and supplied knowledgeable points of criticism which I much appreciated. Full responsibility for what has been written remains, of course, exclusively mine.

Mr Keith M. Ashfield was most understanding about my repeated failure to meet our agreed deadlines for submitting my typescript. I salute his patience. I should also like to thank Miss Betty Neech for typing the entire manuscript with her usual admirable efficiency and expertise.

The most consistently supportive contribution to the research and writing of this book, however, has come from my wife, Kay. Her interest, encouragement and humour, expressed in a variety of stimulating ways, were very important to me.

Bridge of Allan
January 1982

PETER D. STACHURA

List of Abbreviations

ADGB	Allgemeiner Deutscher Gewerkschaftsbund
AG	Arbeitsgemeinschaft der Nord und West Deutschen Gauleiter der NSDAP
BA	Bundesarchiv (Koblenz)
Bay. HSA: ASA	Bayerisches Hauptstaatsarchiv: Allgemeines Staatsarchiv
Bay. HSA: SAM	Bayerisches Hauptstaatsarchiv: Staatsarchiv München
BDC	Berlin Document Center
BNSDJ	Bund Nationalsozialistischer Deutscher Juristen
BVP	Bayerische Volkspartei
C-V	Central-Verein deutscher Staatsbürger jüdischen Glaubens
DAP	Deutsche Arbeiterpartei
DDP	Deutsche Demokratische Partei
DHV	Deutschnationaler Handlungsgehilfen-Verband
DNVP	Deutschnationale Volkspartei
DSP	Deutsche Staatspartei
DVFB	Deutschvölkische Freiheitsbewegung
DVFP	Deutschvölkische Freiheitspartei
DVP	Deutsche Volkspartei
EW	Einwohnerwehr
GVG	Grossdeutsche Volksgemeinschaft
HJ	Hitlerjugend
IfZG	Institut für Zeitgeschichte (Munich)
KPD	Kommunistische Partei Deutschlands
KV	Kampfverlag
KVP	Konservative Volkspartei
NSAB	Nationalsozialistischer Deutscher Ärztebund
NSAG	Nationalsozialistische Arbeitsgemeinschaft
NSBO	Nationalsozialistische Betriebszellenorganisation
NSDAP	Nationalsozialistische Deutsche Arbeiterpartei
NSDStB	Nationalsozialistischer Deutscher Studentenbund
NSF	Nationalsozialistische Frauenschaft
NSFB	Nationalsozialistischer Freiheitsbewegung Gross-Deutschlands
NSFP	Nationalsozialistischer Freiheitspartei
NSLB	Nationalsozialistischer Lehrerbund
NSS	Nationalsozialistischer Schülerbund
RM	Reichsmark

ROL	Reichsorganisationsleitung
SA	Sturmabteilung
SAK	Staatsarchiv Koblenz
SPD	Sozialdemokratische Partei Deutschlands
SS	Schutzstaffel
Uschla	Untersuchungs- und Schlichtungsausschuss
VB	*Völkischer Beobachter*
VfZG	*Vierteljahrshefte für Zeitgeschichte*
VKV	Volkskonservative Vereinigung
VnS	Verband nationalgesinnter Soldaten
V-S-B	Völkische-Sozialer-Block
WPA	Wirtschaftspolitische Abteilung
ZSg	Zeitgeschichtlicher Sammlung

Introduction

The collapse of the Weimar Republic and the concomitant rise to power of the National Socialist movement form one of the most dramatic episodes in the history of Europe in the twentieth century. The repercussions of Adolf Hitler's appointment as Chancellor of Germany in 1933 on the world at large can hardly be overestimated in view of the unprecedented catastrophes in terms of human misery, extermination and destruction that subsequently befell civilisation. The Weimar Republic thus projected on to a broader scenario the fundamental crises its politicians were unable to solve; in the Third Reich, Germany's problems eventually became everyone else's. The reasons for the political and socio-economic disasters which overcame the Republic, particularly in its latter years, have been analysed in countless studies,[1] as indeed have the preconditions and dynamics which made possible the inconceivable – the advent and widespread acceptance, in one of the most industrially and culturally advanced countries in Europe, of a comprehensively negative and nefarious *Weltanschauung*. These explanations for National Socialism,[2] however, must not be allowed to obscure the axiomatic point that people ultimately shape the destiny of democratic parliamentary nations – ordinary citizens exercising their electoral preferences and the leaders whom they install in office.

The Weimar era was singularly lacking in decisive, inspiring leaders. Only a few stand out from the mass of mediocrity who controlled public life, of whom Gustav Stresemann is perhaps the best example. The frustration which this poverty of leadership engendered in many Germans, especially of the younger generation, during these years was poignantly captured in the celebrated slogan, 'Make way, you old ones, your time is up!'[3] The author was relatively unknown. He was, after all, only a member of a peripheral, extreme right-wing party which in the mid 1920s, when the slogan was coined, was of no political importance whatsoever. His name was Gregor Strasser, at that time propaganda chief of the National Socialist German Workers' Party (NSDAP). Strasser was most decidedly a representative of the anguished 'Front Generation' in the Republic, articulating the disillusionment of young Germans with the postwar situation as well as the aspirations and ideals for a better future. Konrad Heiden once described him as 'the anonymous German from the trenches',[4] the voice of the young and vigorous against the old and arthritic. The *Machtergreifung* was, of course, in many respects, a youthful revolution. The NSDAP and its various ancillary organisations were supported in substantial measure by young Germany. Strasser is symbolic, therefore, of a powerful stream of thought and action in the Republic which made an indispensable contribution to the triumph of National Socialism. As such, he is an eminently suitable subject for an intensive scholarly investigation.

The case for examining Strasser's career in detail becomes even more compelling when it is realised that, although he was without doubt the most important and influential NSDAP leader after Hitler, he has remained a curiously neglected figure in the voluminous historiography of early National Socialism. While biographies of other prominent party leaders, including Hitler, Goebbels, Goering and Himmler, abound, Strasser is the odd man out in having little attention specifically focused on him. Although the very broad outlines of the career of this arresting, if somewhat shadowy, Nazi stalwart are well enough known, he is invariably relegated even in more general studies of the early development of the NSDAP to a position of secondary significance.[5] He is mentioned usually with regard to the crises involving the 'northern faction' in 1925–6 and his own personal situation at the end of 1932. Even so, these episodes – particularly that of 1932 – have been discussed for the most part on the basis of incomplete information. Other aspects and phases of Strasser's career have, until very recently,[6] been virtually ignored. The inevitable consequence of this neglectful and fragmentary approach has been a serious absence of proper appreciation of Strasser's role during a crucial era of modern German history and, further, a degree of ignorance and misunderstanding of him, as man and politician, which is as astonishing as it is unjustified. A whole series of leading questions pertaining to his character, ideas and beliefs have not been systematically evaluated in wholly satisfactory terms. For instance, in what sense was Strasser a 'socialist', the leader of a 'Nazi Left' or 'Strasser Wing' within the party, as many contemporaries and later historians suggest?[7] What were the reasons for his resignation in late 1932? Was he ever a serious challenger to Hitler for the leadership of the party? Did he ultimately offer a non-Hitlerian brand of National Socialism? When these and other issues are assessed on the basis of hard evidence, rather than on half-truths and myths, our overall understanding of a significant early National Socialist, of the NSDAP and of the Weimar Republic must be considerably enhanced.

Strasser, after all, was held in high esteem by many contemporary politicians outside the NSDAP, and by prominent luminaries of the Weimar cultural scene. Few would have accepted Count Starhemberg's ridiculous impression of him as 'a North German type, incorporating all the most repulsive characteristics of the Prussian' (sic!).[8] Rather more flatteringly and accurately, he was described by the British ambassador in Berlin as 'the ablest of the National Socialist leaders',[9] by the distinguished American journalist Knickerbocker as a possible future German chancellor,[10] and by Oswald Spengler as 'the cleverest fellow' he had ever met, with the exception of industrial magnate Hugo Stinnes.[11] The Social Democratic Party leader, Wilhelm Hoegener, a noted critic of the NSDAP, saw

Strasser as 'the most trusty and deserving' of its leaders,[12] while in the Reichstag during the early 1930s he was the one National Socialist who commanded the respect of deputies of all persuasion.[13] Within the NSDAP itself, he was regarded as Hitler's undisputed right-hand man by party officials,[14] as the veritable 'Crown Prince of the Party',[15] and to his closest colleagues was known as 'Gregor the Great'.[16]

These accolades from diverse quarters lucidly indicate that by the early 1930s Strasser was a well-established and solid political figure in his own right and, as a result, seen also by many, to use Rauschning's words, as 'the great adversary of Hitler' in the NSDAP.[17] It is true that, in stark contrast to most other top National Socialists, Strasser was for long periods never entirely mesmerised by Hitler's charisma. Accordingly, the Führer could not bring himself to trust him fully, and may even have harboured secret fears that his gifted lieutenant might one day supplant him as leader. The ill-disguised tension between the two men was a salient feature of party development throughout these years.

A further measure of Strasser's standing in Weimar politics came at the end of 1932 when his resignation from his party offices created a major sensation, attracting sustained public debate and press comment. His subsequent murder, in 1934, underlines the distinct element of tragedy in the man; his career, once so promising, was abruptly curtailed, and his life brutally snuffed out by his bitter enemies. Rosenberg's comment that Strasser was the 'unique, tragic star' of the period appropriately conveys the intrinsic meaning of an eventful, prestigious but truncated life.[18] Strasser was cut off in his prime.

Examining Strasser is a task whose difficulty is not to be underestimated, for he was an ambivalent, enigmatic figure, full of contradictions in some important ways, and not easy, therefore, to situate in a settled model of interpretation. A great many myths and legends surround him, making the exercise of establishing the truth about him more complex. Disagreements about his motives and ambitions, differences of opinion about his achievements, become unavoidable. He was a person of bewildering contrasts: built of large frame, he could appear physically intimidating with his shaven head, stentorian voice, and deep reserves of determination and courage, brawl successfully with political opponents, and act ruthlessly towards undesirable elements in his own party. Yet underneath this coarse exterior lay a surprising sensitivity, human warmth, idealism, friendliness, humour, and a capacity for literary appreciation. He could mix with artists and writers, such as Spengler and the Baltic lyricist Otto von Taube, just as easily with fellow-politicians, and when not issuing directives or delivering speeches on behalf of the party found delight in reading Homer and other classics: a unique, impressive, not unattractive man on the one hand, a dedicated, occasionally brutal National Socialist on the other. Any evaluation of Strasser must try to strike a balance between these two extremes.

The present study, generally originating from my wider research into the phenomenon of National Socialism, advances an in-depth critical analysis and interpretation of Strasser's career, with the aim of closing the gap in our knowledge of an interesting and important influence on the Weimar era. It is not a biography in the conventional sense, concerned with a chronological, everyday, detailed description of what Strasser did, said, ate or wore. The kind of material required for that type of book simply does not exist in this instance because most of Strasser's private papers, including those dealing with some of the more dramatic events of his life, were seized and destroyed by officials of the party and the Gestapo following his murder. Neither his widow, who was still living in Munich when the early research for this book was being undertaken, nor surviving members of his wider family circle possess anything other than mundane papers, snippets of gossip, and general information. Even Strasser's intimate advisers in the party, like Paul Schulz, had comparatively little documentation in their hands that was useful.[19] Instead, this work is concerned first and foremost with the evolution of Strasser as a political animal, assessing his contribution to the NSDAP before 1933 in his capacity as organiser, ideologue, propagandist, public spokesman, and chief executive. The book is based in large part on a wide-ranging selection of previously unpublished primary documents gathered from many central and provincial archives in West Germany and the United Kingdom.[20] The vast secondary literature available for National Socialism and the Weimar Republic as a whole in the form of books, monographs, memoirs, diaries, autobiographies and documentary collections, published before and after the war, has also been consulted, as have the extensive publishing output of the NSDAP – newspapers, periodicals, speeches and pamphlets – and the multifarious publications of the Strasser-owned Kampfverlag (1926–30).

A certain section of the secondary literature which directly concerns Strasser has paved the way for this study. Obviously, some parts have been more valuable than others. The two biographies of Strasser which were written during his lifetime are totally unsatisfactory in that they provide only a very brief, uncritical description of some aspects of his career.[21] In particular, the account by 'Geismaier', a pseudonym for Otto Strasser, is little more than an unashamed eulogy, serving to perpetuate several myths about Strasser. Indeed, the principal aim of Otto Strasser's numerous other writings, in so far as they deal with Gregor, is to establish within an apologetic framework the 'socialist' and anti-Hitlerian credentials of his elder brother.[22] He is at pains to depict Gregor as 'a martyr for the idea of a "German Revolution"',[23] which is, in fact, untrue. Otto's works, as other scholars have discovered, have to be treated with great care, even circumspection, because they abound in factual errors, half-truths and outright misinterpretations. They often serve only further to obfuscate and distort a real understanding of Gregor's political history. Otherwise, Otto is mainly concerned in his writings to accentuate his differences with the leader he split off from in 1930, to exaggerate his own political significance, and to build an image of himself as a feasible alternative to Hitler. In effect, he merely succeeds in confirming the notion that his own highly egocentric and ambitious personality was devoid of real political weight. At the same time, it has to be acknowledged that Gregor's own statements in speeches, newspaper articles and pamphlets do not consistently enlighten or elucidate his outlook and opinions, for they are usually characterised by an infuriating degree of nebulosity, vacuity and demagoguery.[24] His words, therefore, cannot always be taken at face value. Selectivity in their use is essential. The brief work on Gregor and Otto by a third brother, Paul, later named Father Bernhard of the Benedictine Order, is interpretatively weak and unrewarding, failing to extend beyond a short factual narrative of their lives, and depending far too much for information on Otto's dubious books.[25]

The years 1924–6 are by far the most thoroughly documented of Strasser's activities in the party, and several works provide a sound basis for broader consideration of this segment of his career in the present book.[26] A number of other studies, while not specifically devoted to Strasser, have attempted to create terms of reference within which his role can be ascertained. Both Kele and Kühnl, for example, discuss the so-called 'Nazi Left' and its peculiar brand of German socialism, and furnish interesting detail about the ideological and organisational development of this alleged stream of National Socialist outlook.[27] But both works have fairly obvious limitations: Kele grossly exaggerates and misrepresents the nature and extent of 'socialism' in the NSDAP, while Kühnl halts his account at the Otto Strasser crisis in 1930 and, more damagingly, overestimates the ideological and organisational unity of what he erroneously accepts as a 'Nazi Left'. He also wrongly supports the conventional interpretation of the crisis in December 1932 as a last stand by Gregor Strasser for 'socialism' in the party.[28]

In a different category stand the works by Dixon, Wörtz and, most recently, Kissenkoetter, because all three are primarily oriented towards an assessment of Strasser's achievements in the party.[29] Dixon's dissertation is the least successful of these efforts: it is based on very limited archival sources and essentially only restates in a compact form an uninformed view of the major stages of Strasser's career. For example, Dixon depicts him as the steadfast socialist and as the acknowledged leader of the 'Nazi Left', thus ignoring his developing contacts with personnel and groups outside the NSDAP from 1930 onwards, and his consequent crucial changes in ideological and political vision. A straightforward narrative in the main, Dixon offers few insights into Strasser's personality or evolving political ideas. On the other hand, Wörtz's study, published at the same time as Dixon's, is altogether a more penetrating analysis, despite using a rather narrow range of primary and secondary sources, and despite a certain conceptual imbalance (the subtitle includes the term 'Strasser Circle', which was non-existent). To his credit, Wörtz questions several of the old wisdoms about Strasser, though his counter-arguments generally lack conviction, mainly because they are not adequately sustained by relevant empirical evidence. Moreover, his interpretation of crisis-points in Strasser's development – for example, in 1930 – are mistaken, and he fails to perceive Strasser's increasingly flexible view of politics during the early 1930s, and its implications. Still, as a whole, this study takes a step in the right direction towards establishing a more thorough and veracious appraisal of Strasser.

Building on this advance, the first full-scale biography of Strasser has attempted an all-embracing diagnosis of the National Socialist leader. The results are mixed. Though this is hardly the place to write a critical review of Kissenkoetter's work, it can be stated that, while there are certainly a number of similarities and points of agreement between it and the present book, there are also a host of considerable differences relating to fundamentally important issues, including: Strasser's role in the 'Nazi Left', the nature and significance of his 'socialism', the crisis of December 1932, Strasser's relationship with Hitler, and the range, character and stages of Strasser's contacts outside the NSDAP. In more general terms, Kissenkoetter, in concentrating heavily on Strasser's activities in 1932, gives a rather perfunctory and unsatisfactory treatment of developments in the 1920s, and fails, therefore, to provide the necessary balanced perspective for his subject. This criticism immediately prompts the question: what specifically does the present study set out to do, and what are its principal arguments?

The book begins by describing the home and family background in which Strasser spent his formative years, and explaining why a person of his apparently conservative, Catholic, Bavarian upbringing should have found National Socialism attractive enough to join. While the influence of school and parents, who were interested in politics, was important, of greater consequence was the experience of the First World War. As a young soldier at the front, Strasser was profoundly impressed by the feelings of comradeship, co-operation and solidarity which he found there. An indelible mark was left on him, especially with regard to the development of his romantic, emotionally laden concept of 'socialism'. As remarked previously, Strasser is an excellent example of the 'Front Generation': patriotic, militant, in search of a deeper cause which, in his case, was expressed during the 1920s in a striving for a synthesis of nationalism and a curious non-Marxist German socialism. The sense of duty, courage and responsibility which army service stimulated in him was carried over into civilian life after demobilisation. The notion of the 'political soldier' – a theme referred to so much in Weimar politics – was given substance, perhaps unconsciously, by Strasser as he attempted to become reconciled to Germany's defeat and to construct a new existence.

Like many former soldiers, however, he found it difficult to return to the normal conventions of society. Thus, although setting up his own pharmacy, getting married and raising a family, he soon became involved in local paramilitary organisations of the Right in Bavaria. Strasser's qualities of leadership allowed him to play an increasingly active role in these groups and, in due course, led to his political involvement with the fledgling NSDAP. The reasons why he joined Hitler, and why he was able to come into rapid prominence as a Stormtroop (SA) leader are discussed. However, it was not until after the failure of the Munich *Putsch* in November 1923 that Strasser was allowed the opportunity to become politically influential in NSDAP circles. The *Putsch* marked a watershed in the early history of the party, just as it did in the career of Strasser. An entirely new and demanding period in his life now began as he exerted more and more influence on fellow National Socialists while the party attempted to rebuild on fresh foundations. From this vital segment of his career Strasser emerged as a young, capable and ambitious politician.

Strasser particularly made his name in re-creating the party in northern Germany, where he emphasised for the benefit of the large concentrations of workers there a distinctly social-revolutionary brand of National Socialism. This was a radical departure from the bourgeois and chauvinistic lines on wich the NSDAP had prospered in Bavaria before 1923. Just as Hitler may be said to have pioneered and consolidated the party in southern Germany, so much the same was true of Strasser in the north. Strasser's success there clearly identified him as the man next in importance to Hitler, and his standing helps explain why in 1925–6 he could effectively mobilise many of the northern National Socialists, including Goebbels and Karl Kaufmann, in a trial of strength against the Munich clique. The confrontation was most crucial in this period of National Socialism, for it encompassed basic matters of ideological orientation, organisation, tactics, and possibly leadership. Strasser was the guiding spirit of the 'northern faction', and he even put his authority behind a draft 'socialist' programme of action as an alternative to the one endorsed by Hitler for the party in 1920 which was supposed to be immutable. Historians disagree on the exact substance and extent of this 'Strasser challenge'; presented here is the argument that he never totally accepted Hitler's charismatic leadership, that he maintained a certain ideological and personal independence of the Führer's autocratic will from this time onwards. For this reason Strasser, although rebuffed, even humiliated, in this early party crisis, remained a potential threat to Hitler's position. He was the only member of the party who could conceivably muster a following, in the 1920s at least, for his 'socialist' ideas. During these years of obscurity for the NSDAP,

Strasser controlled the barometer of radical anti-capitalist feeling, showing that concern for 'socialism' was a politically live issue within the movement. The source, nature and relevance of Strasser's socialistic ideology need, therefore, to be looked at, as does his position *vis-à-vis* the putative 'Nazi Left'. His views at this time differed sharply in many respects from Hitler's – on capitalism, the working classes, foreign policy – and became crystallised in a demand for an equitable synthesis of nationalism and socialism. Strasser thus emerged as an ideologue, the alternative voice in National Socialism during the mid-1920s.

The development of power-bases and the formulation of tactics and strategy were significant considerations for the nascent NSDAP, for after 1925 it desperately sought ways and means of expanding as a mass movement. Hitler had renounced revolutionary, putschist tactics in favour of legal, constitutional methods of capturing control of the state. The party needed to gear itself for successful participation in parliamentary elections. The new approach was not to everyone's liking, and a whole series of disputes and personality conflicts ensued, in which Strasser figured prominently. His relations with other leaders and the expedients he employed to bring his ideas to bear are accordingly assessed. While his colleagues had few lucid ideas of how to advance their cause, Strasser consolidated his recently won pre-eminence and extended his authority throughout the party machine. In 1926–8, despite the disappointment of the Bamberg Conference, the 'socialists' succeeded in having the party as a whole adopting with Hitler's tacit approval an essentially Strasserite tactic to attract support from the German electorate. Until the Reichstag elections of May 1928, the NSDAP pursued a policy designed to appeal to the working classes, in much the same way as Strasser had moulded his campaign in northern Germany between 1924 and 1926. As ideologue and tactician Strasser during the mid-1920s overshadowed Hitler in many practical respects, especially as the Führer was prevented from speaking in public by court order. Operating from his official position as the party's propaganda leader, Strasser stole the limelight to some extent.

The failure of this Strasserite tactic at the 1928 election, when the NSDAP made a poor showing, had the most profound effects on the subsequent strategy of the party. It abandoned the pro-working-class appeal, and now concentrated on winning support from the broad spectrum of the bourgeoisie. The implications for Strasser's own position were equally far-reaching, as his entire ideological and political vista began to change. This occurred simultaneously with his next major contribution to party development, the reorganisation of its central and national administrative structure. His appointment as Reich Organisation Leader in 1928 was one of the most judicious made by Hitler during the pre-1933 period. It gave Strasser the opportunity to display his organisational talent in constructing a machine which for efficiency and effectiveness was unparalleled in Weimar politics, and which was the necessary prerequisite to the NSDAP's meteoric advance in electoral popularity from 1929 onwards. His career enters its most busy and complex period at this time when challenges to his political judgement and personal relationships multiply. The Otto Strasser crisis in 1930 was the first of these, when Gregor had to decide whether to follow his brother into active opposition to Hitler or remain in the party and try to realise his ideals from within. It is a most interesting episode because it revealed openly for the first time Strasser's lukewarm support for 'socialism' and, at the same time, the beginning of his doubt about what kind of party the NSDAP was becoming under Hitler's totalitarian and dogmatic supervision.

The 1930–2 period – the most decisive in the history of the Weimar Republic – sees, somewhat paradoxically, the culmination of Strasser's political career. After 1930, as the NSDAP increased in size and appeal against a background of deepening economic and political crisis, the scope of Strasser's activities widened. While remaining head of the party's organisation, he adopted a very much watered-down version of 'socialism' as he established important connections and friendships with a variety of moderate conservative, nationalist groups and personalities outside the NSDAP. This development took him from being a mere party politician to a national figure whose ultimate concern was the fate of Germany and not the NSDAP. It was a quite astonishing metamorphosis, with far-reaching consequences not only for Strasser himself, but also for the NSDAP and the shape of Weimar politics in general. As for Hitler, he grew more and more resentful of Strasser's manœuvrings, which were often conducted behind his back or at least without his full knowledge, and he became suspicious of his motives. The two men began to quarrel about the direction of the NSDAP, about tactics, about other party leaders, and finally about what the party actually meant and stood for. Ultimately, and perhaps unavoidably, they had their dramatic confrontation at the end of 1932, resulting in Strasser resigning his official duties and retiring from active politics altogether. His departure meant the termination of any effective challenge from within the party to the dominance of Hitler. The Führer's authority and his most outrageous ideas and policies henceforward knew no check. The long-term result was that, in default of Strasser's moderating influence, the face of the Third Reich took shape according to the baser principles of National Socialism. That was the measure of the Strasser Affair.

Finally, we look at the strange world of Strasser from his resignation until his murder in 1934. This last section of his life was filled with sordid allegations against him of political intrigue, of consorting with opposition elements at home and abroad in order to overthrow Hitler. He was also ostracised by former comrades and friends, became the object of ridicule and plotting by Goebbels and Goering, and was the subject of surveillance by the Gestapo. We establish the veracity of these allegations about disloyalty, the reasons for his murder, and the consequences for his family. A concluding section briefly assesses the broader historical significance of Strasser's career as a Weimar personality and NSDAP leader.

The principal arguments of this book's revisionist interpretation of Strasser are: first, that his 'socialism' was vacuous, amounting to little more than an emotionally based, superficial, petty-bourgeois anti-capitalism, that the influences which shaped this 'socialism' were not only his experiences at the front during the First World War, but also his home background and his association with neo-conservative writers and intellectuals; secondly, that this 'socialism', in any case, ceased playing an important role in his ideological and political outlook after the Reichstag election of 1928 and then more obviously following the Otto Strasser crisis in 1930; thirdly, that Strasser did not have his own wing in the party (*Strasser-Flügel*) and cannot be regarded in any meaningful sense as the leader of a 'Nazi Left' because such an entity simply did not exist as a coherent ideological, organisational or political entity; fourthly, that he had an intrinsically reserved relationship with Hitler and never fully fell victim to the Führer cult, although he was sufficiently aware of it in December 1932 to the extent that he failed to carry his convictions to their logical conclusion and lead a revolt against Hitler; fifthly, that the crisis of December 1932 was not a last stand of the party's 'left wing', because it did not exist, that it was in fact caused by Strasser's genuine opposition to Hitler over matters of policy and tactics. During the early 1930s he came to distrust and finally detest the unacceptable face of Hitlerian National Socialism – inflexible, uncompromising, terroristic and, even more, destructive of the very values Strasser cherished. Sixthly, and following on from the previous point, it is argued that from 1930 Strasser was less an NSDAP politician than an evolving Weimar politician of broader horizons, so that by the end of 1932 he was really aligned with a neo-conservative nationalist outlook which put country before party.

1 *The Early Years, 1892–1923*

Background

Gregor Strasser was born on 31 May 1892 in the small Upper Bavarian town of Geisenfeld near Pfaffenhofen an der Ilm, the eldest of a staunchly Catholic family of four sons and a daughter. The Strassers were originally an old peasant family from the Chiemgau district, but Gregor's father, Peter Strasser, had broken with family custom by entering the bureaucracy of the Bavarian royal house, the Wittelsbach. He occupied the lower ranks of secretary and then chancellery adviser (*Kanzleirat*) at the court-house (*Amtsgericht*) in Windsheim and Deggendorf, both picturesque but obscure small towns in Bavaria.[1] Gregor's mother, Pauline (*née* Strobel), originated from a middle-class civil-service family in Dinkelsbühl (Franconia), where her father was warden of the famous 'German House' museum, and married Peter Strasser in August 1891.[2] A second child, Paul, was born in 1895; after serving in the First World War he joined the Benedictine Order as Father Bernhard.[3] Otto, the third son, was born in 1897, and of course went on to become politically active during the Weimar era and beyond.[4] The family was completed by Olga[5] and by a late arrival, Anton, who became a lawyer in Berlin but who during the Second World War went missing at Stalingrad.[6]

Gregor attended primary school in Windsheim (Franconia) and then received his secondary education at the Prog-Gymnasium in Traunstein and the Gymnasium in Burghausen, in Bavaria.[7] He was a lively child whose naturally inquisitive mind was encouraged by his Jesuit teachers, and later on in political life Gregor was teased, much to his displeasure, about the jesuitical streak in his thinking.[8] The atmosphere at home nicely complemented Gregor's formal school training, for it not only provided warmth and security[9] but also stimulated a keen interest in contemporary social and political matters. Lying around the house were many newspapers and periodicals, such as Maximilian Harden's *Die Zukunft*, which took a critical look at society. Peter Strasser, who was once condescendingly described by Goebbels as being 'not exactly stupid',[10] was instrumental in bringing to the attention of his eldest sons the need to appreciate the imperfections of the Wilhelmine Reich and to think about solutions. He often committed his ideas to paper and occasionally had them published under a pseudonym – in deference to his civil-service status. In what might be considered his major work, *Das neue Wesen* (The New Way), published in 1912 under the name 'Paul Wegr', Peter Strasser adumbrated his blueprint for a future German society based on the principles of socialism, nationalism and Christianity.[11] The influence of Friedrich List, Adolf Wagner, Adam Smith and Friedrich Naumann was apparent in this small brochure, which was in a rather vague manner a statement on a type of 'German socialism'. It specifically condemned hereditary monarchy and capitalism, and argued that the working classes be given a more just status in society. Gregor's subsequent ideological outlook, which was usually associated with 'German socialism', was undoubtedly influenced to a considerable extent by his father's ideas. Father Bernhard Strasser believes *Das neue Wesen* 'contained the core of the cultural and political aims which Gregor and Otto were to represent and champion later on'.[12] Gregor consciously underlined the link when he dedicated his first published collection of speeches to his father.[13] In essence, Peter Strasser was advocating an ill-defined brand of nationalist neo-conservatism which was growing in popularity during the last years of the prewar Reich, and which flourished in the Weimar Republic. This neo-conservative dimension was never far from Gregor's thought, even during his period of full-blooded 'socialism' in the mid-1920s. His home environment and the influence of his father left a permanent mark on Strasser, and his experiences as a soldier in the First World War served to strengthen his evolving social-nationalist *Weltanschauung*.

Strasser's original intention had been to become a doctor, but his parents' modest financial circumstances were insufficient to sustain the lengthy period of training involved. After taking his school-leaving certificate (*Abitur*), therefore, Strasser chose instead to become a chemist, which entailed fewer years of study, and he began his apprenticeship in the small town of Frontenhausen in 1910 at the age of 18. During this time he earned pocket money by writing short articles on various subjects for the local newspaper in his mother's home town of Dinkelsbühl. He was a conscientious student and completed his three-year apprenticeship with the award of a first-class certificate. Further study was required at university level, however, and by the time war broke out he had already taken courses at the University of Munich.[14] There was always a tinge of regret in Strasser that he did not make it to medical school, and years later, in a speech clearly coloured by his own experience, he criticised the German educational system for discriminating against the less well-off, and thus for failing to develop talent and ability among a majority of the nation.[15] In 1914 the outbreak of war immediately disrupted his studies, for he volunteered for army service along with his two brothers, Paul and Otto. A decisively formative period in Gregor's life was about to begin.

Strasser joined the First Bavarian Foot Artillery Regiment on August 18 1914 and during the next four years saw substantial service at the front, fighting in a number of major battles, including Vimy, Lens, Verdun, Lys and the Somme.[16] He was a brave and popular soldier, being awarded several high decorations, among them the Iron Cross First and Second Class, in

August 1918 and May 1917 respectively, and the Bavarian Military Service Cross, Fourth Class with Swords, in October 1917. Rising from the rank of corporal in May 1915 to junior officer four months later, and then to lieutenant of the Reserve in January 1916, Strasser suffered fairly serious wounds which continued to trouble him right into his political career.[17] He was held in high regard by his comrades and superiors not only for his courage but also for his exemplary patriotism, humour and devotion to duty. In a glowing testimonial, his last battalion commander, Captain Fürholzer, described him as being of

> smart military appearance. A complete character, who fully proved himself in the field in every possible way . . . and especially distinguished himself by his personal *élan*, energy, faithfulness to duty, and ability. He discharged every aspect of a lieutenant's responsibilities in outstanding fashion . . . I can only express my highest praise of him for the special skill with which he handled the most difficult, galling and dangerous tasks. There was no job too laborious or too dangerous for him to undertake on a voluntary basis. To his subordinates Strasser was a just, kindly but also resolute master. In officers' circles Strasser was, on account of his particular gregariousness, very popular. For me personally, he was for a whole two years a close, congenial colleague whose intelligent advice I listened to willingly and whose cheerful disposition often took us through difficult moments.[18]

In later political life Strasser repeatedly looked back to his 'Fronterlebnis' years as the best of his life, emphasising their importance in shaping his political beliefs.[19] They reinforced the nationalism and social awareness which he learnt at home. He felt the comradeship of the trenches could be translated into a true socialist community in civilian life, in which class differences and privilege no longer mattered and in which the principle of achievement (*Leistungsprinzip*) determined an individual's status. He remarked in 1932:

> . . . it was a real experience getting to know people in trenches at the front . . . we, like Hitler and so many others, we were volunteers, we were a team, and remained so in a way which would not happen in peacetime. . . . There was comradeship. . . . In the war it did become clear to me: with a person whom one understands absolutely, and with whom one has thrown back a hundred attacks, must we become deadly enemies on account of differing economic interests?[20]

Strasser was not unique among National Socialist leaders, of course, in acknowledging the importance of the war to the subsequent ideological and spiritual basis of Nazism. The war was the first and most crucial political event for many in the NSDAP, strengthening an already existing authoritarian outlook and a belief that might was right.

The war convinced Strasser of the rottenness of the Wilhelmine Reich. He criticised its failure to evolve 'a united concept of the state', its perpetuation of social and class tensions, and its inability to integrate the workers into society.[21] Consequently, he argued that neither the Hohenzollern monarchy nor the social and political structures which had underpinned it could ever be restored:

> ... we young ones had nothing to do with this old system. In the fiery breath of the war we young ones fearfully realised how empty were the concepts of this system ... We young Germans of the Great War had nothing, nothing at all in common any more with the rotten world of the old system and saw it fall apart without regret.[22]

On another occasion, he was equally blunt:

> ... any attempt to restore the old 'quiet and order' of 31 July 1914 is partially stupid, partially criminal, in any case, useless and reactionary, since on 1 August 1914 a revolution broke out which ... will bring forth a new world.[23]

His concept of a 'second revolution' which would complete the beginning made by the events of 1914 in doing away with the old Empire frequently turned up in his speeches during the 1920s as a further manifestation of his antipathy to the prewar state.[24] This 'second revolution' meant not so much a violent overthrow of the Weimar Republic as a spiritual transformation in the hearts and minds of Germans which would witness the eradication of the materialistic urge in society. In this context, the November Revolution of 1918 was denounced in equally vehement terms by Strasser:[25] 'We hate that day and despise its supporters (just as we hate its fruit, the present state!).' It was not a proper revolution, he added, but a mere revolt 'born out of cowardice, depravity, incompetence and treason'. He hated it 'because it betrayed, consciously betrayed, the national interests of the German people ... we hate this revolt ... and we know that the form and spirit of this revolt of 9 November 1918, and its fruit, the present state, must be thoroughly rooted out by a German revolution ... '.

Strasser, like other NSDAP leaders, later displayed an acute awareness of the interaction between the November Revolution and the ordinary man in the street, and in the Third Reich the regime was constantly alert to the dangers for Germany's ambitions in foreign affairs which might arise from a disaffected population, particularly from its working-class segment.

As a thoroughly convinced nationalist, Strasser spoke out just as sharply against the ultimate indictment, as he saw it, of the Kaiser's Reich, the Treaty of Versailles, which he pledged his 'whole life and death' to destroy,[26] and its war-guilt clause, a stain 'burdening every single German and robbing him of his honour'.[27] But there was at least one aspect of those troubled years of the war which Strasser found a perpetual source of inspiration – the performance of the 'front generation', and the consequent hope that it would lead the way to Germany's resurrection.[28] He once remarked that 'every national leader, minister and parliamentary deputy must be a front soldier',[29] and liked to describe the NSDAP in the early 1930s as being 'disciplined like the old army'.[30] As a result of his own military experiences, Strasser remained an unashamed militarist, arguing throughout his political career that the values of the front soldier were morally and ethically superior to those of ordinary civilians.[31] He made this viewpoint abundantly clear on numerous occasions. Speaking in the Reichstag in 1928 during the debate concerning the construction of a new battle-cruiser, he stressed his total support for the army and the virtues of Prussian militarism, announcing 'National Socialists are militarists'.[32] In a later speech he affirmed that 'the coming dictatorship will be the dictatorship of the front soldiers',[33] a view consistent with his belief that 'for a man military service is the most sincere and valuable form of participation in the state'.[34] Strasser took care in later years to ensure that 'as a party of front soldiers' the NSDAP catered for the interests of former soldiers and war-wounded, reacting indignantly to reports that certain branches were not treating this section of society with due respect and understanding.[35]

The loss of the war, the abdication of the Kaiser and the November Revolution ushered in a prolonged period of social, economic and political upheaval in Germany which was made worse by escalating inflation and the outrage felt at the terms of the Treaty of Versailles in 1919. As central government desperately sought to impose its control over the situation, revolutionary and counter-revolutionary trends set in, causing widespread confusion and anxiety. It was not an attractive prospect for the millions of demobilised German soldiers who swarmed back into a generally unappreciative society. Unemployment, displacement, despair and often even ridicule were the lot in store for many of them. Strasser was one of the many thousands of ex-servicemen who felt acutely alienated from the new Germany. His sense of disorientation following his discharge from the army in December 1918 was underlined by a petty but rather poignant incident which took place on the day he and his company of men returned home. Strasser recounted what happened when a representative of the Landshut Soldiers' Council approached him, in these words:[36]

> There he stood, the ragamuffin [*Haderlump*], and chattered and chattered on with his stupid swine grunts that he had learnt by heart about the International, the victorious proletariat, the bloodthirsty

generals and warmongers, the sweat-squeezing capitalists and stock-brokers. I sat up there on my nag, which I furtively nudged against the fellow so that he was always having to step backwards again and again, and I said nothing and slowly collected a whole mouthful of spit. Finally, he was finished and yelled out: 'Give up your weapons! Tear down your flags and cockades! Vote for the Soldiers' Council!' And by then I was ready: I let him have the whole mouthful of spit right in the middle of his face. I flooded the rascal away. And then I gave the order, 'Battery . . . trot!' and we marched back into Landshut the same way as we had marched out in 1914.

This was quintessential Strasser – rough, tough, even coarse, but not without a touch of vulgar humour.

Towards Hitler

Peter and Pauline Strasser were delighted to have their sons return safely from the war and did everything possible to help them rebuild their lives on new foundations. Gregor was encouraged to continue with his studies and early in 1919 resumed his interrupted pharmacy course at Erlangen University. In the spring of that year he passed his final examinations with distinction.[37] Shortly before he did so, however, the political situation in Bavaria, which had been fundamentally unstable since the end of the war, reached new heights of crisis when the Soviet Republic was established by the extreme Left in Munich in April 1919. Conservative and nationalist circles in Bavaria were outraged and quickly mounted a counter-attack spearheaded by various Freikorps formations and Reichswehr units. Strasser's deep anti-communist and patriotic views disposed him to break off his university studies for a brief time so that he could join up with the Freikorps under the command of Ritter von Epp. Together with his brother Otto, Gregor took part as a company leader in Freikorps Epp in the ruthless destruction of the Soviet Republic in May.[38] From Strasser's stance the action was simply an extension of his military service and duty to the Fatherland, but the event was also a pointer to his pending involvement in right-wing politics.[39]

Following his exploits in Munich and the completion of his studies, Strasser took up employment as an assistant in a chemist's shop in Traunstein, where he had once gone to school. But unable to ignore the contentious issues dominating political life, about which he read widely, Strasser soon became active in the paramilitary sphere. By mid-1920 he was leader of the Landshut branch of the *völkisch* Verband nationalgesinnter Soldaten (VnS),[40] an ex-servicemen's group which had been set up immediately after the Kapp *Putsch* in early spring 1920 by Captain

Ehrhardt, the well-known Freikorps leader, and Major Franz von Stephani, the former commander of the Potsdam Freikorps, in response to the dissolution of the Freikorps units throughout Germany.[41] The VnS was 'a national political organisation of patriotic and German sentiment' whose objectives included 'the re-creation of a mighty German Reich, the sponsoring of things German . . . and the establishment of the old bond of confidence between the civilian population and the army'.[42] The organisation, which soon boasted some 150,000 members, was also inspired by a form of 'front socialism'. This element no doubt had a particular attraction for Strasser, who built up his 950 Landshut men, many of whom had served beside him in the war or in the Freikorps Epp, into an excellently disciplined formation. In his capacity as a VnS local leader Strasser came into contact with General Erich Ludendorff, the overall protector of these right-wing paramilitary and ex-veterans' groups in Bavaria, during one of the numerous parades held in the summer of 1920.[43] It was the beginning of a bond between the two men which in due course formed the basis of an important political relationship.

By the autumn of 1920 the VnS was disappointing Strasser's hopes for a realistic and vigorous campaign against anti-national forces, and he came to believe that his Landshut followers could play a more fulfilling role in postwar politics in the Einwohnerwehr (EW), or civil militia, which had sprung up all over Germany in 1919 with the initial purpose of helping to maintain law and order.[44] Ostensibly apolitical, the EW soon became a conservative-nationalist and anti-socialist counter-revolutionary movement composed of volunteers drawn overwhelmingly from the broad range of the bourgeoisie. In Bavaria nationalists were determined to prevent a recurrence of a soviet-style regime and, paradoxically perhaps, received considerable financial backing and encouragement from the social-democratic Hoffmann administration. The Bavarian EW consequently developed under the able leadership of Major Forstrat Escherich and his adjutant, Rudolf Kanzler, into a formidable political and military force.[45] Strasser led his men into the EW in late 1920[46] but, although he was able to make contacts with a number of local leaders which became useful to him once he was active in the NSDAP, he did not attain any prominence in EW affairs. One good reason for Strasser's relatively low profile was provided by significant changes in his private life.

At the age of 28, Strasser married on 15 April 1920 his girl-friend of some years' standing, Else Vollmuth, in the Catholic church in Traunstein.[47] Else, who was born in Landshut in October 1896, was 'a charming, tall, slim and lively woman, good-looking, blond', according to a later admirer.[48] It was from the beginning a happy marriage which was to be a constant source of comfort and strength to Strasser throughout his arduous career. Always a deeply family-conscious man, he took easily to his new situation and understandably allowed politics to recede into the background for most of 1920 and part of the following year as he put his mind to building a home. The arrival of twin sons, Günter and Helmut, on 7 December 1920 convinced him that more decisive steps would have to be taken to secure his family's well-being.[49] His salary as a chemist's assistant was modest, so he decided to start up his own business. In January 1921, Strasser opened his own pharmacy in Landshut, where the family now moved. Among later National Socialist leaders he was to be something of an exception in having behind him a solid, viable middle-class profession. Until he chose to sell his business in the mid-1920s to help raise capital for setting up his publishing house (Kampfverlag) in Berlin, Strasser's financial independence played a not unimportant part in bolstering his opposition on occasion to Hitler.

While Strasser was adjusting to his new family and business commitments, developments in Bavarian and German politics soon exerted significant influence on his career. As the country took stock of the Treaty of Versailles, reparations, left-wing insurrections in the Ruhr and central Germany, and other serious matters, the political temperature in Bavaria dropped a little in 1920 – for the moment anyway – and this, together with increasing pressure from the Allies, led to the *raison d'être* of the EW being called into question. Although in Bavaria the movement held out longer than its northern counterpart, it was unable to avoid dissolution in June 1921. Even before this date, however, the EW was losing some of its younger adherents to the galaxy of radical nationalist groups which proliferated in Bavaria at that time. Among these was the NSDAP.

The NSDAP and other extremist groups of the Right arose in Bavaria after the war because of the traumatic political and social upheavals experienced by the conservative and propertied middle and upper classes. Kurt Eisner, his socialist successors and the Soviet Republic shocked the sensibilities of the bourgeoisie and at the same time fortified their innate anti-democratic and counter-revolutionary outlook. After the spring of 1919, and then particularly after the failure of the Kapp *Putsch*, Bavaria became a citadel of right-wing radicalism, offering sanctuary to even the lunatic fringe of nationalist politics.[50] The NSDAP played an inconspicuous part in Bavarian life during its very early years. When Hitler began to display his organisational and propagandistic gifts, the party was able to lift itself slightly above the morass of extremist groups, including the Germanen-Orden, the Thule Society, and the Deutschvölkischer Schutz und Trutz Bund, which were competing for middle-class support.[51] His incomparably vehement anti-semitism, which he expressed, for example, in a seminal speech in Munich's Hofbräuhaus on 13 August 1920,[52] began to win for the NSDAP a measure of notoriety and hence some public awareness among a certain milieu. Membership, which stood at a mere 1,100 in June 1920, slowly increased, but it was not until Hitler took over as leader in July 1921 that the NSDAP was really put on the map as a political force.

It had not been Hitler's intention on joining the party to prepare systematically for a personal seizure of power, as he later claimed. Before 1923 he saw himself mainly as a 'drummer' for the nationalist cause rather than as the potential leader of a national-racist authoritarian state. He felt the masses had to be convinced of the need to get rid of the Republic and its democracy, and only when this concept seemed endangered by discussions in 1921 regarding the incorporation of the German Socialist Party into the NSDAP did Hitler feel it necessary to assert himself against the old guard of the party leadership. Hitler demanded dictatorial power to shape and lead the NSDAP as he saw fit; the alternative, if his demands were not met, was the likely disintegration of the organisation. Having succeeded in taking over as leader, however, Hitler continued to see his role as essentially that of a propagandist for the nationalist cause. He did not regard the events of July 1921 as the first stage of a long-term strategy to become dictator of Germany. That strategy only evolved after 1925.[53] The party which emerged from the crisis of 1921 was quickly better equipped all round to stake an important place in Bavarian rightist politics. It had a programme (February 1920), a progressively efficient and centralised bureaucracy, a loyal and expanding membership, a newspaper (*Völkischer Beobachter*) and, above all, a leader of remarkable if evil genius in Hitler.

The party's message was ultra-nationalistic, anti-Marxist and anti-semitic; it was a militant counter-revolutionary crusade against modern industrial urban society, specifically aiming to abolish the Weimar Republic and its parliamentary system and to replace it with an authoritarian structure. The people drawn to the NSDAP in these early days originated mainly from diversified elements of the lower middle classes.[54] In 1919–20 former army, Freikorps and paramilitary personnel were noticeably represented in the membership, but after 1920–1 the party admitted larger numbers of small businessmen, shopkeepers, lower-ranking civil servants and white-collar staff, artisans, small farmers and skilled workers. Relatively few unskilled blue-collar workers joined and, as a self-consciously *Männerpartei*, women were also considerably under-represented. The party cut a youthful image, which it maintained throughout the pre-1933 period. Munich was the headquarters and focal point of party activities, and before 1923 strong branches were established in Nuremberg, where Julius Streicher was the driving force, and in several other large Bavarian towns. But most of the NSDAP's 55,287 members in late 1923 were resident in rural or small-town areas,[55] and a majority of them were Protestant rather than Catholic. In general terms, therefore, the party already possessed by 1923 many of the major political and social characteristics which came into full focus during the early 1930s. As a negatively oriented movement of radical protest, the NSDAP incorporated that petty-bourgeois mentality and support which during the depression years proved even more dramatically susceptible to the blandishments of fascism. Gregor Strasser was one of those from a lower-middle-class background who found in the early 1920s a natural vehicle for his frustrations and resentments in the party.

It is by no means clear exactly when Strasser joined the NSDAP or SA. Various dates have been suggested but lack supporting evidence. Strasser himself was surprisingly evasive on occasion about the subject. For instance, he did not provide his date of entry to the party in the autobiographical material he submitted for inclusion in the Reichstag Members' Handbook.[56] On other occasions he gave erroneous information. Thus, in November 1931 he informed party headquarters that he joined the NSDAP in 1920 and that he was appointed branch leader of the Landshut branch in spring 1921.[57] The facts appear to be otherwise, as is shown below. In a previous letter to the Reichsleitung, Strasser did not give any dates but claimed to have been branch leader in Landshut.[58] In a brochure on the background of NSDAP Reichstag members Strasser is listed as having joined the party in February 1921, becoming branch leader in Landshut two months later.[59] This information had been taken from a party publication of 1932[60] which was also copied by the *Illustrierter Beobachter* for a feature article on Strasser which would have been published in December 1932 had he not inconveniently resigned his party posts a few weeks earlier. Hans Diebow, Strasser's early biographer, writes that, after hearing Hitler at a meeting in February 1921, Strasser founded the Landshut branch of the party in the spring of that year and shortly afterwards headed the so-called Gau of Lower Bavaria. He further claims that Strasser joined the SA when it was founded in August 1921 and was appointed SA leader of Lower Bavaria in January 1922.[61] Otto Strasser has added his own inimitable brand of confusion to the subject by providing contradictory accounts in his books and by introducing a story of a meeting held in Gregor's Landshut home in autumn 1920 at which Hitler, Ludendorff and he were allegedly present. He writes that Gregor was so impressed by Hitler that he immediatley decided to join the party.[62] Alternatively, Otto tells us that Gregor heard of Hitler in 1920, sought him out, and then joined the NSDAP, without giving dates.[63] Unfortunately, one or other of Otto's accounts has been accepted at face value by reputable historians.[64] The likelihood is, however, that these accounts are spurious. For one thing, Gregor did not live in Landshut in 1920, only moving there from Traunstein when he opened his pharmacy in January 1921. Also, Otto relates how Hitler and Ludendorff arrived for the alleged meeting in a car which parked outside Gregor's pharmacy – the business he did not yet have in 1920! In short, Otto's versions are unreliable, and it is difficult not to agree with the suggestion that he simply invented the meeting in Gregor's house from his colourful imagination.[65] Disentangling these conflicting views is difficult but an answer to the puzzle may lie in a close examination of the development of both the NSDAP and SA in Landshut and Lower Bavaria.

The first NSDAP branch outside of Munich was set up in Rosenheim in March 1920. Kurt Kerlen, who was simultaneously a member of the Deutschvölkischer Schutz und Trutz Bund, played a leading part in this development and it was he who in the summer of the same year began preliminary work for the establishment of an NSDAP branch in Landshut. On 13 October 1920 the inaugural meeting of the Landshut party took place, attended by only thirteen people. A certain Kammermeier was elected branch chairman, and Anton Brandl as secretary. The branch held its first public meeting in the town a few weeks later, on 31 October, when Hermann Esser was the main speaker. Party chairman Anton Drexler was in attendance. By November the branch had attracted fifty-three members, and by July 1921 some 110.[66] The branch was reasonably well organised and expanding slowly but surely,[67] and Strasser had not been involved as an ordinary member, let alone as the branch's founder and leader. When Hitler appeared in Landshut in February and again in March 1921, Konrad Meier was branch chairman,[68] and it is more than probable that Strasser, still an EW leader, was too concerned with his newly acquired business and young family to be bothered with the NSDAP. Indeed, his name does not appear on the party membership list which extends to August 1921,[69] or on a list of NSDAP members in Landshut stretching to 20 September 1922.[70] Moreover, in a list of Bavarian SA leaders, Strasser's date of entry to the party is given as October 1922.[71] The only authentic reference to his status in the party is in a letter which he wrote to the Reichsteitung from Landshut on 14 November 1922 in his capacity as Deputy Chairman of the Landshut NSDAP.[72] This points to Strasser having joined the party in autumn 1922, which is much later than previous accounts of his career have suggested. It is unfortunate that his party membership number is not known because otherwise it would be possible to determine fairly precisely when he became a member. Rudolf Hess, for example, was number 1600, joining on 1 July 1920, while Hellmuth von Mücke was number 3579, having joined on 8 July 1921.[73] What is certain is that Strasser did not found the Landshut branch and did not head a Gau Lower Bavaria in spring 1921, as has so often been claimed.[74] There is a distinct possibility that he did not join until autumn 1922, and the time-scale of his involvement with the SA lends some support to this hypothesis.

Strasser did not found the Landshut SA, nor did he lead it during its earliest years. In autumn 1920 a small *Saalschutz* for the fledgling local NSDAP was set up in Landshut under the command of Klaus Obermeier, and in November of the following year it provided the nucleus of the SA in the town. From that date the unit was led successively by Franz Zirngibl, Franz Schrafstetter and Michael Schachtner before Strasser took over in autumn 1922.[75] In other words, Strasser joined both the SA and NSDAP at the same time. When the EW was dissolved in Bavaria in the early summer of 1921 he did not imitate other young colleagues in following Hitler or any other right-wing organisation such as the Bund Bayern und Reich.[76] Instead, he appears to have taken a little more than a year off from paramilitary and political affairs before deciding to become a National Socialist. Even then, his principal contribution was made in the SA.

By the beginning of 1923 Strasser was already making a favourable impression on the Landshut SA, which he paraded in public for the first time under his command at the NSDAP party rally in Munich's Marsfeld in late January. Hitler dedicated the first SA banners at this meeting to units from Munich, Nuremberg and Landshut.[77] A few months later the Landshut SA was grouped with several other Lower Bavarian units to form the 1st Regiment of the new SA command structure. With his outstanding organisational talent, sure command of men, and the exemplary way in which his Landshut formation was trained, Strasser was an obvious choice for appointment as SA leader of the new Lower Bavarian Regiment in March 1923. At a ceremony in Landshut to mark the event Strasser explained the meaning of the new insignia he now distributed to his men:[78]

> The red colour signifies the social orientation of our party, the white stripe is the symbol of our love for the German fatherland, and the black swastika stands for our struggle against any damned foreign race which consciously tries to pull our country under.

From this point onwards, the SA in general began to overshadow the party as the emphasis in National Socialist activity before the *Putsch* swung from the political to the military. This was certainly the case in Lower Bavaria where Strasser's vigorous leadership of the SA meant a noticeable further decline in the work of the NSDAP.[79] Thus, with his power-base firmly in the SA and not the party, Strasser was before 1923 a paramilitary activist with a resolute belief in the putschist strategy of direct action against the Republic. He travelled extensively in Lower Bavaria, organising new local units, tightening up control and boosting the morale of his subordinates.[80] It was not particularly easy maintaining enthusiasm among his men when there was no real action, and he wrote complainingly to headquarters: 'the periods of quiet preparation are the most difficult for a voluntary organisation, especially where we Germans are concerned'. Another problem for him was the lack of suitable leadership material, while the considerable harassment from police and local government was in a separate category altogether.[81] Strasser took his duties very seriously and was ruthless in excluding from the SA those whom he considered unfit or unworthy of membership.[82] Links were assiduously fostered with other nationalist paramilitary organisations,[83] attendance at most major right-wing demonstrations and parades was kept,[84] and the expertise of local Reichswehr officers was even utilised for the drilling and training of his men,[85] who numbered nearly 900 by autumn 1923. Headquarters in Munich was delighted at the 'exceptionally well-organised' state of the SA in Lower Bavaria and expressed its fullest confidence in Strasser.[86]

Strasser's work in Lower Bavaria was conducted, of course, against a background of rapidly deteriorating circumstances in Germany as a whole in 1923. This was the most perilous year so far in the Republic's brief history, for not only had it to contend with the French occupation of the Ruhr following a default on Germany's reparations payments, but also the inflationary spiral reached unprecedented heights of calamity. Such was the political and economic instability that there was a possibility of the Republic collapsing altogether. That it should fall apart was certainly the intention of the Communists, who mounted a series of insurrections in central and northern parts of the country, and of the extreme right concentrated in Bavaria. Preparations for an assault on the state by the nationalist paramilitary organisations gathered momentum as the year wore on, and the NSDAP and SA were, of course, heavily implicated. There was a growing aggressiveness and militancy in National Socialist ranks, particularly in the SA, resulting in Hitler effectively losing his tight control over it as the Stormtroopers became a crucial segment of the broad paramilitary front. The first clear indication of the violent mentality of the Bavarian Right in general, and of the National Socialists in particular, was given on the occasion of the socialist May Day celebrations in Munich that year. Strasser and his newly formed Lower Bavarian SA were given a rare opportunity to display in the province's capital their antagonism towards the Left and the Republic, but at the same time the event curiously gave rise to a minor scandal which caught up with Strasser some years later in the Reichstag and dogged him almost to the end of his political career.

On 30 April, Strasser received orders from SA headquarters in Munich to report with his men at the city's Oberwiesenfeld the following morning since Hitler had decided on a show of strength against the May Day parade. For some months Strasser had been gathering weapons and he gave them out to his men on the morning of 1 May. As his group travelled in lorry convoy from Landshut they were stopped by police who instructed them to proceed to a nearby army barracks to surrender their weapons. Strasser apparently gave his word of honour to comply, but in the event by-passed the barracks and continued on to Munich.[87] The incident was brought up in the Reichstag on 18 October 1930 by the SPD deputy Wilhelm Hoegener, who charged Strasser with having broken his word, implying that he was not to be trusted. Strasser's reply was typically defiant: he felt compelled to act as he had done in the interests of political expediency. He owed no loyalty to the present system of government and would break his word a hundred times if it would help bring that system down.[88] Writing to Gauleiter Robert Wagner of Baden about this matter Strasser added that 'with regards to orders which deal with the liberation of our people . . . I would give and break my word of honour. I hold the view that a word of honour cannot be taken seriously enough if it applies to personal matters, but where a word of honour relates to questions of my nation's freedom then the mechanical connotation of honour . . . has no validity whatever.'[89] Neither Hoegener nor his SPD colleagues were exactly satisfied by Strasser's obtuse reasoning and they frequently revived the matter in the propaganda war against the NSDAP. For example, in a pamphlet published in connection with the Reich presidential election in March 1932 the SPD described Strasser as 'the one who regards it as the highest honour to break his word *vis-à-vis* the German Republic'.[90] His popularity in the party and among the general public, however, was hardly affected by this incident, which the SPD exaggerated out of all proportion for its own political ends.

The Right's response to the May Day event was stifled by the very firm counter-measures taken by the authorities to preserve order. The 2000 right-wing paramilitaries, of whom over half were National Socialists, were ordered to stand down by Hitler, who disregarded the advice of Strasser and Colonel Hermann Kriebel, the commander of the Munich SA, to take on the police and army there and then.[91] Strasser sheepishly returned with his company to Landshut without further interference by the police,[92] and the Right as a whole had to try to forget a rather humiliating experience. But even worse was to follow six months later.

The Beer Hall *Putsch* in Munich in November 1923 marked the culmination of radical right-wing agitation against the Republic during the early postwar years. With the Bavarian government once again at loggerheads with Berlin over questions of constitutional and legal jurisdiction and the country in a state of profound crisis the nationalist extremists in Bavaria believed conditions were propitious for action. Led by the NSDAP, and acting up to a point in liaison with the conservative Establishment, the putschists struck.[93]

Strasser had become involved in the preparations for this assault when on 23 October he attended a meeting of SA leaders in Munich, chaired by Hermann Goering, the SA commander. Goering stressed the need to build up armed resistance against the Republic and to establish a national dictatorship, while Hitler warned the meeting to stand prepared for a national revolution. Strasser was delighted to hear these words, and he later remarked that this meeting 'was for me perhaps the most beautiful moment since 1918 because from then on I thought things would change'.[94] On 7 November he was instructed to provide protection with his SA men for a party meeting in Freising at which Hitler was scheduled to speak. Strasser did as ordered, but in Freising he received further orders to proceed to Munich to help defend the national government which had just been set up under a triumvirate of Hitler, Gustav von Kahr and Ludendorff. Although aware that a serious crisis was afoot, Strasser had not been specifically told of the plan for a *Putsch*.[95] His company of SA men arrived at the Bürgerbräukeller on the morning of 9 November and was then instructed to guard the strategically important Wittelsbacher Bridge across the Isar. The principal event of that day – the march to the Feldherrnhalle and its subsequent dispersal – passed off without Strasser's involvement or knowledge. Only in the late afternoon did he learn of the fiasco from Captain Ehrhardt, who ordered him to stand his men down.[96] When his plan to escape to Rosenheim, where Hitler had gone, was foiled by police, he marched his group, singing patriotic songs, to Munich's main station where they caught an evening train back to Landshut.[97] On arrival, the men assembled in front of the Rathaus, gave three 'Sieg Heils' for the Führer and Fatherland, and returned home.[98] Strasser, who immediately made himself scarce by travelling to north Germany for a brief period,[99] was later interrogated by the police about his part in the *Putsch* but was allowed to go free. He was not re-arrested until 2 February of the following year, and then not for his putschist exploits but for his attempt to recruit a member of the Landshut police for the banned NSDAP.[100] Described in the arrrest warrant as 'extremely dangerous to the security of the Bavarian State and Reich',[101] Strasser was taken at once to Landsberg prison to await trial. It was the last act of a farcical episode in his life and of an embarrassing and disastrous phase in the history of the NSDAP. For both, however, the black clouds did not last too long.

2 *New Opportunities, 1923–5*

Aftermath of the Putsch

For Strasser the *Putsch* had been an opportunity not only to eradicate the hated Republic but also to ensure that the sacrifices of his 'front generation' during the First World War had not been in vain. It was a sort of nationalist martyrdom in the service of Germany: there was no question in his mind of the putschists having been criminals or traitors, as he emphasised in a fiery speech in 1924:

> The undertaking of 9 November . . . is not, as far as we are concerned, high treason, rather it is and was for us an attempt to pull our Fatherland out from the present morass. . . . We wanted only to help our people, and the people understand this desire. . . . You have no right to call us criminals and traitors, and you have no right to throw hundreds of us into jail. . . . The deed of 9 November was not a crime. . . . I ask you if you can show a day in the history of mankind when men were killed for a movement, for the ideals of a movement, as on 9 November. . . . That was something of such colossal greatness, that sacrificial courage and sacrificial death of all those men, that we will not in any way entertain, or ever will entertain, any right to question our national outlook, our patriotic motives.[1]

Self-justification aside, what Strasser and his fellow National Socialists had to face up to was that the *Putsch*, in broad terms, signalled an important turning-point in the development of both the NSDAP and Weimar Republic. It was an obvious break between the hectic uncertainty and dislocation of the early postwar years and the relative calm and consolidation that overtook Germany during the mid-1920s. The ending of the Ruhr crisis, the failure of the radical Left and Right to dislodge the parliamentary system, and the economic recovery symbolised by the stabilisation of the currency and by the marginal easing of the reparations problem through the Dawes Plan allowed the Republic to recover some confidence and composure and the Germans to regard the war and its implications with more detachment. The first wave of political radicalism was over, and the groups which had been involved had to take stock and rethink their future. The Communist Party (KPD) abandoned its revolutionary strategy and prepared for a period of readjustment and of working within the parliamentary system. A parallel development is noticeable on the part of the NSDAP. The catastrophe of 1923 convinced Hitler in time that violent methods could not succeed in achieving his aim of getting rid of the 'November Criminals' and their alleged 'Jewish Bolshevik' allies, particularly if he did not have the support of the army. He calculated that he could be successful only if the army were at the very least neutralised as an oppositional factor, and so he took great care henceforth to emphasise the patriotic ideals uniting it and the NSDAP.

Democracy had to be defeated by legal, constitutional methods, Hitler concluded, which entailed a thorough reconstruction of his movement – not on revolutionary, élitist lines, as before 1923, but on a broad, mass popular base. As a result, the *Putsch* marked the end of one kind of tactic and the beginning of a new one – an evolutionary, parliamentary tactic in which preparation for, and winning of, elections at local, provincial and national level were necessary.[2] In due course, this new approach was reflected in significant changes in the NSDAP's organisation, propaganda and character as it got ready for the next round of struggle against its enemies. For Hitler personally, the *Putsch* was a watershed, for he abandoned the role of 'drummer' in nationalist politics in favour of a resolutely individualistic policy. He now began to see himself in a different, more exalted light: he determined ruthlessly to continue his career as leader of the radical nationalist opposition front against the Republic. He had lost faith in the old conservative-nationalist lobby. They were no longer to be trusted, for he had felt shoddily let down by them when he needed their help most, and he was unwilling to make himself vulnerable like that a second time. If he were to succeed, he would do it alone: the 'national revolution' would be National Socialist in nature, under his autocratic leadership. Alliances with right-wing paramilitary and nationalist organisations, like Ludendorff's Tannenberg-Bund, were to be avoided. In this way Hitler believed his freedom of action would be maintained, with control of his own and the party's destiny entirely in his hands. This was the only realistic option, he felt, and it was steadfastly adhered to through numerous crises until 1933. He was Führer of the NSDAP, aiming to become dictator of Germany.[3]

Over the next few years the implications of the *Putsch* for the party's everyday struggle became abundantly clear. Within the organisation there was increasing stress on centralisation, tight discipline and the *Führerprinzip* on the one hand, and development towards a broader structure in the party's national character on the other. With mass support crucial to success, the party took the initiative in, or at least encouraged, the establishment of a series of ancillary groups catering for youth, university students, women, lawyers, doctors, factory workers, and others. In effect, the NSDAP broadened its organisational basis to accommodate its evolving parliamentary strategy. This expansion was complemented after 1925 by the party's more adventurous penetration of areas outside Bavaria, thus acquiring a national identity in place of the provincial image it had before

1923. Munich remained the spiritual and administrative 'Hauptstadt der Bewegung', but the party swept into northern, central and eastern Germany in decisive fashion where, in the early 1930s, it received its greatest support.

Strasser's future in the National Socialist movement was directly affected by one further, vital change made by Hitler. He decided that the SA should be divested of its formally paramilitary style and be more stringently subordinated to the control of the party. The SA, in keeping with the new anti-putschist strategy adopted by the NSDAP and also with Hitler's concept of all-embracing power-control, was to serve political rather than military ends within the framework of National Socialism. In brief, the balance of power between the two principal arms of the movement was now to be reversed to the advantage of the party. What happened in practice was sometimes contrary to this intention, for it was not easy to convince the Stormtroopers that the NSDAP was more important, as the episodes of tension and revolt (Stennes 1931, Röhm 1934) lucidly underlined, but Hitler by and large managed to achieve his objective. In Strasser's case, this changing relationship between the SA and NSDAP epitomised the transformation which occurred in his own position. Until 1923 his standing in the movement had been built on his many talents as an SA leader, whereas after that date it rested on his capabilities as a party politician. Accordingly, Strasser's period of limited importance in the movement and of obscurity in Germany as a whole gave way to an era of fundamental significance and even popularity in both spheres. Despite his deep interest in his family and profession, he now took a calculated decision to become a politician.

Shortly after the *Putsch* Strasser began to give his reasons for joining the National Socialist movement in the first place – a theme he returned to several times thereafter. In August 1924 he remarked:

> How does one come to National Socialism? Let me take myself as an example, since I spent four years at the front, doing my duty like millions of others. After returning home to revolutionary Germany I experienced the collapse of everything for which I had fought for four years, the collapse of everything which was sacred and dear to me. . . .

This stimulated in him a hatred for 'the men who destroyed Germany because of their international outlook, making her a plaything of her enemies, and bringing us into the present political and economic misery'. He resented being branded a traitor in the same way as the communists were, and added:

> 'What are we National Socialists, therefore, what do we want, what makes us different, and what is the innermost core of our being? We do

> not want any shouting of hurrah, we do not want any soulless, purely power-based, custom-built nationalism. We see a chance for our nation to rise again only if national needs are recognised, and only if it is understood that only morally responsible social policies can arouse the national spirit and maintain the national spirit among the people.

This approach would bring forth 'a *völkisch* social state'. He ended: 'The great decisive battle for Germany is, in my opinion, not primarily the fight against France' but 'between the Germanic-ethical *Weltanschauung* and Jewish Bolshevism'.[4]

This speech intimated the foundations of an essentially nationalist-racist and vaguely 'socialist' philosophy which was still not yet fully developed. The influence on Strasser of his father's 'social' ideas, his own experiences in the war, and his dismay at the political and social condition of Germany after the war are all evident in this speech. Elaboration on these influences came in subsequent pronouncements. Strasser recalled one occasion during the war when one of his men asked him the meaning of 'Fatherland'. Strasser was deeply moved when the fellow answered his own question by saying that, although he had fought for Germany for three years, neither he nor his father owned any property and had often gone hungry and jobless. Why should he sacrifice his health, and perhaps even his life, for such a country?[5] The episode helped convince Strasser of the need to liberate the German workers from their basically anti-national attitude and bring them into the body of the nation again. National Socialism offered prospects of relieving these goals, he believed, for it alone could be successful in the struggle to eliminate the forces responsible for leading the workers astray – above all, the Jews and Marxists. Very much the same line of thought is perceptible in perhaps Strasser's most expansive speech on his reasons for being a National Socialist:

> In the war we became nationalist, that is to say, from that vague feeling that the Fatherland had to be defended, that it was something great and sacred . . . from this vague notion . . . we became nationalists on the battlefield. When I saw all the nations of the earth rushing against the German trenches with bloodthirsty destruction, when the international stock exchange armed one country after another and set them going against the solitary Germans in the trenches . . . it became clear to me: if Germany wants to survive, every German must know what it means to be a German and must defend this idea to the limits of self-sacrifice.

Hence, he continued:

> Because we had become nationalist in the trenches, we could not help becoming socialists in the trenches, we could not help coming home with

> the brutal intention of gathering the whole nation round us and teaching them that the greatness of a nation depends on the willingness of the individual to stand up for this nation. . . . We could not help coming home from this war with this resolve: Those who have fought together with us and who are hostile towards the nation because it has not bothered with them must be set free so that in future Germany will be strong and the master of her enemies![6]

However incomplete these ideas and aims were during the early 1920s, when other influences such as the neo-conservatism of writers like Spengler and Moeller van den Bruck had still not made their full mark, Strasser the man and his character had reached maturity. He was a large, balding, powerfully built man, speaking with a thick Bavarian accent, and partial, despite suffering from mild diabetes, to good eating and drinking: an imposing if not exactly a refined figure. But he possessed many qualities which were soon widely appreciated by friend and foe: he had an indefatigable capacity for hard work and was extremely diligent, reliable and sensible, though given to an emotional impulse which sometimes clouded his powers of rational thought. Strasser was first and foremost a man of action, preferring to deal with practical problems rather than abstract or theoretical propositions; he was intelligent without being a profound thinker. His honesty, straightforwardness, and not least his optimism, friendliness and good sense of humour allowed him to establish and maintain contact with people fairly easily. He could be trusted; and helpful in this respect was his ability to compromise, to appreciate the other man's point of view. Balancing this were his considerable reserves of determination and courage, independence of mind, and a certain pugnacity. A close associate describes him as a genuine Bavarian (*Urbayer*), above all, shrewd.[7] A man of contrasting, sometimes contradictory parts, Strasser was externally rather coarse, but inside was a man of sensitivity and deep pride. A gifted organiser, he was also a natural leader of men, who could command both respect and affection from his subordinates. A genuine, strong personality, he was both ambitious and idealistic, though on occasion too naïve for his own good. Kurt Ludecke captured something of the curiously appealing side of Strasser when he wrote of his meeting with him in 1924:

> He seemed most genuine and of almost touching simplicity and modesty. . . . He was an odd sight, this big man in his home-made breeches, black woollen stockings, and heavy shoes, with a little Tyrolean hat perched like a plate atop his head, completely out of harmony with his broad and massive features. But at the same time, he impressed me with his calm strength, his pithy humour, and robust health, suggesting at once something oaken and powerful.[8]

Strasser was a rather unusual character, therefore, among the types who came to prominence in the NSDAP as leaders. He was, for all his faults, engaging and wholesome in a way which the likes of Goebbels, Goering, Röhm, Streicher, Himmler, Rosenberg and, of course, Hitler were not. Strasser certainly shared some similarities of background with Hitler: they both came from the small-town lower middle class, their fathers were petty civil servants, both served with some distinction in the war, they were born Catholics, and were roughly the same age. But the Bavarian was of an altogether different mould. These points of difference, personal as well as political, came into sharper focus before long.

In immediate terms, the *Putsch* of 1923 had a devastating impact on the National Socialist movement. Having been prohibited in Prussia as early as November 1922, it was now banned also in Bavaria, while its organisational and leadership structures broke up into various pieces.[9] Bitter internecine strife, occasioned sometimes by disagreement over ideological and programmatic issues, but too frequently by personal rivalries and jealousies, characterised the entire *völkisch* camp over the next year or so. Divisions also appeared between northern National Socialists and their Bavarian counterparts which brought to the surface traditional confessional and regional animosities in German society. In effect, the disintegration of the *völkisch* movement during the *Verbotszeit* ultimately emphasised that the only one capable of bringing a semblance of order to it and of stamping his authority on fractious supporters was Hitler. Whatever else this hiatus in the history of National Socialism may have shown, it is undeniable that it underscored the indispensability of the Führer to a coherent movement. In the absence of his unifying influence there seemed little prospect of the NSDAP remaining anything other than a political nonentity. None of the other personalities who emerged during 1924 appeared to possess the requisite skill. Although enjoying substantial prestige in *völkisch* circles, General Ludendorff was really a figurehead who lacked the necessary guile for successful political leadership, while other established figures of the pre-1923 era, such as Rosenberg, Esser and the DVFP leader Albrecht von Graefe, failed to inspire. None the less, with Hitler in prison and the NSDAP in disarray, opportunities were opened up for some of those members who before the *Putsch* had not been politically significant to achieve a foothold in radical right-wing politics. Strasser was the most notable example of this new development.

Into Politics

At a meeting of National Socialist and *völkisch* groups in Salzburg in January 1924, Strasser played a not unhelpful part in preparing for a merger of Bavarian National Socialists and the DVFP into what transpired in Bavaria as the Völkische-Sozialer-Block (V-S-B), for the purpose of contesting the Landtag elections in the spring of that year. He argued forcefully that *völkisch* supporters, whether in the NSDAP or not, should set aside their differences and unite to confront the real enemy, the 'Red' Republic.[10] His belief in the need for the *völkisch* movement to participate in elections ran counter, of course, to the strictly anti-parliamentary strategy pursued by the NSDAP before 1923, which Hitler continued to uphold until after the forthcoming elections. Strasser's insistence in 1924 on a policy of unity and co-operation in the *völkisch* movement was hardly successful, but it was a foretaste, albeit in inchoate form, of the broadly based strategy of alliance with conservative and nationalist circles which he came to advocate in the early 1930s. Meanwhile, his advance into the Bavarian Landtag as the *völkisch* member for Lower Bavaria in spring 1924 allowed Strasser to begin constructing his initial and all-important political foundations, particularly as he was also elected leader of the *völkisch* faction by his twenty-two colleagues.[11]

While Strasser's success had been helped by his own popularity in Lower Bavaria as a result of his paramilitary exploits there during the early 1920s, the *völkisch* breakthrough in the Bavarian Landtag and Reichstag elections at that time had been made possible by several factors. A large degree of public sympathy had been evoked by the *Putsch* and, more important, by the trial for high treason of Hitler and others which took place in Munich in February and March 1924. Hitler turned his trial into a triumphant *tour de force* and became a *völkisch* hero overnight. The *völkisch* cause was also enhanced by the situation in Germany as a whole in early 1924, for by campaigning on a racist-nationalist and anti-capitalist platform[12] the V-S-B attracted the votes of many of those urban lower middle class who had been severely hit in a variety of ways by hyper-inflation: loss of savings, closure of small businesses through bankruptcy, and redundancies and salary cuts in the civil service. These people of the traditional *Mittelstand* consequently deserted their customary allegiance to the established liberal and conservative parties.[13] In Bavaria, most of the V-S-B's 17.1 per cent of the vote came from these classes in small-town Protestant areas in Franconia.[14] Another source of support, though not nearly on the same scale, was that of disaffected non-unionised blue-collar workers employed in small manufacturing and family enterprises. These trends were amply confirmed in the Reichstag elections in May when the developing rightward shift in the electoral preferences of sections of the *Mittelstand* became manifest on a nationwide basis for the first time, as the combined NSDAP–*völkisch* list attracted nearly 2 million votes (thirty-two seats).[15] In the early 1930s these trends turned into a panic-stricken avalanche when the same essentially petty-bourgeois constituency formed the backbone of the NSDAP.

Strasser was not regarded by the authorities as sufficiently important either as an NSDAP leader or as a participant in the *Putsch* to be tried for high treason along with Hitler. He was tried along with lesser figures at a separate trial shortly after the main one was over, and when found guilty on 12 May of aiding and abetting high treason he was sentenced to fifteen months' imprisonment and fined a small sum.[16] He was sent to Landsberg prison, but after a few weeks there his election to the Landtag allowed him to be set free.

Strasser's short period of service in the Landtag was eventful, even rather turbulent. He quickly earned a reputation as an outspoken critic of the Bavarian government, and his colourful language of vituperation led on one particular occasion, on 19 November, to his expulsion from the chamber. During the debate about Hitler's possible release from prison, Strasser lost his temper after being described as 'too young and stupid' by BVP deputy Professor Stang,[17] and shouted out that 'a vulgar bunch of pigs govern Bavaria'.[18] Though his outburst was not appreciated by the President of the chamber, the *völkisch* faction roundly congratulated Strasser for supporting their cause so well.[19] More memorably, he was the first National Socialist to deliver a speech in a German parliament, on 9 July 1924.[20] Indeed, it was his first formal public speech as a member of the NSDAP. Unfortunately, it was not an especially distinguished effort, being prolix and rather prosaic, with a low level of argument. But the speech was also characterised by its proclaimed vision of the future, by its intimation of the kinds of issue and priority that Strasser, and the NSDAP generally, were to follow in the years immediately ahead to a large extent. Herein lies the speech's significance. Strasser was noticeably scathing in his observations about 'international Jewish capitalism' and its alleged concomitant, the 'spirit of materialism':

> The whole history of the last hundred years shows that this so-called democracy was nothing other than a mask concealing the domination of big business ... no action of the state can be undertaken nowadays without the approval of the big banks and stock exchange bosses. ... The materialist outlook of the entire epoch is being systematically strengthened, and whole generations are being influenced by the current nonsense that economic interests take precedence over ideas of honour and of the Fatherland.

He criticised the 'betrayal' of German workers by the 'Jewish-controlled' SPD, and in the same breath denounced 'Jewish Marxism' and the Jews themselves:

> Marxism has shown itself to be a destructive doctrine, an anti-German and anti-cultural system; it does not mean a struggle for great social ideas, but an overt power struggle of international high finance, led by

> Jewish agitators, against the national and economic independence of all nations . . .

Strasser had little time, either, for the major Weimar parties of the Right and Centre. The DNVP was dismissed as being 'reactionary' and insensitive to the social question, which was not altogether untrue, while the Catholic parties were accused of fostering sectarian-political divisions among the German people. In place of all this Strasser called, principally, for a restoration of national values and honour (without saying how this was to be achieved), the abolition of the Treaty of Versailles, and, in a cursory reference to 'socialism', demanded the nationalisation of the big banks. He ended on an impassioned note:

> We know that we will be hated by all those who do not want a *völkisch* Greater Germany; but we also know that there will be a time in German history when that handful of men will be spoken of who, amidst the most shattering circumstances of defeat, did not lose faith and courage, and who fought for the preservation of the German people, their revival and their freedom.

Similar speeches of denunciation and piteous self-justification were given by Strasser and his colleagues throughout the course of 1924 in the Landtag, interspersed by vehement pleas to the authorities to release Hitler and to lift the ban on the party. These endeavours were not always taken too kindly by Hitler because they threatened to upset his delicate relationship with the powers that be who were making serious inquiries into the possibility of returning him to his native Austria. But at least Strasser's appeals to the patriotism of the government in deciding the future of the party could not be faulted for effort. He thundered:

> People who do not understand our movement pursue it with hatred . . . they want to place us . . . on the same level as the Moscow traitors, to place Hitler, the destroyer of Marxism in Bavaria, on the same level as Kosmanowski, who is described by the editors of *Vorwärts* in their own newspaper as a clown. How much longer are we to suffer this irrational policy of wiping out the national spirit in our people, how much longer are we to have police cudgels used against our movement . . . ?

He implored the authorities 'not to be the grave digger of a patriotic movement, a great national movement of struggle! . . . Lift the ban on the National Socialist German Workers' Party . . . !'[21]

Strasser's experience as a Landtag deputy was invaluable preparation for his career in the Reichstag, to which he was elected as *völkisch* member for Westphalia North in December 1924. It was a substantial boost to his prospects as a politician at a time when the *völkisch* cause in general slumped in popularity as the Republic stabilised on the political and economic fronts.[22] The fact that Strasser was on the *völkisch* (NSFB) Reichstag list of candidates, and indeed in third place behind Ludendorff and Graefe, bore testimony to the rise in prestige and influence he had earned for himself during that year.[23] He had campaigned hard for the election, speaking mainly in Bavaria and the Ruhr,[24] and made clear the vital importance he attached to the result:

> Elections stand before us whose outcome will be decisive for the political destiny of Germany for years to come . . . these elections have the express aim of breaking National Socialist and *völkisch* influence throughout the Reich and saving the seriously troubled dictatorship of treason . . . from final bankruptcy.[25]

It was legally possible for Strasser to hold both his Landtag and Reichstag seats at the same time but he was, in principle, against this. He chose to go to the latter where he could not overlook the greater scope for advancement it offered, or indeed the comfortable salary and free first-class rail-pass which went with it. He found some irony in the fact that he was now to be paid by the state he had sworn to help destroy.[26] By the time he departed for Berlin, Strasser's reputation as a leading National Socialist was secure, and due also in considerable degree to his activities in *völkisch* politics that year.

Strasser's good standing with General Ludendorff, which had been formed during his time as a paramilitary leader in Bavaria before 1923, and his emerging talent as a politician following his election to the Landtag soon gave him another vital opening in the *völkisch* movement. To maintain the momentum begun by the *völkisch* electoral alliance that spring, the Nationalsozialistischer Freiheitspartei (NSFP) was set up by Ludendorff and Graefe and, in the absence of the incarcerated Hitler, Strasser was called by the General into its leadership (Reichsführerschaft). These moves caused further reactions in the *völkisch* camp, especially in Bavaria where Rosenberg, Esser and Streicher of the Grossdeutsche Volksgemeinschaft (GVG) protested vigorously, and in northern Germany where diehard anti-parliamentarian National Socialists loyal to Hitler had grouped in the North German Directory under leaders Adalbert Volck, Reinhard Sunkel and Ludolf Haase. Arguments about whether Strasser had been endorsed by Hitler or not, whether he was the Führer's designated representative, raged tiresomely for some time, and merely underlined once again the arresting pettiness of *völkisch* politics during this low period in their fortunes.[27] Hitler himself added to the confusion in this matter. Having initially agreed to Strasser's appointment to the Reichsführerschaft, he subsequently changed his mind because Strasser, in his view, had allowed himself to be pulled into the heart of the quarrelling in the *völkisch* camp.[28] Consequently, Hitler abandoned his alleged plan to appoint Strasser deputy leader of the NSDAP.[29] The Directory in northern Germany took its cue from Hitler's attitude and refused to recognise Strasser's authority in the NSFP, 'his excellent qualities notwithstanding'.[30] Hitler's further decision in summer 1924 to retire from politics until his release from prison did little to soothe matters. An important meeting on 20 July in Weimar, which Strasser helped chair as the 'Treuhändler Hitlers', as he described himself, failed to resolve these differences, though there was enough support from the delegates for the formal endorsement of the now named Nationalsozialistischer Freiheitsbewegung Gross-Deutschlands (NSFB) and its unity strategy at a second meeting in Weimar the following month (15–17 August).[31] The GVG and the north Germans refused to join and instead indulged in a barrage of unceasing recrimination against the new party. Strasser, for his part, was unmoved and stoutly defended the NSFB at a meeting in Munich in October. While Hitler remained in prison, he argued, the work for the *völkisch* aims had to continue and leadership was required to give guidance and take decisions. He stressed the need once again for all *völkisch* followers to unite in the NSFB.[32]

The party's programme had been drawn up for the Reichstag elections in May and was not altered during the year.[33] The programme, over which Strasser appears to have exercised some, but not important influence, was typical of the erratic *völkisch* outlook at that time: it incorporated a hodgepodge of racist resentments, denunciations of Germany's alleged enemies (Jews, Marxists and liberals), and was bereft of clear, realistic alternatives to existing political and socio-economic policies. However, electoral participation was held as the most effective means of destroying the Republic from within. In attacking both Marxist socialism and high-finance capitalism, but at the same time recognising the existence of private property and the rights of small farmers and businessmen, the programme articulated ideas typical of the siege mentality of the petty bourgeoisie during the Weimar period. In this respect, the programme was not unlike the draft alternative programme presented by Strasser in 1925 (see Chapter 3). Clearly, whatever his talents as a party organiser, he had few as a theoretician, and it was in the former capacity that he consolidated his position in the *völkisch* movement during 1924.

Strasser's work as an organiser took him all over Germany, especially to his native Bavaria and, significantly for the future, into the Ruhr and other northern areas.[34] Despite the continued hostility of the Directory and its successor, the NS Arbeitsgemeinschaft (NSAG), he built up many personal contacts in the north which provided the basis for his influence and popularity there after the NSDAP was refounded in 1925. He was in demand as a public speaker, for having overcome an initial diffidence his abrasive, combative style of delivery was eminently suited to his predominantly lower-middle-class audiences. Naturally, however, as an increasingly successful politician, he made bitter personal enemies, particularly among those National Socialists who opposed his policy of co-operation with Graefe and other conservative *völkisch* elements, such as Fritz Saukel[35] and Artur Dinter in Thuringia,[36] and Streicher and Esser in Bavaria. While the latter accused Strasser of betraying the NSDAP, he rejected their sterile policies and abhorred them as individuals. Both had deservedly acquired unsavoury personal reputations which, to Strasser's mind, only did the NSDAP and the *völkisch* cause a grave disservice.[37] He was instrumental in having Streicher expelled from the *völkisch* faction in the Bavarian Landtag[38] and did his level best to have both excluded altogether from the movement.[39] Here Strasser had to admit failure because of the following Esser and Streicher had gathered around them in the GVG and, more significantly, because Hitler valued their loyalty to him.

With his stretching workload as Landtag deputy, NSFB leader and *völkisch* propagandist, Strasser decided in summer 1924 to employ a full-time secretary. His choice fell on his former adjutant in the Landshut SA, Heinrich Himmler.[40] The arrangement worked to the advantage of both men in the short term. Strasser had a dutiful and competent factotum who was quite happy to travel around Bavaria on a motor-bike carrying out assignments, while Himmler was given the opportunity to carve out a career in the NSDAP where he benefited from the patronage of an influential master. His later appointment as Reichsführer of the SS may also have been partly at Strasser's instigation.[41] In the longer term, the partnership brought calamity to Strasser, for his friend and one-time errandboy turned out to be one of those involved in his murder.

While Ludendorff's role in 1924 was useful in providing some element of integration in the mainstream of the *völkisch* movement, Strasser's contribution was arguably just as important. By his constant prompting and tireless activity he did a good deal to retain a reasonably sound basis within the NSFB which later served as a springboard for the NSDAP. In doing so, Strasser developed an awareness of his own ability as a politician and of his significant position within the National Socialist–*völkisch* movement. His innately independent outlook and self-will were both strengthened during 1924 to the extent that, although he was loyal to Hitler, it was not an unconditional submission. His capacity for critical assessment of both Hitler and his colleagues was sharpened by his own success; and, while it would be an exaggeration to say that in 1924 his 'aim was to push Hitler aside and replace him',[42] Strasser had made clear his right to be accorded due and proper respect as an individual leader. If there was any doubt about this point, it was dispelled when the NSFB and other *völkisch* groups took account of their situation when Hitler was released from prison just before Christmas that year.[43]

Hitler's reappearance and the setback suffered by the NSFB at the Reichstag election in December 1924 produced something of a crisis in the party, which was exacerbated when the Führer began privately announcing plans early in the New Year to revive the NSDAP. Thus, although the NSFB was not officially dissolved until February 1925, a power vacuum opened up which increased the pressure on Strasser, who was recovering from one of those periodic bouts of illness which peppered his career,[44] and his associates to reach a decision about their future relationship with the NSDAP. For various reasons a small minority, including Graefe, declined to follow Hitler, but most members of the NSFB and other groups fell into line. Strasser's attitude was crucial to the emergence of this favourable majority, as even the Bavarian government was aware when it tried to lure him into the BVP with the offer of a ministerial post.[45] Although a notable absentee from the inaugural meeting of the NSDAP on 27 February 1925 in Munich, speculation that Strasser was uncertain whether to join Hitler, or that he stayed away to show his disapproval of Esser and Streicher, is unfounded. The explanation is that, prior to this meeting, Strasser, having resigned from the Reichsführerschaft on 12 February, had reached agreement with Hitler about his future role in the NSDAP. At a private meeting, held in Munich perhaps on 17 February,[46] or at least sometime between the NSFB's dissolution on 12 February and 22 February when he chaired an important meeting of National Socialist leaders in Hamm (Westphalia), Strasser pledged his support to Hitler, emphasising that he was rejoining him as a 'colleague' (*Mitarbeiter*) rather than as a 'follower' (*Gefolgsmann*).[47] The distinction was a real one, reflecting Strasser's important status as well as giving notice in an oblique way of his potential rivalry. Hitler, no doubt wary of Strasser, accepted these terms of support and gave him full authority as his plenipotentiary to organise the party in the north as he saw fit. There was much sense in this arrangement because not only had Strasser made himself known and liked in the north, but also he was based in Berlin where he could use both his free rail-pass and his immunity as a Reichstag deputy to the advantage of the NSDAP.[48] Moreover, the two most powerful figures in the party would avoid working in the same area, Bavaria. Hitler needed time and freedom to sort out his power-base in Munich, while Strasser would be virtually his own master in the north.

Strasser lost no time in going about his difficult task. The Hamm meeting was the first step, and his involvement in further meetings and party activities accounts for his non-appearance in Munich for the meeting on 27 February. Two days previously he had formally enrolled in the party and, as a further mark of the esteem in which he was held, was awarded a low membership-number, nine.[49] His task in the north was eased by the fact that many local NSFB groups formed ready-made starting-points for the new NSDAP, while many leaders were on hand to be confirmed by

Strasser, subject to Hitler's final sanction, as local and district leaders of it. A meeting called by Strasser in Harburg on 22 March was another crucial step forward in this regard. He was under no illusions about the scale of the problems lying ahead, though he could hardly have anticipated the drama which shortly unfolded.

3 *The 'Socialist' Years, 1925–8*

The Northern Challenge

The period stretching from the refoundation of the NSDAP in early 1925 to the Reichstag elections of May 1928, when crucially important changes took place in the party's character, organisation, propaganda and social bases of support, constitutes a distinctive phase in the history of National Socialism and in the development of Strasser's personal *Weltanschauung*. Hitler was immediately confronted in 1925 by the problem of restoring some semblance of order among his followers and of constructing the basis of an organisational and administrative structure that would allow him to assert his authority as Führer. It was a formidable undertaking in view of the deep schisms which had been opened up in the broad National Socialist–*völkisch* movement during his imprisonment. The situation was further complicated by the need for Hitler to give his party a lead in ideological and propaganda matters now that it was developing a quasi-legalistic parliamentary road to power. Hitler had to take account of the fact that Weimar politics by the mid-1920s had settled into a pattern in which socio-economic status and confessional inclination largely dictated electoral preferences. While the SPD and KPD cornered the working-class vote, at least in non-Catholic industrial-urban areas, the DNVP, DDP and DVP appealed to different sections of the bourgeoisie. Only the Centre Party and its Bavarian sister, the BVP, succeeded in cutting across class lines because of their Catholic bias and outlook. Every party involved in the democratic process had, therefore, to decide to which particular groups of society it should project its appeal. The NSDAP's dilemma in this respect was intensified at the outset because of a certain dichotomy in its own ranks: the conflict implicit in the emergence of a northern section of the party committed, however vaguely, to a form of 'socialism' and to attracting blue-collar industrial workers, alongside the southern end of the party, based in Munich, which pursued an essentially national-racist anti-semitic and anti-Marxist course. Hitler's problem in 1925–6 was to reach an accommodation between these two viewpoints, but this necessitated, of course, facing up to his northern supporters, whose leading spokesman was Strasser.

Although appointed leader of NSDAP *Kreisverband* Lower Bavaria in March 1925, and shortly thereafter Gauleiter of Lower Bavaria,[1] Strasser delegated most of the everyday running of the Gau to his deputy, Himmler,[2] and tended to restrict his appearances there to district meetings and the occasional public speech.[3] His Reichstag duties took up some of his attention in Berlin, but it was his interest and enthusiasm for the work of disseminating National Socialism in northern Germany which demanded most of his time. Indeed, he was reprimanded and fined RM800 in the summer of 1925 by the Reich President's office for being absent for too long a period from parliament and for holding public meetings during that time.[4] The year 1925 saw Strasser fully complete his transformation into a politician of the NSDAP, and simultaneously it witnessed a flowering of his organisational talent and ideological outlook. Having lost faith in Ludendorff's abilities as a political leader after his disastrous showing in the Reich presidential election in March 1925,[5] though retaining his friendship with the General,[6] Strasser travelled extensively throughout the north helping to establish local branches, appointing or confirming leaders, and making speeches. Of the ninety-one public speaking engagements he held that year, the overwhelming majority took place in industrial parts of north-central Germany.[7] Through this intense activity Strasser consolidated his earlier good impression among northern National Socialists,[8] and despite his Bavarian Catholic background he very quickly became finely attuned to the interests, attitudes and sensibilities of his associates. He became an attractive figure, capable of bringing into the party new, restless blood excited by his seemingly radical approach. Strassser gathered around him during this year a number of personalities who later became well known and influential in the party: Josef Goebbels, who grew fond and admiring of his master and spoke highly of his vigorous policies,[9] and others like Ernst Schlange, Karl Kaufmann, Erich Koch, Hellmuth Elbrechter, Hinrich Lohse and Friedrich Hildebrandt, who all shared his radicalism and became his close friends.[10] Strasser also contrived to bring members of his own family into the party: his father and, after much persuasion, his younger brother Otto, as well as his brother-in-law, Rudolf Vollmuth, who later became his secretary/adjutant in the Reich Organisation Leadership.[11] Although not having to begin the rebuilding of the party in the north totally from scratch, Strasser was the one leader there who possessed a sure overview of the entire picture. He provided the necessary vision and perspective to the daily struggle and thus became in the course of 1925 the person to whom the others could turn for advice, assistance and even inspiration, for the Munich headquarters and Hitler were somewhat detached and distant. Strasser was on the ground in the north, in touch with all activities, and therefore was the only party leader with a realistic appreciation of what was going on there and in the *völkisch* movement as a whole.[12] If any confirmation were needed of this position, it was provided by the nature of the ideological standpoint which he was in the process of completing in 1925.

Strasser's primary concern in 1925, whether speaking in the Reichstag or in the country, was to attack from an anti-capitalist stance the corruption of the Weimar Republic, the betrayal of the workers by the SPD and KPD, the Dawes Plan and, from an anti-Western position, the Locarno

Pact and the League of Nations. He described the Dawes Plan as Germany's 'second Versailles'[13] and the Locarno Pact as her 'third Versailles', both selling out the national interest to the capitalist West. Germany's impending full admittance to the League of Nations meant for him that 'the politics of English imperialism and American Jewish finance capitalism have succeeded in harnessing Germany to the service of the West against the East.[14] Although at pains to emphasise that for 'we National Socialists . . . the struggle against Marxism in its every form is a sacred task' and that there had to be no suspicion that 'we sympathise with the Marxist Soviet Republic and its Jewish leadership', Strasser believed at this time that Russia and Germany, as oppressed nations, had broadly similar interests. The road to friendship and alliance with Russia, he insisted, had to be kept open despite the ideological cleavage. His notion of a 'Bund der unterdrückten Völker' (League of Oppressed Nations) was a rather fanciful extension of his anti-colonial and pro-Eastern outlook,[15] but Hitler's strongly anti-Bolshevik and anti-Russian animus and, above all, the concept of eastward expansion (*Lebensraum*), which was clearly expressed in *Mein Kampf*, put a decided dampener on this particular aspect of Strasser's ideology. Following the Bamberg Conference in February 1926 and the publication later that year of the second volume of *Mein Kampf*, Strasser changed his views on foreign policy and accepted Hitler's argument for a German alliance with England and Italy.[16] What did not change was Strasser's antipathy to capitalism in whatever shape, and to its concomitant, as he saw it, materialism:

> We National Socialists have recognised that a fateful and causal relationship exists between the national freedom of our people and the economic liberation of the German working class. We have recognised that the capitalist economic system with its exploitation of economic weakness, with its theft of the work-power of the working class, with its immoral valuation of people according to possessions and money instead of according to their inner virtues and achievement must be replaced by a new, properly collectivist economic order, by a German socialism.[17]

And further:

> We National Socialists want the economic revolution involving the nationalisation of the economy! In this nationalised economy the employee will be no longer mainly a wage-earner, work slave, but a co-owner, co-adviser and co-master. . . . We want in place of an exploitative capitalist economic system a real socialism, maintained not by a soulless Jewish-materialist outlook but by the believing, sacrificial and unselfish old German community sentiment, community purpose and community feeling. We want the social revolution in order to bring about the national revolution![18]

Strasser attempted to practise what he preached by introducing a motion in the Reichstag on 10 August 1925 aimed at taxing stock exchange profits, but it received little support.[19] However, such sentiments became standard components of Strasser's ideological posture in the mid-1920s; for example: ' . . . we National Socialists are fighting passionately not only for the national freedom of our nation but also fanatically for social justice, for the nationalisation of the German economy'.[20] Some of what he said was sheer demagoguery, calculated to make the headlines and cause a stir, though there was an underlying honesty in what he believed in. Strasser's concept of 'German socialism' was already laden with emotion rather than reason, and appeared to mean little more than a utopian desire for a return to the Middle Ages with their corporative crafts and gilds.[21] He tried to explain the difference between his socialism and Marxist socialism in this way:

> What distinguishes us from . . . Jewish-led Marxism is not only a fervent national outlook, but something deeper: the rejection of the materialistic world view. . . . We hate from the bottom of our souls the levelling, comprehensively idiotic Marxist ideology! Socialism does not mean the domination of the masses, the levelling of achievement and reward, but rather socialism is the deeply felt Prussian German idea of 'service to all'.[22]

One of the few reasonably positive ideas he expressed at this time, and to which he adhered throughout the remainder of his career, was that of Germany's need to develop economic autarky. Freely acknowledging the influence of Friedrich List, he called for a 'national German economy', but signally failed, unfortunately, to define properly what he meant by this term.[23] For Strasser autarky was simply another weapon to be used against the alleged control of the economy by international capitalism. He did not propose any concrete formulas for implementing autarky, merely restricting himself to demanding protectionist tariffs to safeguard German industry and agriculture. Not only were his ideas ill-defined and unsatisfactory on this theme,[24] but they were also almost certainly supplied in large measure by the unacknowledged inspiration of Otto Strasser, who held a doctorate in national economy studies. Otto's influence is also evident in his brother's ideas on the need for a new tariff structure for agriculture because some of the technical details in the proposal required a certain understanding of and familiarity with such matters, which Gregor lacked.[25] Otto was generally intellectually superior to Gregor and had a liking for dealing in ideas, which the latter did not. Even in these early days, therefore, a pattern was appearing, which was strengthened later on, of Gregor acting as a mouthpiece for certain views whose authorship was someone else's. The influence of Otto obviously began before he officially joined the NSDAP, and it was to be again apparent in connection with the alternative Draft programme presented by Gregor to his northern colleagues in autumn 1925 (see below).[26]

Strasser's ideology in 1925 amounted to an unclear, unexplained vision of 'socialism' which had its roots firmly in the confused world of petty-bourgeois politics in the Weimar Republic.[27] A neo-conservative dimension had been added to the influence of home background and war experience, and a number of individuals had clearly impressed Strasser. These included the Sudeten German NSDAP ideologue, Rudolf Jung, who published *Der nationale Sozialismus* in 1919, and the leading Weimar neo-conservatives Moeller van den Bruck and Oswald Spengler, whose *Prussianism and Socialism* (1919) conveyed to Strasser a distaste for materialism and monetary values as well as an idealisation of the peasantry's role in standing against proletarian revolution and modernism.[28] It was no coincidence that Strasser tried earnestly in 1925 to enlist Spengler's services for the party and in doing so made no secret of his long-standing admiration for the writer's work as well as underlining the similarity between many of their ideas.[29] Strasser also complimented Spengler's recently published book, *Der Neubau des deutschen Reiches*, in which the NSDAP leader perceived 'a far-ranging relationship with our aims'. In turn, Spengler expressed his high regard for Strasser, describing him as 'the cleverest fellow' he had ever met (after Hugo Stinnes, the industrialist).[30] None the less, he felt he had to decline the offer to become directly associated with the party and its publishing activities, basically on account of his profound reservations about *völkisch* politics as a whole. Strasser reluctantly but gracefully accepted Spengler's decision, though stressed that there were real differences between the conventional *völkisch* movement and his concept of a 'national Socialism' which aimed for 'a German Revolution through a German socialism':

> It is a question of none other than the realisation that this social German revolution is the prerequisite for the re-establishment of Germany's freedom of action in foreign affairs and, conversely, this external freedom of Germany is the only security for this German socialism.[31]

While Spengler is unlikely to have been overimpressed by Strasser's customary lapse into insubstantive jargon, he could not help feeling some warmth for his honesty and seriousness. Strasser may not have made a National Socialist of the distinguished theorist, but he at least made an admiring friend.

Strasser's concern about the overall ideological orientation of the party, the need he felt to have its political-philosophical terms of reference clarified, lay partly behind the gathering frustration with Munich among northern leaders in autumn 1925. The northerners were perturbed at the lack of directed development in the party, by Hitler's apparent lack of interest in them and in organisational matters generally, by their resentment of the Esser–Streicher group, and by emerging differences of attitude and emphasis over certain domestic and foreign issues. Despite renewed bouts of illness which forced his absence from official duties between 25 May and 29 July,[32] Strasser inevitably became the spearhead of the growing discontent in the north and, having overcome the temporary mood of resignation about Hitler's leadership he experienced at a meeting of party leaders in Weimar on 12 July,[33] it was he who took the initiative in calling the northern Gauleiters to a meeting in Hagen (Westphalia) on 10 September to discuss matters. At an earlier meeting in Elberfeld, on 20 August, Strasser had outlined a plan to organise a 'Westblock' to counterbalance the power of Munich,[34] and now in Hagen that strategy was taken a step further. Among other decisions, it was decided in Strasser's absence[35] to set up the Arbeitsgemeinschaft der Nord und West Deutschen Gauleiter der NSDAP (AG) under Strasser's leadership, and to publish bi-monthly the *NS-Briefe* as its organ.[36]

For most AG members their organisation was little more than a pressure-group with limited aims, as its statutes clearly indicated.[37] The AG was not a *fronde* directed against Hitler as party leader; his position was not being called into question. From Strasser's personal viewpoint, on the other hand, the AG may have represented something rather more: he may have seen it as a potential weapon to reduce Hitler's power in the party, to undermine the fascist concept of *Führerprinzip* in favour of the traditional *völkisch* idea of organisational democracy, and thus secure a stronger position of authority for himself and his northern colleagues in the party. It is also possible that Strasser saw an opportunity to displace Hitler as leader, even though he never admitted to this ambition either in private or public conversations. Scholars are divided on the nature of Strasser's role in the AG and on the extent of his ambition.[38] Despite the absence of documentary evidence, a case can be made out, based largely on an understanding of Strasser the man in 1925, that he might well have moved against Hitler for the party leadership had conditions been right.

In the first place, Strasser's natural independence of mind and belief in his own abilities as a leader of men had been enormously strengthened by his success in the north. His judgement of people and situations in 1925 had been very sound in the main and he enjoyed the esteem and trust of a great majority of his colleagues and fellow party members. A Saxon SA man later wrote of that period:

> We instantly liked Strasser. He stood in our midst, with his hands buried deep in his trouser pockets, throwing out banter on all sides in his deep bass voice. He was exactly as he had been described. Something paternal emanated from him. Perhaps it was his deep voice or his powerful figure.

At any rate, we had immediate confidence in him. He was a man of the people, in an entirely different sense than Hitler, who seemed so unapproachable to us.[39]

Strasser complained bitterly and often about the unsatisfactory situation of the party in Munich: he criticised the 'low level' of the *Völkischer Beobachter*,[40] the continuing influence of Esser and Streicher,[41] and Hitler's irregular attendance at headquarters.[42] From his correspondence with Goebbels it is clear that both saw the AG as the beginning of something novel and exciting, referring to it almost as an independent entity within the party. Moreover, this was an NSDAP which was still in a rather disorganised state and, therefore, vulnerable. For a man of Strasser's ambition there had to be some temptation to assert himself and take over. He was largely immune to the slowly gathering Führer cult emanating from Munich[43] and benefited from the fears of some of his colleagues of the 'Roman influence' in Munich and murmurings against 'Pope' Hitler. It has been suggested that some of these leaders would have welcomed Strasser taking over as leader, with Hitler assuming the powerless role of honorary chairman,[44] but no effort was made to bring about such an arrangement. None the less, in the autumn of 1925 Hitler's position as the unchallengeable charismatic party leader had still not been fully established. Strasser, in any event, put the 'idea' of National Socialism before and above anyone,[45] and harboured doubts about Hitler's capacity to be a great leader. He resisted any suggestion that Hitler or anyone else had an automatic right to be regarded as the party's permanent leader; he had to demonstrate his worth just like everyone else. It is hardly surprising, in view of Strasser's opinions, that tension between the two men surfaced that autumn, though there were brief periods of open friendliness. Following a meeting he had with Hitler in Hamm at the beginning of November, for instance, Strasser informed Goebbels that 'recently a much better relationship' had developed.[46] Despite some surprise, Goebbels expressed his pleasure at their new-found cordiality,[47] but it was no more than skin-deep. Strasser's innate coolness towards the Führer was still strong and, believing in himself, he might well have seen the possibility of emerging as Hitler's successor. He believed he had the necessary qualities to make a successful leader of the party. Hitler's reputed 'most intimate adviser'[48] – which, in fact, was not the case – was watching developments very carefully that autumn, weighing up the chances of upsetting the balance of power in the party.

If these were Strasser's thoughts at the inauguration of the AG, however, they were soon dispelled once he saw that as an ideological or organisational unit it had little coherence and, therefore, offered no likelihood of serving as his power-base for a challenge to the party leader. Even the hope that the AG would bring about a new 'socialist' party programme came to nothing. The fissiporous character of the AG became clear when the alternative Draft programme came up for discussion.

The Draft, which was drawn up under Stasser's supervision, reflected the essence of his ideas as he had been expounding them during the early 1920s, but it was not written exclusively by him.[49] Otto Strasser undoubtedly contributed much of the detailed economic sections dealing with industry and agriculture,[50] while Goebbels may have exercised a marginal influence.[51] Gregor, as he was to do often in the early 1930s, acted very much as a front man, a spokesman for the Draft. He was the obvious person to put his name to it, of course, because of his authority and status in the party, but he simply did not have the necessary breadth of knowledge for formulating such a wide-ranging, if vague and naïve, document. Any expectations he may have had of a uniform and favourable response to his proposals from his colleagues were dashed, however, at meetings of the AG in Hanover on 22 November 1925 and, more decisively, in the same location on 24 January of the following year. This happened despite the establishment by Strasser within the AG of a close but loosely organised circle of friends, including most probably Goebbels, Otto Strasser, Kaufmann and Elbrechter among others, whose purpose was to act as his 'intellectual General Staff'.[52] However, Strasser's failure to keep Hitler informed of developments until virtually obliged to do so after Feder had got to know of the Draft was an embarrassing *faux pas* which did not augur well for the Draft's success.[53]

The Draft did not differ fundamentally from the original party programme: it amounted to a relatively more precise and emphatic reaffirmation of the 'socialist' or, more accurately, the anti-capitalist parts of the 1920 statement. Prominent sections of the Draft upheld a brand of extreme racist-nationalism and pan-German imperialism to which no one in conservative Munich, let alone Hitler, could reasonably object. Perhaps to please the Führer, the Draft included a demand for the return of Germany's lost colonies – a peculiar aim of so-called 'socialists' – while the only new proposal in foreign affairs was for a United States of Europe and a customs union. Furthermore, the Draft's anti-semitism, though not attaining the high standards set in *Mein Kampf*, was, by demanding the deportation of all Jews who had entered Germany since the beginning of the First World War, and the withdrawal of German citizenship from all Jews who remained, consistent with the NSDAP's and *völkisch* movement's general attitude towards the 'Jewish problem'.

The Draft failed lamentably as a 'socialist' document. Its proposals on nationalisation, worker participation in industry, profit-sharing and co-ownership, and its agrarian reform ideas, involving the break-up of the largest estates into small peasant holdings, were tentative, woolly, and characteristic merely of the AG members' roots in a utopian–romantic version of lower-middle-class anti-capitalism.[54] This was a manifestation of reactionary anti-capitalism, a 'socialism' made specious from the start by its obsession with racist chauvinism and anti-semitism. Envisaged was a vaguely defined form of mixed economy in which all property belonged to the nation but where private citizens would still own property on a lease basis from the state. This was the principal method by which the Draft sought to deal with the problem of the redistribution of wealth in German society – a theme which Strasser had been speaking about quite frequently during 1925. His ideal was a 'Not-Brot- und Schicksalsgemeinschaft' (a community of need, bread and destiny), which was simply yet another of his typically bombastic slogans devoid of real meaning and sense. In effect, the ostensible subjects of the Draft's concern, the industrial working class and landless agricultural labourers, were given scant consideration, whereas the interests of important sections of the old *Mittelstand* – small businessmen, artisans and small farmers – were well catered for. This feature was also brought out in the Draft's political suggestions. In spurning the concept of both proletarian and capitalist domination of the state and its institutions of power, the Draft contained the notion of a medievalist-slanted, fascist-corporative structure based on a hierarchical, authoritarian 'national dictatorship' of the type which had been extensively debated in neo-conservative circles since the early 1920s.

The Draft was viciously attacked from a number of quarters within the AG. Franz von Pfeffer denounced its egalitarian-liberal-democratic character and advocated instead an élitist approach based on the concept of achievement (*Leistungsprinzip*). Ludolf Haase and Hermann Fobke were likewise alarmed at the Draft's levelling tone and lack of *völkisch* content,[55] while Dr Wolfgang Harnisch of Göttingen dismissed it as 'Marxist'.[56] Others, including Goebbels and Kaufmann, also had their reservations, and from outside the AG Feder's voice was predictably raised in protest.

From an ideological viewpoint, the Draft cannot be taken seriously as indicative of the existence of an authentic 'socialist' or 'left wing' in the NSDAP during 1925–6. Similarly, it was soon discovered that the AG had no meaningful organisational or personal integrity: it was a shakily constructed body of various northern leaders who, as it transpired, had differing views on the one theme which supposedly united them, 'socialism'. Strasser's personal friendship with many of his northern colleagues was not necessarily a guarantee of their substantive political alliance. The AG was torn by a series of personal animosities, in fact, dating from 1924. Some former NSAG members still felt bitter about Strasser's role in the NSFP, and the AG had essentially brought together a coalition of groups and personnel who had been in conflict with one another only a short time previously. Differences over important issues such as electoral participation and foreign policy contributed to these divisions. The AG's democratic organisational form, the curiously insipid leadership given by Strasser, and the equality among the Gauleiters meant that each member had the option of disregarding or defying points of AG policy. Each Gauleiter jealously guarded his right to independent action. In Westphalia, for example, Pfeffer made clear his determination to put the interests of his Gau before and above those of the AG.[57] In other words, the whole idea of a 'Nazi Left' in the NSDAP at this time has little meaning. The northern National Socialists were disunited organisationally, ideologically and personally. The degree of unification in these respects that would justify the use of the term 'Nazi Left' as an identifiable entity within the party did not exist. The term is simply one of convenience, a way of alluding to the relatively small number of National Socialists who were anxious to give greater weight to ideology in the party's make-up, particularly to an ideology that was not exclusively based on racism, anti-semitism and pan-German imperialism. Those who displayed this indistinct and intellectually poverty-stricken form of radical anti-capitalism in the mid-1920s were conditioned by the comprehensively anti-Marxist outlook embraced by the petty bourgeoisie in Weimar Germany. They feared a severe loss of economic and social prestige at the hands of big business and organised labour and reacted hysterically to any change suggestive of proletarianisation. Notwithstanding the undeniable sincerity with which Strasser propounded his 'socialism' at this time, the objective political role in the NSDAP of these 'socialists' was demagogic, tactical and propagandistic. By its very definition, fascism, especially when successful, excludes the possibility of a geniune 'leftist' opposition within its ranks. The erroneously labelled 'Nazi Left' and 'Strasser wing' did not exist in concrete terms, but were only one more expression of petty-bourgeois panic in the Weimar Republic.

Strasser's initiative in having the AG set up and an alternative Draft programme formulated came unstuck, therefore, within a matter of months, and crushed all ambitions of challenging Hitler for the leadership of the party. For Hitler's part, he was at this stage indifferent to ideological questions: what mattered to him was the maintenance and consolidation of his power. He tended to see the various squabbles and bouts of in-fighting within the NSDAP in terms of how they affected his objective of developing a mass totalitarian movement on the predicates of charismatic leadership and the *Führerprinzip*. Throughout the autumn of 1925 he displayed extraordinary tolerance towards his northern comrades so long as they appeared not to question his authority. Hitler only decided to intervene directly when he began to feel that the matter might move on from the level of ideological and tactical discussion to his own position as Führer. He was fully alert to the stature enjoyed by Strasser in the north and he also knew enough of him to harbour a suspicion about the range of his ambition. By early 1926, when he received news of the Draft, Hitler, prompted by Feder and others of the Munich clique, felt under attack. His delayed reaction was swift and triumphant. Having met Strasser in early February, when he secured a promise that the Draft would be withdrawn, Hitler arranged the Bamberg Conference on 14 February at which he re-asserted his total dictatorial control of the party, forcing Strasser to eat humble pie and promise the dissolution of the AG.[58] The NSDAP was to be a united *Führerpartei* led by Hitler, or nothing at all. That was the message at Bamberg, and Strasser, through his important differences with Hitler in succeeding years, never forgot it.

Hitler followed up his success by publishing that spring a series of directives which appreciably increased his centralised control of the party, and a new mechanism was established (Uschla) for maintaining internal discipline. Strasser and his colleagues tried to put as brave a face on it as possible and shrug off their humiliation. A meeting of AG Gauleiters in Hanover the day after the Bamberg Conference supported Goebbels' view that Munich had won only a pyrrhic victory and his admonition to 'work, get strong, then fight for socialism'.[59] A meeting of Gau Rhineland North and Westphalia in Essen on 6–7 March showed there was plenty of heart still in the north, and Strasser went ahead and implemented his plan to fuse the two Gaue into one united Gau Ruhr under a Kaufmann–Goebbels–Pfeffer triumvirate.[60] Encouraging also for the northerners was the exclusion of Esser from the Reichsleitung in April following discussions between Hitler and Strasser.[61]

Strasser's personal pain and disappointment after Bamberg were distracted somewhat when he was seriously injured. On his way to a meeting in Buer (Westphalia) on 10 March his car collided with a goods train at a level crossing at Altenessen, and he was confined to bed for several months.[62] In addition to the many expressions of good wishes and regret at this absence from the movement which he received, Strasser was delighted by a surprise visit to his home in Landshut by Hitler. As he wrote to Goebbels: 'Last week Hitler was here with a giant bunch of flowers; it was very nice.'[63] For a man of Strasser's energy the confinement was exasperating, but it afforded him the opportunity to get over his recent setback in private and to gather his thoughts for the future. By the time he appeared on crutches at the party's annual general members' meeting in Munich in late May he was reinvigorated and nearly ready for the fray. Having decided neither to surrender nor to break with Hitler, Strasser opted for a third way: to repudiate any suggestion that Bamberg had stopped 'socialism' in its tracks, and to continue more determinedly than before the campaign to carry his beliefs into the party as a whole. He concluded that the character and spirit of the NSDAP were far more crucial than arid discussion about programmes. He believed that an important cause of his failure to carry either the northern Gauleiters in their entirety or Hitler along with him was the still inchoate nature of his ideological outlook, and during the next few years he tried to intensify his commitment to what he continued fancifully to call his 'socialism'. He had lost a battle, but the war was far from over – that was Strasser's post-Bamberg message.

Strasserism

It cannot be said that Strasser enlarged upon his philosophy in a way which would make it more comprehensible. As before, his 'socialist' ideas remained nebulous and eclectic, and they continued to be put over in a popular fashion. Strasser himself appears to have been partially aware of the problem, but his unencouraging answer was that 'rational thought corrodes the foundations of life itself'.[64] His style more than anything else determined the nature of his thought: emotional, simplistic and unproblematical. He frequently invoked the concept of a 'national Socialism'[65] yet did little to explain systematically what he meant by this term. What he continued to offer instead was an abundance of fundamentalist honesty and sincerity; he actually believed, in contrast to some other NSDAP 'socialists', in what he was saying. But, of course, as previously noted, Strasser's forte was not theorising, and so his vehement anti-capitalist and anti-bourgeois rhetoric, however crudely articulated, was about the extent of his 'socialism' during the mid-1920s. Even then, his ideas were for the most part derivative; he himself contributed very little that was his own. In essence, Strasser gave forcible expression to a form of resentment peculiar to his fellow lower-middle-class *enragés* in the Weimar Republic. For him, National Socialism offered a unique, idealistic kind of socialism designed to return to the working class dignity of labour and a place in the national community.

There are many examples from Strasser's statements during this period which amply illustrate these observations about the character of his 'socialism', but there were two occasions in particular when he was given a perfect opportunity to give his message an explanatory as opposed to a revelatory dimension. While recuperating from his serious accident in spring 1926, he wrote his 'Gedanken über Aufgaben der Zukunft' ('Thoughts about Tasks of the Future'), which was designed as a comprehensive definition of his beliefs. Unfortunately, the chance was missed: the themes remained unchanged, and the superficiality was still blatant:

> We are Socialists, are enemies, deadly enemies of the present capitalist economic system with its exploitation of the economically weak, with its injustice in wages, with its immoral evaluation of people according to wealth and money instead of responsibility and achievement, and we are determined under all circumstances to destroy this stystem! . . . It seems obvious to me that we have to put a better, more just, more moral system in its place . . . .

What kind of system, what basis and direction this system should have is not made clear. All Strasser can say is:

> . . . it is not enough to change a system, to replace one economic system by another; necessary above all is a change of spirit! This spirit which is to be overcome is the spirit of materialism!! We must achieve an entirely new kind of economic thinking, a kind of thinking which is free from the present conceptions rooted in money, in property, in profit and false success! It is an indication of the Marxist, the false Socialism, that its way of thinking is exactly that of capitalism.

He condemns what there is, but what was his alternative?

> National Socialism, which stems from organic life itself, casts aside the mendacious words of a theory remote from the world, as well as the dead ideas of a declining civilization! We have to learn that in the economy of a people it is not profit, not gain, which are important, but only satisfying the needs of the members of this people!! This and nothing else is the task of a 'national economics'.

He continues:

> We have to learn that work is more than property! Achievement is more than dividends! It is the most unfortunate heritage of this capitalist economic system that all things are evaluated according to money, according to wealth, property! . . . Selection according to property is the mortal enemy of race, of blood, of life! . . . Achievement is the only valuation we recognise!! We emphasise achievement not dividends, and we recognise responsibility, not riches or splendour, as the zenith of human striving.

Strasser's anti-materialist diatribes remained a permanent part of his ideology into the early 1930s when other aspects of his thinking underwent significant change. On radio in June 1932, for example, he severely criticised the 'spirit which puts the highest priority on economic profit, on thinking in terms of money', advocating instead 'loyalty, honour, decency, cleanliness and responsibility'.[66]

One point which Strasser did make clear in his 1926 statement was his belief in the inequality of the human race. Perhaps influenced by Pfeffer's recently stated views on *völkisch* élitism, Strasser dismissed as liberal–Marxist nonsense the concept of equality:

> . . . we have realised that the idiotic belief in the equality of man is the deadly threat with which liberalism destroys people and nation, culture

> and morals, violating the primordial sources of our existence. [And further] we have to reject with fanatical zeal the frequent lie that people are 'basically equal'. . . . People are unequal, they are unequal from birth, become more unequal in life and are therefore to be valued unequally in life and . . . in their positions in society and in the state! But this inequality in turn has only one standard, can and must have only this one standard: the achievement of the individual for society, for the nation, for the state!!

In determining the standard of selection, however, Strasser leads himself into the hocus-pocus world of distorted racialist–militarist thinking which can only be dismissed as absurd and totally impracticable. He gets carried away into an unreal world of fantasy in this article, involving, among others, incredible prescriptions for better motherhood!

Strasser's incapacity for measured argument in lucidly exemplified here: ideas run into one another with gay abandon and are left dangling in suspended animation. The whole exercise degenerates into boring prolixity. He missed another chance to explain himself in early 1927 when he briefly became involved with Alfred Rosenberg in a discussion about the meaning of 'National Socialism'. Rosenberg relegated 'socialism' to a position secondary to nationalism in rank of importance, arguing that it had an essentially supportive, tactical function in the party's appeal.[67] Strasser took quite the opposite view in his reply,[68] but he failed to open up the ideological debate publicly in the party because his arguments followed the familiar pattern of vacuous slogans and catch-phrases. In the end Rosenberg remained unconvinced and expressed his regret at both the superficial content and polemical style of Strasser's response.[69] Strasser's inability to add content to his definition of 'socialism' was never corrected, and at times made him appear rather foolish. In 1932, for instance, he talked of 'the anti-capitalist yearnings of the German people', yet signally failed to develop what he really meant by this before his Reichstag audience.[70] Even worse was to follow in his radio speech a few weeks later:

> We understand by socialism . . . Baron von Stein's liberation of the peasants, the incorporation of the corporative system into the ossified organism of the present state, the principles of achievement of the Prussian officers and of the incorruptible German civil servants, the walls of the town hall, the cathedral, the hospital of a free imperial city – all that is the expression of German socialism as we conceive and demand it. These ideas have nothing, absolutely nothing to do . . . with internationalism, pacifism and class struggle.[71]

In the mid-1920s Strasser's earlier emphasis on the rights of workers was continued: 'The emancipation of the German workers will be accomplished by their participation in profits, participation in ownership, participation in achievement.'[72] But how this aim was to be realised he left unanswered. Strasser admitted that the class struggle was a reality but this was so only because, in his view, 'Jewish' Marxism had duped German workers with internationalist ideas, and only because of the failure of the national camp to create a true community incorporating the workers.[73] Resulting was a division between a property-owning bourgeoisie and a propertyless working class.[74] But Strasser's analysis of Germany's social problems went no further than this level. Since his appreciation of what had caused these problems in the first place was simplistic, if not erroneous, then, naturally, his solutions carried little conviction. He was invariably reduced to denouncing the incapacity of the bourgeoisie for any constructive tasks in much the same way as Hitler in *Mein Kampf*.[75] Strasser's concept of class was, therefore, far from clear and in some respects was contradictory. He rejected the idea of a 'dictatorship of the proletariat' in a Marxist sense, yet wanted to enlist the help of the workers to destroy capitalism. The dilemma was not confronted: instead Strasser fell back upon the entirely negative tactic of criticising the left-wing parties for failing to change society for the good of the workers.[76] In fact, despite his claims to be a revolutionary, 'what we National Socialists want is revolution or, better said, the attainment of a German future by the ruthless implementation of all measures which are necessary for the establishment and consolidation of national freedom, social justice and *völkisch* recovery,[77] Strasser was as counter-revolutionary in his thinking as the German lower middle classes as a whole. This was shown in his repeated denunciations of the French Revolution and its 'decaying, immoral ideas' which National Socialism would destroy: 'The aim of the NSDAP is victory over the French Revolution and its offspring, which are: liberalism, capitalism, Marxism and pacifism.'[78]

The negativism with which Strasser discussed a large part of his ideological perceptions went hand in hand very often with a decidedly apocalyptic view of Weimar politics. He was at his most pessimistic at the beginning of 1926 when he remarked:

> The outlook for 1926? What I have shown in another place . . . to be the inexorable fate of Germany will be fulfilled. After the death of the middle class through inflation and revaluation will come the extinction of the farmers through pressing debts and insufficient prices, then will come the end of the independent manufacturer and businessman through shortage of money and market crisis, and along with that the crushing of the civil servant and the worker through retrenchment, dismissals and lock-outs.[79]

Against this gloom, Strasser revealed himself to be a fervent eschatologist, with a firm belief in the righteousness of the National Socialist cause and in final victory, regardless of the odds:

> Out of the gloom of need proceeds the realisation, out of the agony of hopelessness the faith is formed, and out of the death anxiety of suffering and out of the yearning of the soul for formation breaks forth the will, passionate and great, fanatical and certain of victory! We National Socialists are fighters, fighters with passionate hearts and cool heads!... We have no fear of the necessary struggle... since we know before God and our conscience that our aim is peace. ... And we know with a certainty that comes from the blood and from the brain that our path is right.[80]

If Strasser's beliefs were ill-defined yet sincerely felt and sure in his own mind at this mid-point of his career, his attitude to race has to be seen as further confirmation of the unbridgeable gulf separating him from Marxist socialism. While not subscribing to the virulent, biologically inspired racist anti-semitism of Hitler, Streicher or Rosenberg,[81] it cannot be denied that Strasser was a convinced anti-semite throughout his life, openly acknowledging the virtues of *völkisch* principles. He stated his acceptance of 'the enormous importance of the racial question'[82] and confessed: 'We are... not only "national Socialists" but also "anti-semites".... '[83] At times, he called for fairly stringent action, including racial protection for Germans from Jews[84] and the demand that marriage should take place only between racially suited partners.[85] The link here with the later notorious Nuremberg Race Laws (1935) is obvious. His alternative Draft programme incorporated calls, as we have seen, for deportation and withdrawal of citizenship from Jews. He frequently fulminated against the 'Jewish spirit' and influence in the capitalist economy and against its presence in the leadership of the socialist and labour movement:

> The Jew used the workers' movement... in order to destroy the state. ... The Jew has not taken over the workers' movement out of compassion but out of self-interest.... The German workers' movement was betrayed to Marxism by the Jews.[86]

But Strasser stopped short of threatening physical harm, let alone extermination, against Jews. His most consistent demand later in his career, which represented a modification of his earlier views, was for the exclusion of Jews from the media and cultural life[87] and other important branches of public life and the professions:

> We want no persecution of Jews, but we demand the exclusion of Jews from German life. We demand a German leadership without a Jewish or foreign spirit, without Jewish backers and Jewish capital. ... We demand the protection of our cultural inheritance from Jewish presumption and encroachment.[88]

He promised his followers that the full significance of his thoughts on the Jewish question would be shown when the party came to power: 'A National Socialist government will mean that the domination of Jewry in Germany is finished, that is, the exclusion of Jewry from all spheres. . . .'[89]

In the rough and tumble of everyday politics in the Weimar Republic where the tense atmosphere produced clashes of personalities all too easily, and where the trading of insults, defamation of character and slanders were freely exchanged among political opponents, Strasser was not exceptional in being deeply involved. He often spoke disparagingly of individual Jews, and on one occasion was severely reprimanded by the President of the Reichstag for calling a KPD deputy a 'Jew-boy'.[90] Rudolf Hilferding, the SPD economics spokesman and former Reich Finance Minister, was dubbed by Strasser 'that Galician Jew',[91] while Ruth Fischer, the KPD leader, was 'that fat Galician Jewess'.[92] Further opprobrious epithets such as 'Jewish cheats' and 'Jewish hyenas'[93] peppered Strasser's radical invective, and consequently he was taken to court on various occasions on charges of libel and slander by several Jewish organisations, notably the Central-Verein deutscher Staatsbürger jüdischen Glaubens (C-V). As responsible editor for the Kampfverlag publications, he also had to stand accused for the anti-semitic outpourings of his colleagues.[94] Small fines or brief periods of imprisonment sometimes ensued. He was certainly saved from more numerous court appearances by the Kampfverlag's greater concern for the impending 'social revolution' which tempered or reduced in frequency the anti-semitic element of its campaign.

Ironically, in two of the bitterest personal quarrels in which Strasser became involved during the 1920s, the Jewish question reared its ugly head in a rather unusual manner. In an aggressively anti-semitic party such as the NSDAP the vilest insult one member could throw at another was that he had Jewish blood in his veins, and this is exactly what happened in Strasser's conflicts with Goebbels and Artur Dinter, the Thuringian religious fanatic. The simmering antipathy between the Strasser brothers and their erstwhile 'socialist' comrade in arms, Goebbels, broke out into the open less than a year after he had taken over as Gauleiter of Berlin in the autumn of 1926.[95] The infamous article written by Erich Koch, but inspired by Otto Strasser, and entitled 'Consequences of racial mixture',[96] predictably outraged its intended though unnamed target, Goebbels, while Gregor added salt to the wounds by claiming that the Gauleiter's club-foot was proof of his Jewishness.[97] Not to be outdone, Goebbels countered by alleging that Gregor's mother and wife were Jewish, while Otto had a Jewish appearance to boot.[98] Behind this unsavoury business was the Strassers' feeling of having been 'betrayed' by Goebbels over the socialist campaign in the party, the friction inevitably caused once both sides became active in Berlin, and the increasingly desperate situation in the Berlin Gau whose difficulties were capped by its temporary prohibition by the police in May 1927. Last but not least was the Strassers' fear that their newspaper monopoly in Berlin and Brandenburg would be broken by Goebbels' *Der Angriff*, which commenced publication as a weekly in July 1927: there was money as well as personal grudges at stake.[99] The Reichsleitung, through the offices of Rudolf Hess, the Führer's private secretary, and General Bruno Heinemann, the organisation leader, became embroiled in the affair to some extent, and eventually an uneasy truce was arranged,[100] though the bitterness on both sides was hardly attenuated. In later years, Otto attacked Goebbels unmercifully in his Black Front newspapers, and Gregor continued to make extremely unflattering remarks, while Goebbels, in the immediate aftermath of the resignation crisis in December 1932, revived his earlier, unfounded allegations about Gregor's Jewish background.[101]

Strasser and Dinter had been enemies for some time (see Chapter 2), and when Strasser played a leading role in securing his expulsion from the NSDAP in October 1928[102] the response was a stream of slanderous vituperation from the pages of *Das Geistchristentum*, a publication which in its pseudo-religious way was as perverse as *Der Stürmer*. Dinter wrote that 'the name Strasser is a good Jewish name . . . a look at Herr Strasser's nose and his characteristic business and combat methods . . . confirm without doubt this racial connection'.[103] No one, least of all Strasser, took much notice of this obscene crankiness,[104] even when it was reported with glee in the opposition press.[105] None the less, these two sordid and distasteful episodes revealed part of what went on in the murky backwaters of the party. Noticeably, on both occasions, Hitler did not do a great deal to help Strasser; he probably derived a degree of satisfaction from the momentary discomfiture of his rival.

The Dinter affair's real significance lay in the fact that it underscored once again the party's determination to stay outside religious controversy of any type, and to reaffirm its official policy of neutrality *vis-à-vis* the Christian churches. Hitler had shown no time for General Ludendorff's anti-Catholic tirades in Bavaria in 1925, and repeatedly stressed his party's commitment to an unexplained 'positive Christianity', as intimated in the 1920 programme. In 1930, for instance, he declined to allow the party's endorsement of Alfred Rosenberg's *magnus opus*, *The Myth of the Twentieth Century*, partly because of its strong anti-Christian bias. Strasser's support for Hitler's line of argument in this sphere was one of the reasons for his alienation from Ludendorff after 1925. The previous year, while still in the Bavarian Landtag, Strasser had pointed out that the NSDAP had both Catholics and Protestants in its ranks and that it was vital not to engender sectarian rivalries or to allow the party to identify with one or other of the major Christian denominations.[106] A few years later he told the Reichstag:

> We want no agitation against religious denominations and no persecution of the Christian churches, but we demand the honest co-operation

of the churches in the renewal of German culture, without which the churches would also become spiritually arid and empty. From the clergy we want no party politics, but instead service for the peace of the human soul, for the moral improvement of the masses. . . . Finally, we demand of the servants of the Christian denominations that they do not weaken the God-given instinct of national self-determination and that, in the spirit of early Christianity, they will not permit religious differences to become a political danger to the German people.[107]

Strasser reiterated his guarantee of non-persecution of the churches in 1932[108] and as Reich Organisation Leader made it clear that the confessional background of members was of no importance whatsoever:[109]

I have never as Reich Organisation Leader inquired about a person's religious viewpoint when appointing him to a Gauleiter's post, and will never do so in the future. In Halle-Merseburg party comrade Jordan's membership of the Catholic Church[110] was stressed either by idiots or by our enemies and trouble-makers. Within a sound, intact organisation, no one thinks of such things . . . it is the standpoint of the Reichsleitung that any assessment of people according to confessional allegiance is to be rejected.

Strasser stressed the value of Christianity to an individual's sense of security and fulfilment and conceded no essential incompatibility between Christian and National Socialist principles. During the mid-1920s, therefore, he usually described himself as a '*völkisch* Catholic', repudiating any suggestion that the *völkisch* idea could only be accommodated within Protestantism; he for one was not prepared to be regarded as a 'second-rate *völkisch* follower'.[111] As if to underline this point, Strasser fully supported the strong opposition of the *Kampfverlag* circle to the political involvement of the Catholic Church through its unofficial representatives, the Centre Party and BVP. He drew a distinction between religion and its use for political purposes, and from this angle denounced the Concordats agreed during the 1920s between the Catholic Church and the governments of Bavaria and Prussia,[112] while lambasting the Lateran Accords between Mussolini and the Vatican in 1929 as 'papalism'.[113] The Catholic bishops were not infrequently on the receiving end of a tongue-lashing from Strasser for meddling in politics,[114] and the Centre Party, in particular, he usually dismissed as the lackeys of Rome.[115] When Heinrich Brüning of that party became Chancellor in 1930 it confirmed Strasser's worst suspicions that Germany was about to be sold out by the unlikely combination of the Papacy and the 'Golden International':[116]

So now we see the political troop of Rome, the Centre Party, operating

> shoulder to shoulder with the political troop of Jewish world finance . . . with the aim of setting up a Roman–Jewish fascism, represented in the Reich by the Brüning dictatorship, and in Prussia by the Braun dictatorship,[117] both supporting and balancing each other.

The statement was, of course, false and only illustrated Strasser's continuing penchant for raucous rabble-rousing no matter which area of debate he happened to be in. More interestingly, as the 1930s got under way and Strasser's political outlook became less narrow in certain respects, his outspoken attacks on the political power of the Catholic Church ceased, and his attitude to the Centre Party changed so much that in the summer of 1932 he was the foremost advocate within the NSDAP of a coalition alliance in government with that party (see Chapter 5). By that time, Strasser, having forsaken his anti-Catholic associates in the Kampfverlag, was demonstrating more respect for the church as an institutional force, accepting that the NSDAP would have to come to terms with it rather than attempt to reduce or even eliminate its influence.[118] The support and encouragement he gave to the extremist neo-pagan German Christian movement within the Evangelical Church and then in parish elections in the Old Prussian Union in November 1932[119] were motivated by his concern to extend the party's influence into organised religion and not by any personal disillusionment with orthodox Christianity. Until his death Strasser remained a Catholic, though he could never be counted amongst the most devout or militant of the church's following.[120]

The church's conservative attitude towards the role of women in society helped shape the final ingredient of Strasser's thought under review here. As a stridently male chauvinistic movement, National Socialism preached that women had no place in politics and should devote themselves exclusively to certain areas of activity epitomised by the holy trinity of children, home and church. The party had few female members before 1933, but the extensive electoral support given it by women in the early 1930s forced a certain degree of rethinking on the part of its leadership. Acting under such pressure, Strasser, as Reich Organisation Leader, was instrumental in establishing the first coherent official women's group within the NSDAP, the NS-Frauenschaft (NSF), in autumn 1931.[121] With his eye firmly set on potential female electoral support, Strasser not only urged party leaders in the provinces to lend assistance to the new organisation, but also made a number of public statements promising women a responsible and honourable role in a future National Socialist state.[122] But, despite his protestations to the contrary,[123] Strasser's ideas on women hardly deviated from traditional party doctrine, and even when there were marginal differences they were dictated by the desire for political advantage. In the early days when there were no such political incentives, his views on women were sublimely ridiculous – as in 1926, for example, when he equated motherhood with military service.[124] By and large, Strasser upheld the NSDAP argument that despite the changed circumstances produced by the industrial-mechanised age as many women as possible should leave employment so that men, as in pre-industrial times, could revert to their old role as the only breadwinner.[125] As events after 1933 were to show conclusively,[126] this was a wholly impracticable notion, rooted as it was in a regressive utopianism. Strasser's endorsement of the NSDAP's anti-feminism must ultimately be seen as another illustration of the hollowness of his 'socialism', for it was the genuinely socialist parties and organisations which canvassed most determinedly for women's rights in the Weimar Republic. Strasser had no claims to be included in that progressive movement.

Taken as a whole, Strasser's ideological position was shallow and intellectually mediocre. Certain elements he consistently adhered to in later years, others he modified or even abandoned under changing political and personal circumstances. In the mid-1920s, however, as the NSDAP was rebuilding, it was the central core of his thought, the anti-capitalist and anti-bourgeois orientation, which effectively determined the nature of the party's character and appeal. The theory had to be put into practice.

Propaganda Leader

The NSDAP's commitment to ideology was always unsure, if racial anti-semitism and *Lebensraum* are excepted. It was above all a pragmatic, opportunistic party which responded as political circumstances dictated. The advantage of being flexible was that ideology became part of the tactics of any given situation in the political power game. Hitler had no interest in programmes: what mattered was action, discipline and will-power. The NSDAP was a thoroughgoing activist party which disdained theoretical discussion and could carry a whole range of ideological propensities – chauvinism, anti-semitism, pan-Germanism, anti-Marxism and so on – without paying too much attention to inconsistencies or contradictions in its appeal. But the emphasis in its propaganda, which it did regard as important, did vary considerably from time to time, reflecting calculated shifts in strategy and tactics. In the mid-1920s 'socialism' became a conspicuous aspect of its image, allowing the party an opportunity to break into the industrial working-class electoral constituency. Hitler went along with this approach without ever explicitly approving it. In keeping with his more cautious outlook on politics since the failure of the *Putsch*, he preferred to keep his options open until the pattern of German political life had taken more definite shape. He never had a serious regard for socialism in any form; it was a Jewish swindle, as far as he was concerned. The Führer had little interest in the socio-economic problems of the workers;

their interest for him lay simply in their votes. They were a temporary political expedient, a useful instrument, perhaps, in the fight for power. Hitler never moved out from his quintessentially petty-bourgeois frame of mind; he steadfastly upheld the rights of private property and supported entrepreneurial capitalist enterprise.[127] With the adoption of an electoral strategy after 1925, however, and in view of his burning resentment against the upper *Mittelstand*,[128] he was predisposed towards the masses as a way of building up support for the party. If this involved giving them socialist, anti-capitalist rhetoric, he was prepared not to disagree. Hitler's attitude made Strasser's objective of constructing the party along proletarian lines by instilling nationalism rather than class-consciousness among the workers a lot easier. During the mid-1920s, therefore, the character and spirit of much of the party and its ancillary organisations were fashioned according to Strasserism, and Strasser himself took advantage of Hitler's partially enforced absence from the public eye[129] to project an image of being the principal motor behind this direction.[130] The appeal that had proved comparatively successful in northern Germany in 1924–5 was carried over into other parts of the movement as the essential component of an 'urban plan',[131] and meant that the NSDAP was set up in open and often violent confrontation with the SPD and KPD as it also sought the working-class vote.[132]

The establishment of the Kampfverlag in March 1926 by Strasser with money raised from the sale of his chemist's shop in Landshut[133] and from his brother's own resources[134] gave the party's 'socialists' an indispensable forum for the propagation of their views. Weekly and daily newspapers published by the Kampfverlag quickly penetrated northern, central and eastern parts of the country and aimed at an industrial working-class readership in towns and cities.[135] At the same time, the more intellectual *NS-Briefe* allowed discussion of ideological matters to be continued among the leaders and active supporters despite Hitler's reiteration in May 1925 of the immutability of the 1920 programme.[136] Strasser spent much time and effort encouraging the widest possible circulation of his newspapers 'with all means and the greatest intensity', as he remarked to Goebbels,[137] and before long had been nicknamed the 'newspaper king of National Socialism'.[138] The impact of the 'socialist' assault was soon apparent. In Berlin, Goebbels took the fight into the poorer districts to the north and east of the city, and the party faithful were appropriately dubbed 'Hitler proletarians'.[139] A similar trend emerged in the Ruhr, Rhineland, Hamburg, Thuringia, Saxony, Lower Saxony and Baden,[140] and many contemporaries were convinced the NSDAP was a revolutionary, proletarian party representing a kind of national Marxism.[141] This image was strengthened by the character and composition of some ancillary groups. In the NS-Students' League (NSDStB), Reichsführer Wilhelm Tempel imparted a radical social-revolutionary outlook aimed at the less well-off of

Germany's university students. He was a willing and enthusiastic follower of Strasserism and encouraged Strasser to stay in regular contact with the group's leaders, speak at its meetings, and generally take an interest in its development.[142] Similarly, in the Hitler Youth (HJ), Kurt Gruber, whose background in 'Red' Saxony was significant, gave his youths a socialist orientation which, although somewhat naïve and lacking in depth, was pursued with a potent mixture of ebullient idealism and romantic nationalism. Consequently, a majority of its rank-and-file members were young workers.[143] In the SA the same sociological make-up of most ordinary members[144] produced a rowdy radicalism which contained vague elements of an anti-capitalist, anti-bourgeois *élan.*

It was no accident that the main inspiration of this campaign was also chief of the party's propaganda office for much of this period. Strasser appears to have taken the lead himself in securing this appointment, which became effective from 16 September 1926 and extended until the end of December of the following year.[145] He suggested to the Reichsleitung that the party needed a more streamlined propaganda operation, which was, of course, an implicit criticism of that office's previous incumbent, Esser. After talking matters over with Hitler, Strasser accepted the responsibility with considerable enthusiasm and lost no time in getting down to business.[146] In his first communiqué as Propaganda Leader he promised that his office 'will not merely be involved in a great deal of paperwork . . . it will conduct, within the confines of the very slender means at its disposal, a forward-looking propaganda, which is the second most important task of the movement'. Presumably, organisation was the first. His aim would be 'to eradicate the poisonous and destructive ideas of Jewish Marxism and to break the power of its devilish propaganda'.[147]

Strasser at once embarked on a punishing tour of inspection of branches in northern Germany in order to co-ordinate their propaganda effort as far as possible.[148] Before long, he had undoubtedly brought for the first time in this sphere of party activity an admirable degree of professionalism and energy. He was responsible for introducing the basic ingredients which later came to characterise NSDAP propaganda: fanatical zeal, ruthless determination, extravagance, commitment. Some observers described his approach as 'Marxist' and, of course, he did learn and borrow from his hated opponents quite freely. One of his most constructive moves was the setting up of an inventory of party speakers which helped centrally to control their appearances throughout the country. Strasser's achievements did not go unnoticed by the authorities. The 'very well prepared and thoroughly organised propaganda' and 'lively publicity' of the party,[149] particularly in industrial-urban areas, was noted, and by late 1927 it was suggested that he had succeeded in devising an 'extraordinarily comprehensive and activist' propaganda machine,[150] and all done on extremely limited funds. Above all, he had considerably advanced the cause of rationalisation and co-ordination, despite the many regional differences he had to face.

Despite Strasser's efforts, the NSDAP's 'socialist' image at this time was not absolute. Running alongside the Strasserite urban strategy was the notion that the party, unlike its competitors, was not tied to specific social and economic interests. It aspired to the status of a broadly based popular movement, incorporating a synthesis of nationalism and socialism. But this approach, which was theoretically sound in terms of broadening the appeal of National Socialism, was unconvincing because it produced a crop of anomalies and contradictions when everyday political problems intruded. One of the most glaring and damaging of these was the party's failure to back the SPD-KPD sponsored campaign for the state expropriation of the property of the former royal houses (*Fürstenenteignung*). Although Hitler may have feared losing financial subsidies from several monarchist and royal benefactors, his decision was dictated more by his refusal to be associated in open partnership with parties from which he hoped to entice popular support. In any case, the prospect of aligning, albeit temporarily, with the Left, was anathema to him. Hitler may also have been sensitive to the possibility of other party stalwarts, notably Strasser, being permitted to display too much influence over policy since this might reflect adversely on his own position as Führer. For motives which had little to do with ideological purity, therefore, the NSDAP failed to vote for the expropriation motion when it came up in the Reichstag on 6 May 1926. None the less, it was unbecoming behaviour for an allegedly 'socialist' party.

Further shadows must also have been cast by the spectacle of Hitler's contacts with industrialists in 1926 and 1927 and by his statements in favour of private enterprise.[151] Contemporaries were not to know that in fact the party received insignificant funds from industry during these years and was financially self-supporting to a large extent.[152] Similarly, the appearance of a few middle-class-type ancillary groups, the NS-Teachers' League (NSLB) and Kampfbund für deutsche Kultur did not help sustain the party's 'socialist' credentials, even though these groups were small in membership and uninfluential. Infinitely more damage was done by Hitler's negative attitude towards the frequently mooted idea of a National Socialist trade union organisation. In view of the pro-working-class appeal it seemed only logical, if not essential, to have such an organisation. But Hitler's strictures in *Mein Kampf* prevailed,[153] and the most he was prepared to allow was informal discussion of the subject among interested party members. Given this opposition, radicals like Strasser and Goebbels were unwilling to take up the issue seriously in the mid-1920s, though they were aware that the credibility of the 'socialist' appeal was impaired. The omission was certainly one reason for a final paradox in the party's situation at this time. Despite its proletarian inclination, the NSDAP remained a predominantly lower-middle-class affair. The disintegration of many *völkisch* and right-wing paramilitary groups brought a large number of new middle-class recruits into the party, whose membership rose from 521 in April 1925 to 85,464 in March 1928. On average, only 7 per cent were workers, though in selected urban centres such as Berlin, the Ruhr and Saxony the percentage reached as much as 20 or 25 per cent.[154] Specifically local conditions, including peculiar social and economic structures, the scale of small or family businesses, the non-existence of unions and socialist organisations, usually accounted for these exceptions.[155] The groups most heavily represented in the membership were artisans, small businessmen and white-collar commercial employees, who were reacting to unemployment, bankruptcy, poor salary-levels and diminishing promotion prospects. Lower-grade civil servants, especially younger ones living in small towns and countryside, were also becoming increasingly susceptible. To these discontented sections of the lower *Mittelstand*, Strasserism appeared an attractive third way between capitalism and Marxist socialism, as it did also to the DVFB Reichstag deputies Reventlow, Kube and Stöhr, who defected to the NSDAP in February 1927 because they perceived in the party a social-revolutionary dimension lacking in their own.[156] As it happened, the defection coincided with Strasser's withdrawal from the amalgamated *völkisch* faction in the Reichstag following a bitter dispute with DVFB deputy Jürgen von Ramin which eventually ended in court.[157] The hair-splitting pedantry of the *völkisch* movement was once again brought to public attention.

In addition to its failure to attract many workers, the Strasserite approach was also manifestly unsuccessful as an electoral bait. In a series of local and provincial elections which the party fought on a 'socialist' platform in Saxony, Thuringia, Mecklenburg-Schwerin and other areas,[158] the results were profoundly disappointing, and by 1928, after three years of electioneering, the NSDAP was independently represented in only four state parliaments: it had one seat in Prussia, six in Bavaria, and two each in Saxony and Thuringia.[159] The same strategy was doggedly persevered with, however, and the party looked on the Reichstag election in May 1928 as its first really important test. Despite Strasser's absurd assertion that 'we National Socialists have no direct interest in these elections and their outcome', being only interested in observing 'how widely the National Socialist ideas of freedom are already embedded in the people',[160] the election, in fact, assumed crucial importance for the party, for it would produce a definitive answer as to the feasibility of the urban strategy which was now given a final opportunity to prove its worth. Success in the election would certainly mean a continuation in an intensified form of the plan; failure would result in its abandonment for good.[161] The party still entertained high hopes of doing well, and the vigorous campaign it mounted was not disturbed by Strasser's removal from the propaganda office.

From 2 January 1928, Strasser took over as Reich Organisation

Leader.[162] The changeover inevitably produced a spate of rumours in the opposition press about a rift between him and Hitler,[163] but there is no evidence to suggest that Strasser was anything other than delighted to move into what he regarded as the top position in the party after that of leader. Besides, with his influence so extensive over the NSDAP's propaganda direction and character in the mid-1920's, Strasser's relationship with Hitler had improved, even if there remained a distinct element of coolness and reserve on both sides. In 1927, for example, Strasser made one of his most fulsome statements about Hitler which came as close as he ever did to identifying him with the idea of National Socialism:

> The sincerest devotion to the idea of National Socialism . . . is bound up with a deep love of the person of our Führer. . . . The tremendous superiority which the NSDAP has as an instrument of struggle compared with all other formations . . . is due to the fact that we have the outstanding leader, who holds not only supreme power but also the love of his followers. . . .[164]

The statement stopped short of making Hitler synonymous with National Socialism, and it was something of a theatrical gesture for public consumption, but it was without doubt an arresting salutation from the Führer's most critical colleague. Also, at the time of his new appointment both men went out of their way to deny that there was any disagreement between them. Hitler issued statements thanking Strasser 'for the extraordinary services which he had rendered in his position hitherto in the movement'[165] and referring to 'the extraordinarily successful leadership of the Propaganda Department'.[166] For his part, Strasser stressed his commitment to the party and its leader in unequivocal terms, particularly in his speech at the Hofbräuhaus just before Christmas.[167]

Strasser's appointment was one of the most judicious made by Hitler in the party before 1933. With his sure eye for administrative detail and his capacity for hard work he was an eminently apt choice. In any case, given General Heinemann's somewhat inattentive attitude to the job, Strasser had already gained experience in organisational matters by taking on responsibilities which an efficient organisation leader would normally have performed. In addition to his propaganda, Reichstag and Gauleiter duties, therefore, Strasser usually chaired important party meetings, played a major role in preparing the party rallies of July 1926 in Weimar and August 1927 in Nuremberg, and acted as a troubleshooter in local party disputes, including those in Hamburg in 1926 when he removed Gauleiter Klant from office,[168] in the Austrian branch in March 1927,[169] and in East Prussia and Silesia in 1928.[170] He entered his new office, consequently, with a sense of realism, but any major changes in the structure and practice of the party's organisation he postponed until after the forthcoming election.

The NSDAP contested all thirty-five electoral districts with a vigour which seemed incongruous amidst a generally placid campaign,[171] which was a reflection of the Republic's economic progress since 1924 and its more secure position in international affairs following its admission to the Locarno Pact and League of Nations. Strasser, always in heavy demand as a public speaker,[172] was to the fore in denouncing the Republic's 'lack of true socialist achievement' and 'subservience to capitalism', though in some agrarian parts of the country the party was beginning to be aware of the potential support among the increasingly disgruntled community of small farmers. Hitler's last-minute alteration to point 17 of the party programme was a blatantly opportunistic move designed to pacify small farmers' fears about the NSDAP's attitude to private property. A total of thirty-six names were on the party's electoral slate (*Reichstagswahlvorschlag*) which was headed by General Franz Ritter von Epp, a recent convert from the BVP. Strasser, like Kube, Goebbels and a few others, figured prominently as a candidate in many areas so as to enhance the chances of election under the complex system of proportional representation.[173]

Contrary to the opinion of some authorities,[174] the result of the election was a severe disappointment for the NSDAP. By capturing only 2.6 per cent of the vote (809,771) and twelve seats (Strasser being elected for Franconia), the urban strategy had been dealt a fatal blow.[175] The appeal to industrial workers floundered ignominiously, while the SPD and KPD both increased their support. For the moment, the Republic's democratic parliamentary system appeared reasonably stable. However, upon closer analysis the election indicated a crisis in middle-class politics in 1928 which could be exploited by a party sufficiently equipped and attuned to the underlying fears of the bourgeoisie. The traditional middle-class parties, DNVP, DVP and DDP, had all lost ground, the *völkisch* movement had collapsed, and the relatively new smaller middle-class groupings such as the *Wirtschaftspartei* had made a promising showing. On its own account, the NSDAP's limited appeal had been concentrated in rural, small-town Protestant areas in Bavaria, Schleswig-Holstein, Lower Saxony, Hesse-Nassau and the Pfalz, thanks to the radicalised peasant vote, as well as in parts of Saxony and Thuringia. These results intimated that the way forward for a party of the Right was not among the proletarian masses, but amongst the most unhappy segment of the electorate, the Protestant *Mittelstand*. For the NSDAP to become that party a dramatic reorientation would be necessary in its organisation, propaganda and ideological emphasis. Otherwise, it faced the prospect of remaining totally insignificant as an electoral force. The lesson was not lost on Hitler, nor on Strasser as he viewed disconsolately the ruins of a strategy which had been initiated and sustained largely by him. For both the NSDAP and Strasser a profound crisis had emerged which required immediate and drastic resolution.

4 *Reorientation, 1928–30*

Organisation Leader

Between the summer of 1928 and the beginning of the 1930s the NSDAP was well on the way to becoming a party of the Protestant small-town and rural-based *Mittelstand*, located for the most part in northern, central and eastern Germany. The shock of disappointment at the Reichstag election result had immediately run deeply through the rank and file,[1] and the theme of reorientation was avidly taken up and discussed in influential party circles. Emphasis was put on the NSDAP's position as the only remaining viable representative of the *völkisch* idea, and the 300,000 who had voted for the decimated *völkisch* parties at the election were identified as a primary future target for the NSDAP.[2] This would mean a conscious swing to the right for the party because these *völkisch* supporters were drawn overwhelmingly from the middle classes. Leading party spokesmen like Alfred Rosenberg and Wilhelm Frick called for a new alignment with the conservative Right and its organisations now that the industrial-urban strategy had failed to attract more than a handful of blue-collar workers.[3] An important editorial in the party press, which was undoubtedly inspired by Hitler, gave official backing to the new line of thought.[4] The Führer's leadership was obviously being put to severe test as only he could assess the implications of the election result and make a definitive statement about the party's future strategy.

While reaffirming his determination to continue following a parliamentary course of action and trying to reassure his despondent followers that the election was only a temporary setback,[5] Hitler fully understood the position and the necessity of changing course. He now appreciated the futility of the basically petty-bourgeois NSDAP trying to develop into a mass movement with the support mainly of the industrial proletariat. It was clear to him that the urban strategy had been a salient manifestation of the party's confused, faltering state of mind in the mid-1920s as it attempted to re-create an identity. As a result, the NSDAP had been naïve and unconvincing. In deciding in 1928, therefore, to begin a new phase of development as a middle-class party, the NSDAP was simply acknowledging at last its inherent social and political substance. To prepare for the opening to the right, that is, to begin a systematic courting of the bourgeoisie, the party required a more traditionalist, conservative and chauvinistic character. In practice, this not only involved abandoning the failed urban strategy and toning down drastically expressions of 'socialism' in the movement, but, more positively, it also meant identifying the NSDAP with politics, attitudes and priorities which were dear to the hearts of the German *Mittelstand.* As in the aftermath of the 1923 *Putsch*, the party's inordinate capacity for opportunism and flexibility greatly facilitated these major changes which most other political organisations would have found extremely difficult, if not impossible, to achieve. Having decided in conceptual terms on this radical transformation in the party's image and appeal, Hitler took the first steps towards a practical implementation of the new strategy at the important meeting of leaders in Munich in late August and early September 1928.

The meeting was designed to provide a frank and sober analysis of the party's position, to re-examine its whole organisational and propaganda approaches and to discuss fundamental questions of political campaigning for the future.[6] Hitler set the tone for the meeting and for the flavour of the strategy about to be adopted by demonstrating a resolutely nationalist line of argument: in essence, the German people had to be educated to fanatical nationalism by the NSDAP. Noting that in the recent election the party's successes had taken place in rural-agrarian areas, it was now decided to switch the emphasis in its propaganda and organisational drive from urban to country regions, adjusting their content to appeal to small farmers and other nationally minded groups. The themes which were to receive priority henceforth were nationalism in the broadest sense, anti-Marxism, anti-semitism, militarism, law and order, and pan-German imperialism, with particular stress on the injustice of the Treaty of Versailles and the Dawes Plan in so far as they were deleterious to national interests. Hitler himself soon gave the lead in his speeches and writings, which after 1928 were concerned more and more with foreign policy and the alleged misdemeanours of Foreign Minister Stresemann. In the early summer of 1928 Hitler wrote his 'Secret Book' where, with an eye on conservative-nationalist circles, he paraded his very best national credentials in discussing foreign affairs.[7] The book was an unequivocal indication of the party's new pro-bourgeois nationalist strategy: 'socialism' was increasingly restricted in the party's appeal to large industrial centres in Berlin-Brandenburg, the Ruhr-Rhineland, Hamburg and central Germany.

Gregor Strasser was given his first clear-cut opportunity at this meeting to cut his teeth as the party's recently appointed Organisation Leader. Shortly after the election he had drawn up a plan to reorganise the party's administration at both the national and the provincial levels, with a view to encouraging trends towards centralisation and rationalisation.[8] The plan was meant to ease the adoption of the new strategy, and met with the unanimous approval of the meeting. The party's provincial organisation was redefined to correspond to Reichstag electoral districts, and the internal structure of the Gaue was streamlined, with the powers of Gauleiters increased in their respective districts, particularly with regard to the appointment of leaders. In the long term, of course, the position of the Gauleiters was progressively weakened not only by the party's conflict with the SA, which Strasser could not control, but also by the organisational changes involved in the NSDAP's emergence as a mass movement. These changes involved the appearance of officially recognised ancillary groups and the increasing degree of specialisation in party administration. New organisational structures emerged which impinged on areas of competence formerly within the exclusive jurisdiction of the Gauleiters. Strasser was aware of what was happening, and his aim was to encourage a parallel development which would allow them to act as supervisors and co-ordinators of the party's various activities within each Gau. He made clear his backing for the Gauleiters, but in return expected them to be willing subordinates rather than independent agents of the Reichsleitung.[9] The brooding, ubiquitous presence of Hitler overshadowed these arrangements, however, as during the early 1930s he intimated to everyone, including his Organisation Leader, that the Gauleiters were primarily his personal agents in the field. Strasser's progressively complex bureaucracies were not to be permitted to come between the Führer and his chief lieutenants.

Strasser's plan resulted in the Reichsleitung tightening its control over the party's disciplinary procedure, while headquarters was itself remodelled into two main departments as an efficiency measure. The overall objective was to give the party the kind of organisational structure that would allow it to contest elections in a more positive and disciplined way within the new scale of priorities. Correspondingly, Strasser also made it his business to concentrate the direction of all party propaganda in the hands of the Reichsleitung, where Himmler contributed his own share of streamlining by devising the saturation method of propaganda in selected areas over a short period of time which soon became the hallmark of NSDAP activity in this sphere. As Organisation Leader, Strasser was able to follow up these changes by making a series of new top appointments which resulted in some personnel coming into office who were his close associates or even personal friends.[10] Thereafter, he had a determining influence on all important leadership appointments.[11]

The NSDAP's determination to cherish middle-class values after 1928 was epitomised by a certain change in Hitler's life-style in late 1929 when he 'abandoned the pretension of being the leader of a working-class party'[12] by moving from his shabby small flat in Munich to an elegant, expensive apartment in a fashionable *haute bourgeois* part of town. But more concrete and significant signs of the party's rightward shift quickly came into view. The ancillary groups which emerged in the late 1920s were all specifically geared to attracting bourgeois support: the leagues for lawyers (BNSDJ), doctors (NSAB) and grammar-school boys (NSS). At the same time, there were perceptible right-wing trends introduced into those existing ancillaries which until 1928 had been close to Strasserism: the NSDStB was brought into line with the conservative-nationalist strategy after its leader, Tempel, was replaced by Hitler's protégé, Baldur von Schirach, in July 1928. His boyish-romantic attachment to the notion of a classless *Volksgemeinschaft* notwithstanding, Schirach determined to make his organisation successful by appealing to Germany's predominantly conservative and nationalist student population. On this basis, he effected a dramatic change in the NSDStB's fortunes, for already by 1930–1 it was the dominant body in student affairs at many universities.[13] He also tried to bring the social-revolutionary HJ into line: at a special meeting at the 1929 party rally in Nuremberg, Schirach's plan for a merger involving the HJ and several right-wing *Bündische* youth groups just failed and he had to wait until autumn 1931 before finally getting rid of Reichsführer Gruber, who encouraged the HJ's radicalism. The HJ's personality was then toned down, with greater weight given to recruiting middle-class youths. The drive to the right was clear enough, though the HJ fought off Schirach's influence for a while and retained its mainly proletarian rank-and-file membership until 1933.[14]

On the broader Weimar political front, the NSDAP's reorientation was revealed in its increasingly serious courting of the small farmers, which in 1930 led to the creation of Walther Darré's specialist agrarian office in the Reichsleitung, and also in its friendly attitude towards the right-wing patriotic and paramilitary organisations – a policy already foreshadowed by Hitler in May 1928 and taken up enthusiastically after the election.[15] Thus, the NSDAP could collaborate with the conservative Right in 1929 in the campaign against the Young Plan, which had been devised as a slightly more flexible arrangement than the earlier Dawes Plan on the vexed question of reparations. As a result of these associations the NSDAP did a great deal to eradicate its former revolutionary image among wide sections of the middle classes by showing that it was now a respectable and trustworthy segment of the conservative-nationalist camp. The party's relationship with big business also improved and consequently laid the foundations for the surge in interest from that quarter which blossomed after the Reichstag election in September 1930.

The NSDAP's orientation towards the right in 1928 was not an isolated phenomenon in Weimar politics; rather, it was but part of a more general development which witnessed a growing anti-democratic intransigence among the conventional middle-class parties like the DVP after Stresemann's death and the DNVP under Alfred Hugenberg's leadership, as well as of an increasing mood of intolerance towards the Republic among broad sections of the bourgeoisie and its representative organisations. Right-wing intellectual circles, youth groups and universities all evinced from the late 1920s a predisposition towards political radicalisation. This development was matched by a similar tendency on the far Left because the KPD adopted its ultra-leftist tactics which identified the SPD as 'social fascists' and hence as the foremost enemy of the working class. Across the entire political spectrum, therefore, there was a clear hardening of party attitudes after 1928. The initial hopes for harmony and stability invested in the 'Grand Coalition' government of Hermann Müller were shortly dashed.[16] Even before the onset of the depression, German politics was already in a severe crisis. Whatever confidence and security had been built up during the mid-1920s were cast aside: extremism, passion and militancy were to prove too much of a challenge for the deliberate, painstaking and compromising ways of democracy. As such, the NSDAP was poised to become one of the principal beneficiaries of these changing times and circumstances.

It was axiomatic that, if the NSDAP were to take advantage of the developing political situation, its organisation would have to be kept in good working order and, of course, this heavy responsibility fell on Strasser. Hitler, being uninterested in administrative detail and everyday problems connected with it, gave him a virtually free hand, and over the next few years Strasser began to display the organisational talent that made him an indispensable party leader as well as a powerful and esteemed figure in his own right. His efforts were largely responsible for giving the NSDAP by the early 1930s perhaps the most efficient and best equipped organisational structure in German politics, thus fully vindicating the view that his appointment to the Organisation Department in 1928 was one of the most significant Hitler made in the party before 1933.

Strasser made strenuous efforts to familiarise himself fully with the way the party operated throughout the country, and to allow the fullest concentration on his new tasks he renounced his position as Gauleiter of Lower Bavaria in March 1929.[17] His methods were those he had successfully employed in northern Germany in 1924–6, and then as Propaganda Leader, only on a larger scale. He travelled untiringly the length and breadth of the country visiting Gaue, conferring with leaders, discussing and solving problems, mediating in local disputes,[18] soothing tempers, conducting detailed correspondence about the most minute matters, and generally stamping his authority on the whole apparatus. He was most anxious to establish a solid and accepted chain of command in the party and did more than anyone else to institutionalise the *Führerprinzip*. He was quick to pounce on slackness or corruption, and a number of Gauleiters found themselves being reprimanded in forthright terms.[19] Strasser's constant watchwords were centralisation and rationalisation, with the goal of promoting efficiency, co-ordination and dedication. This was a continuing and interminable process because of the party's rapid expansion in size, and the extent to which centralisation could be achieved was necessarily limited. He was wary of overextending the party's organisational capacity to the point where his aims would be jeopardised: uncontrolled expansion could have been disastrous for the NSDAP as it was still striving to become a national political force.[20] Hence, while accepting the establishment of ancillary groups for lawyers, doctors and grammar-school boys, Strasser's rejection of a suggestion by Albert Krebs in 1928–9 for a National Socialist group within the right-wing white-collar workers' union, Deutschnationaler Handlungsgehilfen-Verband (DHV), was based on such thinking.[21] This was despite the fact that Strasser had a high regard for the DHV, remarking once that within it the party had potentially its 'best junior officer corps'.[22] In early 1930 he refused to permit the formation of an official National Socialist Economic Association and a group for civil servants for the same reasons of wanting to preserve organisational integrity.[23] He stated that if these two groups were granted recognition by the party 'other occupational groups would demand the same right and one day the great National Socialist movement would be split into special groups and class organisations'.[24]

Although he became immersed in the day-to-day supervision of the party, Strasser was alert to the longer-term implications of his work. He soon developed, in organisational terms, a vision of a future Germany in which the NSDAP would be in control of government. After all, he was drawing what seemed to be the correct conclusions from the party's development in 1928–30. Membership was on the increase, from just over 100,000 at the end of 1928 to approximately 300,000 by autumn 1930, and local branches had reached the 3,400 mark by late 1929.[25] That influx was sufficient by itself to test the effectiveness of Strasser's organisational arrangements, but when it was coupled with a steady rise in electoral success in 1929 and early 1930 the resulting strains required an almost constant adaptation. These were distinct signs that the party was coming in from the political wilderness and thus vindicating already the post-1928 reorientation. Strasser was resolved not only to keep his organisation abreast of this development but also to prepare it for future expansion and greater responsibility. In line with this thinking was his cautionary advice to NSDAP local councillors that they were primarily representatives of the party and its aims and that they had to conduct their business in close co-operation with local party branch leaders.[26] But of more importance was the reorganisation of the party apparatus which he introduced in late 1929.[27]

The division of the Reich Organisation Leadership into two separate but interdependent departments, the first (Angriff) under Strasser dealing with the everyday running of the party, and the second (Aufbau) under Colonel Konstantin Hierl concerned with long-range planning for a National Socialist government, bore ample testimony to Strasser's perspicacity as an organisational expert.[28] The arrangement was consistent with his insistence on making the best possible use of the party's resources, while simultaneously rationalising its operations. Strasser lost none of his authority as Organisation Leader as a result of this change. He retained overall control of the Reich Organisation Leadership and, besides, in Hierl he had found a congenial and loyal colleague. They had become acquainted in 1925 when Hierl was the south German leader of Ludendorff's Tannenberg *Bund* and Strasser was an interested bystander.[29] Their friendship developed even after Hierl parted company with Ludendorff in 1927, for Strasser was impressed by the Colonel's organisational ability, his reliability and his ideas – especially those relating to work service (*Arbeitsdienst*) and work-camps (*Arbeitslager*). Largely at Strasser's instigation, Hierl joined the NSDAP in April 1929, and his appointment as Organisation Leader II was initiated by Strasser himself.[30] He felt confident that by delegating the long-term planning aspect of the party's work to a trusted friend he could devote his energies to maintaining the soundness of its organisational basis as it fought for power.[31] Strasser's standpoint and his choice of Hierl were fully justified. The two men worked closely and fruitfully together until a further major reorganisation of the party in June 1932 abolished the division of the Reich Organisation Leadership. In another sense, Strasser's association with the solidly conservative-nationalist Hierl was symbolic of his own changing political and ideological perceptions after the 1928 Reichstag election, as we shall now see.

Crisis

As the principal architect of the urban strategy Strasser's immediate reaction to its failure was one of understandable disappointment. He himself must bear a large share of responsibility for the situation, for he consistently neglected to develop a coherent interpretation of 'socialism' which would have been attractive to the workers. Strasser's colleagues in the Kampfverlag were similarly ineffectual in clarifying their message, though they probably sought a lead from their mentor. The meretricious style of social revolutionary radicalism was there in abundance, but not the authentic socialist substance. The 'Nazi Left' had been shown to be a myth, a figment of the imagination. Thus, the resilience of the organised and politically schooled proletariat, built up by decades of class consciousness and an evolving sub-culture, was hardly tested by the anti-capitalist rhetoric of the NSDAP. None the less, the reaction of the Kampfverlag circle and fellow-travelling radicals to the election result was defiantly unrepentant. They argued that the poor outcome had been caused by the party's overemphasis on nationalism and anti-semitism and, conversely, its relative lack of attention towards 'socialism': what was needed, ran the argument, was more, not less, of the latter ingredient.[32] Otto Strasser was not unexpectedly vociferous in his criticism of the party. He accused Hitler of emulating the bourgeois methods of the traditional conservative parties and demanded a renewed commitment to the 'socialist' parts of the party's 1920 official programme. As far as he and his friends were concerned, the goal was still the same: the working class had to be converted to the national cause.[33]

One of the most interesting statements amidst the debate came from Dr Erich Rosikat, a former Deputy Gauleiter of Silesia and an expert on peasant-agrarian problems, who had left the party in 1927.[34] As a proponent of '*völkisch* socialism' Rosikat took up forcefully the argument that the appeal to the workers had collapsed in 1928 because Hitler had established a fascist control over the party which had mortally weakened 'socialist' elements. The workers had been right in dismissing the NSDAP's 'socialism' as a fraud. Like Otto Strasser, Rosikat concluded that what the party now needed was an intensification of the pro-worker approach on the basis of a more thoroughgoing socialist platform.[35]

Gregor Strasser shared Hitler's repudiation of such reasoning. He possessed enough political sagacity to realise that as a feasible initiative the 'socialist' period in the NSDAP was over, that the way forward was not on the unwilling backs of the working class.[36] He referred significantly to the 1928 election as signalling the end of an era, and also to the necessity of facing up to 'new tasks and situations' in the future.[37] Never a rigid doctrinaire, Strasser had the character to admit his failure and to adopt a new set of personal priorities in politics. Henceforth, he sought to distance himself from the dwindling band of party radicals who rejected Hitler's new course and pressed on with the same brand of anti-Marxist 'socialism'. Over the following few years Strasser's commitment to his former ideological views grew weaker and weaker as he accommodated himself to a more nationalist line of thought consistent with the NSDAP's post-1928 rightward swing. The evidence for this interpretation of the new phase in Strasser's career is clear and substantial.

His responsibilities as Organisation Leader and his deep involvement in the administration of the party gave Strasser a new appreciation and sense of realism about the practicalities of political struggle. The woolliness of his earlier speeches and their equally ill-considered promises for the future increasingly appeared to him to be a form of loose wishful thinking which did the party's cause and his own personal reputation no good. From the vantage-point of Organisation Leader Strasser was allowed a unique insight into the everyday problems of the party across Germany, real problems of finding suitable leaders, public speakers, sources of finance and so on, which had to be solved if National Socialism were to be in a position to take advantage of the weakening Weimar system. He must have been both impressed and encouraged by the apparent success of the new strategy as the NSDAP increased it share of the vote in a series of Landtag and local elections in 1929–30: these were positive signs that the party was at last making headway, and the development could not be endangered by a resurrection of his previous radicalism. In effect, his new position and authority in the party contributed to a distinct blunting of Strasser's 'socialism' during the late 1920s. Other influences reinforced this trend.

After 1928 he developed, without consciously submitting to the growing Führer cult, a fresh awareness of Hitler's qualities as party leader. It was almost as if the outcome of the Reichstag election had proved Hitler right, while impressing upon Strasser that he would inevitably have to pay the price for being wrong. At any rate, the publication by Strasser in late 1928 of a veritable panegyric of the Führer was a sure sign of the new wind that was blowing at this time across their relationship.[38] In the book Strasser was embarrassingly unstinting in his praise for Hitler and unreserved in his declarations of trust and loyalty in his leadership.[39] More important, to show that these were not empty, meaningless gestures, Strasser was quick to support key elements of the party's strategy after the election. He upheld Hitler's coolness towards the Tannenberg *Bund*,[40] and clearly intimated his unqualified backing for Hitler's policy of reconciliation *vis-à-vis* the right-wing paramilitary groups[41] – a remarkable turnabout for someone who earlier the same year had issued a hearty denunciation of the Stahlhelm as 'the greatest enemy of nationalism'.[42] The following year Strasser played a major role in enlisting the co-operation of the Werewolf paramilitary organisation in Saxony for the party's Landtag election campaign, and he tried very hard to incorporate that group *en bloc* into the NSDAP.[43] Even more arresting indications of his new perception of the traditional Right came also in 1929 when he was a conspicuous figure and Chief Liaison Officer in the party's alliance with the DNVP and other conservative-nationalist associations in the crusade against the Young Plan. Admittedly, Strasser defended his support for this temporary link-up on tactical grounds,[44] as did the party as a whole, and he continued at times to fulminate against capitalism and political reaction,[45] but he took a noticeably less critical view of the alliance than his brother and the Kampfverlag circle, and beat the nationalist drum as loudly as anyone. Strasser told the NSDAP rally in Nuremberg in August 1929: 'The plebiscite creates a clear line between two categories in Germany: on the one side, those who believe in a German future, the Germans; and, on the other, those who, for whatever reasons, are against, the non-Germans.'[46] Strasser's support for the alliance, even if not absolute, and his inclusion in the national executive committee which organised the campaign of action would have been inconceivable a year earlier because of his 'socialism'. That was the dramatic extent of the changes already occurring in his political and ideological outlook, a point further exemplified by the nature of his public statements in 1928–30.

In contrast to the mid-1920s, 'socialist' bombast appeared much less frequently in Strasser's speeches and writings during the last years of the decade. There were still examples of his anti-capitalist and anti-bourgeois radicalism to be found,[47] of course, though they were invariably more moderate in tone and far removed from the blood-and-thunder style of earlier years.[48] It was noteworthy that he took little active interest in a theme debated passionately by the party's radicals after 1928: the question of setting up a National Socialist trade union. Strasser's thoughts were more concerned with subjects of a nationalist nature and usually of particular interest to the middle classes to whom the party was now directing its major appeal. His defence of the army and militarism,[49] and his endorsement of war as a legitimate instrument for attaining objectives in international diplomacy, is a case in point.[50] Also highlighted in his statements were the iniquity of the Treaty of Versailles, Germany's weakness in foreign affairs and the allegedly ineffectual policies of Stresemann – all of which constituted the core of Hitler's pronouncements at that time – while the Weimar Republic's ineptitude rather than the pernicious capitalists attracted most of his attention.[51] Indeed, one of Strasser's most widely noted observations came in June 1929 when he announced a policy of catastrophe to be pursued by the party against the Republic:[52]

> Everything which is detrimental to the existing order of things has our support . . . because we want catastrophe . . . in a word: we are pursuing a policy of catastrophe because only catastrophe, that is, the collapse of the liberal system will clear the way for those new tasks which we National Socialists name . . . everything which hastens the beginning of catastrophe in the present system, thus, for example, every strike, every governmental crisis, every erosion of state power, every weakening of the System . . . is good, very good for us . . . and it will always and constantly be our endeavour to strengthen such difficulties . . . in order to expedite the death of this System.

His stress on the putative enemies of the national interest introduced a rather different sort of radicalism in his public statements, for his targets were now well-known politicians and personalities associated with the Republic, as well as Jews. Strasser's outbursts against them in word or in print pulled him into a long spate of court cases, including a well-publicised one in Oranienburg in August 1929, for libel, slander, defamation and so on. These resulted not only in fines, which he often found difficult to pay,[53] and a few brief periods in prison,[54] but also in the temporary lifting of his immunity as a Reichstag deputy in summer 1929[55] – only the second time this had happened in Germany since 1918.[56] The sobriquet Strasser acquired at this time, 'Terror of the Reichstag' ('Schrecken des Reichstages'),[57] was attributable to his notorious involvement in public controversy and in disputes with parliamentary authorities. He was the first exponent of that disruptive policy (*Tumultpolitik*) which later characterised the behaviour of the NSDAP faction in the Reichstag.

Strasser's heated nationalist and anti-Weimar stance was compatible with the NSDAP's conciliatory moves towards the conservative Right, but there are a few hints that as early as 1929 he believed that the logical extension of this policy was the option of coalition with appropriate partners drawn from the nationalist camp. He did not take up this coalition option in earnest until after the Reichstag election in September 1930, but before that date he was already showing some moderation in his attitude to the NSDAP's opponents. In early 1929 he gave the first clear intimation of what was in his mind when he delivered a remarkable speech entitled 'Der neue Ton' ('The New Tone').[58] Here Strasser urged the party to adopt a more cautious and co-operative attitude towards its opponents, particularly those on the Right. He encouraged his fellow-members not to rely totally on negative polemics but to be prepared to discuss their differences in a constructive, understanding manner; the party should try to convince others by persuasion and reasoned argument rather than by browbeating and violent agitation. In this way, Strasser believed, opponents would come to understand National Socialism a lot better. In short, there was now a case for the party to act more positively in its dealings with opponents: '. . . it has become a pressing necessity to discard more and more the polemical character of our views . . . so that the German people can understand not only the correctness of our arguments but also the necessity of our aims!' The reaction of political enemies was profoundly sceptical: Strasser's words were dismissed as simply another stage of the NSDAP's tactical battle.[59] But there is no denying from an objective standpoint that in this speech he was giving notice of an impending development of fundamental importance in his own outlook which unfolded more poignantly in the years ahead. It was no coincidence, however, that at the 1929 party rally he helped defeat an anti-coalition motion presented by Rudolf Rehm.[60]

It is hardly surprising in view of his changing views that Strasser's connections with the Kampfverlag should have become increasingly tenuous after 1928 as he fell out of sympathy with its radicalism. By the beginning of 1930, in fact, his leadership and control of the press complex were merely nominal.[61] He had taken less and less interest in its affairs, and his contacts with its personnel had become reserved and infrequent, particularly as he now spent a good deal of time when not engaged in parliamentary business in Munich, where he had his organisation office. The overwhelmingly conservative-nationalist ambience of the party headquarters effectively counteracted any influence the Kampfverlag might have exercised on him, for a larger proportion of his daily work was conducted with other members of Hitler's entourage. It is significant, moreover, that his personal relations with his brother deteriorated markedly in the late 1920s, so that it is very doubtful if Otto had as much to do with Gregor's speeches and articles as has been suggested. Not only Gregor's growing disillusionment with the Kampfverlag's 'socialist' outlook, but also a series of petty squabbles with Otto over the ownership of the press brought about a strained relationship between them.[62] It appeared to Gregor that the Kampfverlag was rapidly heading into a political vacuum from which there would be no escape. For all its polemical language, the press still failed to define properly its concept of 'socialism', as the publication of the decoratively titled '14 Theses of the German Revolution' in August 1929 and a book called *Der Nationalsozialismus – die Weltanschauung des 20. Jahrhunderts* clearly demonstrated.[63] Otto Strasser did not attempt a comprehensive statement of his beliefs, in the event, until he was out of the party altogether.[64] Gregor Strasser was drawing the correct conclusions from all this, as a number of episodes soon revealed.

He failed to give any support to Hellmuth von Mücke, the NSDAP luminary in Saxony and associate of the Kampfverlag, when he suggested an NSDAP–SPD–KPD alliance in Saxony following the Landtag election in spring 1929. When turned down by Hitler, Mücke left the party and vigorously campaigned against it.[65] Strasser's attitude in this case further stimulated murmurings among some of the NSDAP's more attentive members about his softening on 'socialism'. One such member complained to the branch leader of Wiesbaden that not only was the party betraying socialism because of its new strategy, but, even worse, Strasser had surrendered to the 'fascist' tactics of Hitler: 'Gregor Strasser was the brightest hope for a socialist NSDAP and now that has been most regretfully lost,' the correspondent lamented.[66] The use of the past tense in the statement is striking. If any additional proof were required of Strasser's new conception of politics, it was uncovered in his response to the crisis concerning his brother in 1930 when he was able to show that his 'socialism' no longer counted as one of his major concerns.

The fundamental cause of the conflict was the Kampfverlag circle's opposition to the right-wing course of the party since 1928 and the corresponding relegation of 'socialism' to a position of relatively minor importance. The occasion was provided by disagreement between Hitler and the Kampfverlag over the party's standpoint *vis-à-vis* the striking Saxon metalworkers in spring 1930, and then, shortly afterwards, towards the question of participation in a coalition government in Saxony following another Landtag election. The NSDAP had previously, in the case of Thuringia, supported the tactic of coalition with the bourgeois parties, thus allowing Frick to secure appointment as Interior and Education Minister in that state in January 1930.[67] He was the first National Socialist to take office in the Weimar government system, and in summer 1930 Gregor Strasser was being strongly tipped for the Interior Ministry in Saxony if negotiations proved successful.[68] He himself was rather looking forward to the experience,[69] but in the event the discussions fell through. By that time, the dispute involving Otto Strasser and his colleagues had reached the point of no return – a deadlock to which Otto's egotistical ambition and inability to respect any kind of authority for long also contributed. Consequently, on 4 July 1930 he led his small group of followers out of the party under the slogan 'The Socialists leave the NSDAP!' If he expected his elder brother to follow him into opposition against Hitler, as seems to have been the case,[70] he was rudely awakened.

Anyone aware of the changes in Gregor's ideological and political outlook could have easily anticipated his decision to remain in the party. Even as recently as April 1930 he had publicly renewed his pledge of loyalty to Hitler, at a birthday celebration for the party leader on 24 April when Strasser spoke on the theme 'Leader and Leadership',[71] a few days later at an official party meeting, also in Munich,[72] and then in Stuttgart when he remarked: 'Hitler is really the kind of man one dreams about. . . . I have increasing respect for him. . . . Hitler in fact is the man who could control the destiny of Germany.'[73] Similar effusive statements of devotion were expressed by him at a series of other party meetings throughout the spring and early summer of 1930. Any differences he had with Hitler he felt confident of ironing out. At this stage, Strasser believed that the Führer was a reasonable, decent leader who was open to discussion and argument and thus capable of changing or modifying his views to accord with the outlook of his Organisation Leader. Strasser sincerely thought that he could win Hitler over to some of his evolving ideas – for example, on the need for the party to co-operate with other groups, depending on circumstances, – and that the only chance of doing so was to work with him inside the NSDAP, not against him from outside it, as Otto advocated.[74]

At Hitler's famous interview with Otto in Berlin's Sanssouci Hotel in May 1930, during which the Führer dismissed socialism and affirmed his belief that the working classes needed only 'bread and circuses', Gregor, who was present at the second of the two meetings, gave no support to his brother.[75] Instead, he demonstrably issued yet another personal declaration of loyalty to Hitler and his policies,[76] and a few weeks later, on 30 June, resigned his leadership of the Kampfverlag in anticipation of a secession from the party by the radicals.[77] When the entire NSDAP Reichstag faction issued its own statement of loyalty, Gregor signed it and even attached another personal oath to his leader in which he expressed his 'sharpest condemnation and opposition' to Otto.[78] In subsequent private correspondence with friends and party colleagues Gregor gave full vent to his embarrassment and disappointment at his brother's action. Writing to Rudolf Jung, the Sudeten German National Socialist leader, he accused Otto of having been 'absolutely disloyal' to Hitler and himself, and criticised his departure from the party as 'pure madness'.[79] To Alois Bayer, branch leader of NSDAP Regensburg who, ironically, later joined the Black Front, Gregor complained that 'my brother has treated me in a humiliating fashion and the party in a treacherous way',[80] while in his letter to a Herr Erckmann he ridiculed Otto's 'subtle theoretical formulations' on socialism as 'a product of his rational, abstract deductions from his work at his desk, enlarged by an extraordinarily strong assessment of his own ability'.[81] To emphasise his complete dissociation from his brother and his continuing commitment to Hitler, Gregor took a considerable hand as Organisation Leader in purging the party of suspected radicals. For his part, Hitler contemptuously described the episode as a revolt of 'rootless literati' and 'chaotic salon-Bolsheviks',[82] and was unworried about repercussions.

By his prompt and unequivocal repudiation of the secessionists, Strasser was not only expressing his considered political judgement, but also hoping to dispel any suspicions on the part of Hitler as to his reliability. Strasser did not want the crisis to injure his standing in the party, for he now enjoyed substantial authority and prestige.[83] Given Hitler's intrinsically untrusting mentality, it was probably too much to expect that the episode had not adversely affected their relationship in some way, but there was certainly no overt sign in 1930 that this was the case. On the contrary, Hitler appears to have been immensely relieved that Strasser stayed with him.[84] Only when his own moment of crisis came did the behaviour of his impetuous brother contribute, albeit indirectly, to the souring climate which dominated their relations at the end of 1932.

The events of that summer inevitably produced a wave of rumour and speculation about what was going on in the NSDAP, and about the relationship between the two Strassers. Scholars have also indulged in this business, often to little effect. The argument, for example, that Gregor chose to remain in the party because he reckoned the odds of persuading Hitler to follow a 'socialist' strategy were higher there[85] rests on the erroneous assumption that in 1930 it was still his aim to continue promoting this line. It is also invalid to assert that he had serious misgivings about not joining Otto in opposition,[86] while his brother's cynical and unworthy remark that Gregor, being financially dependent on Hitler, could not afford the luxury of breaking away, cannot be seriously entertained.[87] Finally, there is not a shred of evidence to uphold the theory that the whole rumpus was a smokescreen to cover a carefully planned operation by the two brothers acting together to undermine Hitler and to prepare for the advent at some later date of an alternative Strasserite movement.[88] The very opposite is true. Gregor faithfully kept a pledge he made to Hitler at this time not to have any further personal or political contact with his brother. This was a private agreement which, therefore, could not prevent stories that the two brothers were in secret liaison cropping up quite frequently during the early 1930s, fuelled by Otto's ability to obtain and publish at regular intervals accurate information about top-level developments in the party.[89] Gregor had to deny indirect inquiries from party colleagues that he was in touch with his brother.[90] Replying to Gauleiter Loeper he curtly commented: 'My personal relationship to my brother is such that an inquiry about it is senseless.'[91] In fact, they did not meet again until the spring of 1933 when Gregor, having relinquished his responsibilities in the party, was no longer bound by his solemn promise to Hitler.[92]

Despite losing some of his financial independence and his own press outlet, Gregor Strasser judged correctly in 1930 that the 'socialist' option was nothing but a passport to political oblivion, as was underlined within a few months, and he was right to endorse fully the parliamentary road to power. His brother's Black Front organisation attracted only a few hundred dissident National Socialists – a clear indication of the Kampfverlag's lack of status in the party as a whole between 1928 and 1930 – and, although it maintained a loud presence in Weimar politics, it exercised little influence.[93] More important, Gregor's decision was vindicated in the autumn of that year when the NSDAP made its spectacular breakthrough on to the national political stage at the Reichstag election.

By the summer of 1930 any lingering doubts that there was no such entity as a 'Nazi Left' had to be brushed away.[94] Those NSDAP 'socialists' with any degree of sincere commitment to their beliefs generally joined either the Black Front or one of the other splinter nationalist groups of a social revolutionary type.[95] It may be true that a few 'socialists' decided not to secede because Gregor, still the recognised leader in many quarters of the putative 'Nazi Left', remained in the party.[96] They were gravely misguided, for they could not yet perceive how his 'socialism' had been fundamentally emasculated or even superseded by other less sectarian, nationalistic political and ideological considerations. But during the early 1930's Strasser's role and activity were to show irrefutably that his 'socialism' was a thing of the past, that he was not the leader of a 'Nazi Left', which did not exist anyway, and that his horizons were opening out on to a rather different landscape.

5 *Party Leader or Weimar Politician, 1930–2?*

The Party Man

As the 1930s got under way Germany quickly began to display symptoms of profound economic and political crisis. The Müller government had been experiencing increasing difficulty in reconciling the divergent interests of its coalition partners, especially where economic and financial matters were concerned, and in March 1930 finally disintegrated over the contending views of the SPD and DVP on the question of unemployment insurance policy. The depression was already accentuating the divide between capital and labour which successive governments in the early 1930s were to find beyond their powers of solution. The collapse of the last authentically democratic parliamentary administration of the Weimar Republic underlined fundamental weaknesses in the constitutional structure and party system which had been threatening disaster for some time. Democracy and its minority of supporters had been unable to make a sufficiently strong case among the electorate at large and had failed to construct a properly sound institutional infrastructure to underpin their beliefs. A heavy price was shortly to be paid for the omission. The path was now open for a vigorous right-wing authoritarian approach, riding roughshod over the dying corpse of the Republic. Dr Heinrich Brüning, the ascetic, scholarly Catholic and leader of the Centre Party's parliamentary faction, was appointed to lead a new-style presidential cabinet which, lacking a majority in the Reichstag for its legislative programme, was obliged from July 1930 to rely on the emergency powers granted President von Hindenburg under Article 48 of the constitution. In a real practical sense, therefore, the advent of the Brüning cabinet marked the end of parliamentary government in Germany and the beginning of that anti-democratic disposition which less than three years later culminated in Hitler's chancellorship.

When his programme of financial retrenchment failed to win the necessary backing in the Reichstag in July 1930, Brüning promptly dissolved the chamber and announced new elections. He was soon to regret his precipitate action. An opportunity was afforded the NSDAP to proclaim its message before a national electorate whose political sensibilities were more alert than at the last election in 1928. The party's reorientation towards the right had been attracting growing middle-class support, but now faced a crucial test. Strasser had intimated to an NSDAP meeting in Württemberg as early as that spring the possibility of a premature election, and he was keen to have his organisational machine ready to swing into action.[1] Having got rid of its 'revolutionary' elements that summer, the party approached the election campaign and its bourgeois targets with some confidence. Strasser cancelled his carefully laid plans for a party rally in Nuremberg in August[2] as all resources were mobilised to achieve a good result. Strasser himself was prominent as usual in the campaign, giving numerous public speeches at meetings all over Germany.[3]

The outcome of the election on 14 September sent shockwaves round Germany and the rest of Europe. Although the SPD remained the largest single party in parliament, the NSDAP astonished everyone, including its own leadership, by emerging as the second strongest, with 107 seats on the basis of some 6½ million votes. The post-1928 change of direction had been completely vindicated because the party's votes came in large measure from former lower-middle-class supporters of the DNVP,[4] while it also drew a sizeable proportion of new young voters as well as previous non-voters.[5] The balance of results denied Brüning the Reichstag majority he had been seeking: the NSDAP, DNVP and KPD were lined up against the government, though the SPD's decision to pursue a policy of toleration eased the situation a little. When negotiations involving Brüning and NSDAP leaders Hitler, Strasser and Frick on 6 October about a possible National Socialist participation in government proved abortive,[6] the Chancellor's minority administration had to function on Hindenburg's emergency decrees. Any doubts that non-parliamentary government was merely a temporary aberration vanished as Brüning stumbled unconvincingly through the next eighteen months or so, then to be replaced by even more authoritarian forces. The overall trend in German politics ran henceforth in favour of extremism, allowing the NSDAP above all to cast a progressively darker shadow over developments.

Between September 1930 and July 1932 the NSDAP succeeded in becoming the choice of approximately one German voter in three and thus the largest political movement in German history. The party's vote grew in almost the same proportion as the losses sustained by the conventional bourgeois parties and a handful of smaller middle-class interest-groups, like the Economic Party,[7] and was bolstered by impressive gains among previous non-voters and the newly enfranchised young. The general reasons for this unprecedented transformation in the party's status are clear enough. The essential background was created by rapidly deteriorating political, social and economic conditions, with its attendant confusion, psychological pressures and despair among the population, and by the inability of government to combat the depression and solve the constitutional crisis. Political opinions became radicalised to a dangerous degree, which suited the two major totalitarian parties. The NSDAP in particular demonstrated a striking aptitude for exploiting the crisis: an efficient organisational apparatus, a skilfully manipulative propagandistic and ideological appeal, and a pseudo-religiously projected charismatic Führer cult combined to produce a telling impact. By continuing to champion ultra-chauvinism, radical anti-semitism and anti-Marxism, and pan-German imperialism, by effectively infiltrating and capturing control of professional interest-groups and using its own ancillary organisations to win over particular sections of society, the NSDAP managed to entice and then integrate disparate elements of the broad German middle classes behind the swastika. As Strasser, among others, frequently asserted, the NSDAP was a spearhead of an anti-modernist, backward-inclined bourgeois mentality, directed against the entire liberal tradition inaugurated by the French Revolution. The bulk of the party's electorate and membership before 1933 came from the small-town or rural-based Protestant new and old *Mittelstand*, particularly the latter, located mainly in northern, central and eastern Germany; only by 1932 did it begin to attract an increasing percentage of the better-off, educated and propertied middle and upper classes. Catholics and the organised industrial proletariat were conspicuously under-represented – often for similar reasons. Both groups developed a deep ideological immunity to National Socialism through traditions of confessional or class consciousness, and through organised and mature societal sub-cultures ranged around the church on the one hand and the SPD, KPD and trade union movement on the other. The NSDAP, therefore, was never a popular movement (*Volksbewegung*) in the fullest sense: it was a predominantly youthful and reactionary *Sammlungsbewegung* of bourgeois integration.[8]

Strasser's career developed in two directions during the early 1930s: he had his onerous responsibilities as NSDAP Organisation Leader and Reichstag deputy on the one hand, and there was his expanding public role as a Weimar politican on the other, which was complex and provides the basis for a new interpretation of his activity and aims.

It was ironic that, coinciding with the arrival and further development of the party as a major parliamentary force after 1930, Strasser's career in the Reichstag should suffer a comparative decline. It was not that he lacked application: he was a conscientious deputy who was highly regarded by his constituents in Dresden-Bautzen (*Wahlkreis* 28) whom he represented between 1930–2.[9] He remained capable also of making thunderous and even dramatic statements to the chamber, beginning with his vehement anti-Republican and anti-Brüning speech in mid-October 1930 and ending with his more famous 'Work and Bread' address in May 1932.[10] But more and more Strasser stepped into the sidelines of party work there and tended to use the Reichstag more as a sounding-board for his ideas. His appointment in 1930 as the deputy leader of the NSDAP faction – his friend Wilhelm Frick was leader – carried little significance for him and, although he was chosen as his party's delegate to the important People's Representational Committee of the chamber[11] as well as to others, he did not take them too seriously. Indeed, he ran into trouble with the Reichstag authorities on that account. In one particular instance, in July 1932, Strasser was reprimanded by Reichstag President Paul Löbe for refusing to call a meeting of the People's Representational Committee, which at that time he was chairing, in defiance of the wishes of a majority on the Committee.[12] When he in turn described Löbe's intervention as 'unconstitutional', Strasser was replaced as committee chairman by SPD deputy Heilmann.[13] Other top NSDAP leaders besides Strasser increasingly imposed their personality on parliamentary proceedings, especially his bitter enemy, Goering, who was elected President of the Reichstag in August 1932.[14] Strasser's reduced presence in the chamber did not mean, however, that his standing and prestige among his colleagues of all parties decreased. But it might have been greater had he not been distracted by other interests outside parliament, and also by his unfortunate habit of becoming involved in well-publicised petty squabbles, such as that with SPD deputy Dr Helmut Klotz in May 1932, which landed him in court on an assault charge.[15] In a clumsy way, the latter episode epitomised Strasser's innate contempt for parliamentary democracy and its institutions, as he had made clear in his October speech:

> We have not come to this house to poison ourselves with parliamentarianism. . . . We have not come either to this house to make political deals with the aim of obtaining ministerial posts. . . . We National Socialists want not reaction but recovery. We want no planless revolution, but a new order in place of disintegration and anarchy. . . . If we think through the consequences of living on under the present state, common sense tells us we are being utopian. A state which can no longer put its own house in order . . . such a state, especially when embodied in its present men, can never under any circumstances begin and execute that sweeping essential task of renewal which is so necessary to the salvation of the German people.[16]

Of more immediate and pressing concern to Strasser was his role as Organisation Leader and solving the manifold problems which the party's rapid expansion produced after 1930.

Strasser's general state of health at this time imposed a certain handicap on his organisational role. It was not so much his old war wounds or his diabetes that was the problem as the severe and painful spinal injuries he sustained in a skiing accident at Oberstaufen in the Swabian Alps at the beginning of January 1931.[17] For a few weeks he lay in hospital with his life hanging precariously in the balance, and his protracted convalescence meant that he had to retreat from everyday matters until April. His first public appearance after the accident did not take place until the end of that month when, still heavily strapped up and on crutches, he briefly looked in on a party Gauleiter meeting in Munich.[18] Even so, he was not fit enough to resume full duties until June, and was unable to travel any distance until later in the summer.[19] For this reason, an earlier idea of his to make a fund-raising trip to the United States in July had to be abandoned, though he indicated to Reventlow that the 'tense political situation' in Germany also helped change his mind. Reventlow was delighted, remarking to him that 'in your capacity as the most valuable man in the movement' (sic!) his place was at home.[20] Once fully recovered, Strasser threw his considerable resources of concentrated effort yet again into this crucial sphere of the party's activity. Given the growth in membership and number of local branches, the demands on him were necessarily greater than ever before, and meant that the party's whole administrative structure and relationships within it had to be kept under careful and vigilant supervision if efficiency and effectiveness were to be maintained at the established high level.

Strasser was clear-sighted about the character of the party's organisational development and by 1930 had established a number of objectives which dominated his approach to the task: first, to further the process of centralisation, standardisation and rationalisation while avoiding a mechanical bureaucratisation of the party – a danger Strasser was acutely aware of[21] – and to extend the evolution of the party as a microcosm of German society, equipped in all essentials for constructive participation in the running of the state; secondly, to encourage further controlled horizontal expansion of the party in response to the surging interest in it by diverse groups of the general public; thirdly, to eliminate corruption and dubious elements in the party; and, fourthly, to afford the greatest possible protection to those whom he had personally entrusted with high office – with Hitler's ultimate approval, of course – and to stamp his own authority on the party bureaucracy, without in any way consciously creating an instrument of opposition against Hitler. Strasser's role and achievements as Organisation Leader can be assessed under these different categories of activity.

The basic framework of organisation which Strasser had set up in late 1929 held good until the major changes of June 1932.[22] Throughout the period his meticulous devotion to the smallest details of organisational practice[23] as well as his grander vision of the party's future in a National Socialist state combined happily to produce an administration which other parties could only envy. Strasser's unrivalled grasp of organisational dynamics gave the NSDAP the necessary direction, substance and thrust in everyday politics which underlay its spectacular electoral success and growing involvement in regional coalition government. He was also aware, however, that only so much planning of the organisation from the top was possible, that this had to be complemented and sustained by organic growth emanating from the daily struggles of the party at the grassroots.[24] His implementation of the inspectorate system in early autumn 1932 was partly designed to bridge the gap between the Reich Organisation Leadership and the party in the country, though its success was limited because of the opposition of some Gauleiters who resented being subordinated to the inspectorate.[25] None the less, by late 1932 few could honestly deny the overall positive impact of Strasser in this area.

The party's organisational base was widened during the early 1930s by the official establishment of not only the NS-Frauenschaft, as previously noted, but also a Foreign Office under Dr Hans Nieland,[26] a revamped youth section,[27] and the NS Factory Cell Organisation (NSBO). All of these innovations were directly inspired by Strasser's goal of pushing the NSDAP's influence into as many areas of societal life as possible without disturbing the general balance of the administrative apparatus. Some of these developments proved less successful than others. For example, the Foreign Office's operations were rather improvised and dilettante, and drew substantial criticism from other party leaders, notably Goebbels. It is worth stressing the fact that the creation of the NSBO in March 1931 was not attributable to any desire on Strasser's part to extend 'socialism' in the party: it followed on logically from his horizontal strategy, and was seen by him mainly as an anti-Marxist initiative in the factories.[28] Typical of the NSBO's blatantly demagogic mixture of chauvinism and crude anti-capitalism was its *Hib-Aktion* (*Hinein in die Betriebe*) in 1931. Moreover, the largely lower-middle-class, white-collar membership for most of the pre-1933 period underlines the absence of a genuinely proletarian-socialist impulse in the organisation. Only in the last few months of 1932 did the number of blue-collar workers among the 294,042 members significantly increase, coinciding with the party's transient display of radicalism when it co-operated with the communists in the Berlin transport workers' strike in November.[29]

On another level, Strasser continued his policy of the party providing aid to members who were sick, in prison or out of work, and at the same time urged a boycott of the facilities given by the state.[30] In March 1931 he set up an *NS-Notwehr* to take care of the increasing number of party members imprisoned for politically motivated offences and members who had been fined or faced legal expenses as a result of court action.[31] The NS Winter Aid scheme was also extended under Strasser's direction,[32] so that he contributed to the development of a specifically National Socialist sub-culture within Weimar society.

Strasser's determination to weed out unsavoury elements in the party had been shown in the early years when he came out as a strong critic of Esser and Streicher. During the early 1930s his clean-up campaign was continued on a larger scale not only in the NSDAP itself, but most notably also in the SA. He had initially welcomed the appointment of Ernst Röhm as SA commander in 1930 in successsion to Pfeffer.[33] But the evidence of deep unrest in the ranks as characterised by the Stennes revolt in spring

1931, which Strasser and his right-hand man Paul Schulz did much to clean up, and of Röhm's notorious homosexuality brought the two leaders into conflict. In the spring of 1931 Strasser attempted to have Röhm removed from his post,[34] and when in March 1932 the SPD published compromising letters written by the SA leader to a homosexual friend from the time of his sojourn in Bolivia the political embarrassment inflicted on the party caused Strasser to try again, with support from Schulz and Hierl.[35] Rumours of plots and counter-plots between the two sides created a tense atmosphere, with Röhm even (wrongly) accusing Schulz of organising an assassination attempt against him.[36] Because he had Hitler's confidence, at least for the time being, Röhm stayed in office, but Strasser's misgivings about him were not assuaged.

On another occasion, Strasser made clear his total opposition to appointing Feder to succeed Gauleiter Peter Gemeinder when his unexpected death in autumn 1931 caused a vacancy.[37] Feder had asked Hitler to give him a Gauleiter position as early as July 1930, suggesting that Hesse, Württemberg 'or at least' (sic!) Lower Franconia might be suitable.[38] The Führer was unimpressed by Feder's rather pathetic sentimental pleas then, and Strasser was similarly unmoved now. Besides, both men had fallen out a few weeks earlier after Feder's refusal to accept for publication in the *NS-Bibliotek* series a piece written by Jacob Sprenger.[39] Strasser wanted to promote talent not mediocrity, and Feder simply did not come into the reckoning. Strasser's opinion prevailed, and the episode clearly illustrates the extent of his authority in the organisational sphere. Undesirables could and did, frequently, join the party ranks, but at the leadership level they could sometimes be kept out, as in Feder's case, or harassed, as the Röhm affair revealed. Corruption of one type or another always existed in the NSDAP, and in general terms Strasser was fighting a losing battle, but at least he was prepared to combat it to the best of his ability.

The corollary of Strasser's anti-corruption campaign was his resolve to defend and protect those in high party office whom he considered were trustworthy and performing valuable service. He was as Organisation Leader an occasionally critical but always loyal taskmaster and no one was more energetic than he in supporting the *Führerprinzip*, the foundation of Gauleiter authority. Strasser assured Gauleiter Schlange of Brandenburg: 'I shall support every Gauleiter so long as I see that his positive work outweighs his negative effect and outlook',[40] and there were many instances in which he proved as good as his word. Erich Koch, Gauleiter of East Prussia, had every reason to be grateful, for Strasser intervened decisively in September 1930 to support him in a bitter power struggle against the Danzig SA,[41] and then again the following autumn when he was in further difficulties. Strasser assured him that the rumours suggesting he was to be replaced were unfounded and gave every encouragement for a continuation of his work.[42] In other situations, Strasser was not slow to issue reprimands if he thought they were needed, as Gauleiters Florian of Düsseldorf and Albrecht of Mecklenburg discovered.[43] Even Reichstag deputies could find themselves being called to account by him: Wilhelm Börger received a sharp rebuke not to make his public speeches too personal.[44] In these various ways Strasser built up a powerful bond of trust with a great majority of Gauleiters, but he did not consciously set out to use them or the party organisation as a bulwark against Hitler, who remained the focal point of the movement, its inspiration and integrative force. It would also be a mistake to assume that Strasser's standing within the organisational sphere was omnipotent: the wrangle over the future of Gau Rhineland in 1931 showed his incomplete control over the Gauleiters,[45] and his failure in November 1932 to have Gauleiter Maierhofer dismissed for inefficiency owing to opposition from Uschla underscored constraints on his position which were not readily appreciated by contemporaries.[46] His influence was very substantial by 1932 and he ran a well-oiled bureaucratic machine, but Strasser never enjoyed an authority independent of Hitler, as the events of the crisis in December 1932 demonstrated. Before that showdown, however, Strasser was given more and more latitude by Hitler in influencing the appointment of Gauleiters and, more strikingly, in selecting candidates for the party's Reichstag election lists.[47] Hitler was increasingly content merely to rubber-stamp Strasser's choice of personnel out of respect for his intimate knowledge of the everyday situation in the party,[48] thus causing the Organisation Leader's status to be compared with that of General Secretary Stalin's in the Soviet Communist Party under Lenin.[49] But there the analogy stopped, for Hitler had made it abundantly clear at the Bamberg Conference in 1926 that he would not entertain rivals for his role as leader in any circumstances.

His success as Organisation Leader gave Strasser vast executive power and also provided him with much of his prestige and popularity in the party as a whole.[50] He implicitly believed in strengthening the party organisation for the good of the movement and could not help but be aware that this enhanced his personal position at the same time. His efforts in this sphere, therefore, did not contradict the evolution of his thoughts about establishing links with political circles outside the NSDAP. Indeed, it is this aspect of his work in the early 1930s which holds the real key to Strasser's political role and personality.

New Friends and Perceptions[51]

The most salient and intriguing feature of Strasser's political interests during the early 1930s is its diversity and increasingly extra-National Socialist dimension. He constructed a veritable network of important contacts and relationships with a broad range of personalities and organisations drawn from different sections of the Weimar political spectrum. Strasser was thus able to develop, while retaining a position of authority within the party, a growing body of opinion and support sympathetic to his ideas outside the NSDAP. At the end of 1932, General von Schleicher, as Chancellor, regarded those allegedly sharing Strasser's views as a vital calculation in his bid to split the NSDAP and bring them into a new, broadly based government. The cultivation of these non-National Socialist links had simultaneously a profound effect on Strasser's political style and disposition. Having abandoned the role of polemical revolutionary by 1930 he developed into a much more moderate and cautious politician whose ultimate loyalties lay beyond Hitler and the NSDAP. An anxious concern for what the political and economic crises of the early 1930s meant for Germany rather than for the NSDAP in particular motivated him. Consequently, for many contemporary observers, Strasser emerged as the only statesmanlike personality in the National Socialist movement, especially after he had delivered his celebrated radio speech in June 1932, 'Die Staatsidee des Nationalsozialismus'.

The metamorphosis in Strasser's politics, already evident in the Otto Strasser affair as noted, was significantly encouraged by his association later the same year with Oberleutnant a.D. (retired) Paul Schulz who, from the moment of joining the NSDAP in October 1930 as Strasser's deputy and Chief of Staff in the Reich Organisation Leadership[52] until the crisis of December 1932, exercised a decisive and eventually tragic influence on his ideas and activities.[53] Born in Stettin in 1898 and described by a friend as 'a Prussian through and through'[54] Schulz was a highly decorated war veteran and Freikorps commander. With Major Ernst Buchrucker he was a principal organiser of the Black Reichswehr,[55] but gained notoriety as the mastermind of the *Feme* murders during the early and mid-1920s. 'Feme-Schulz', as he was popularly known, had been sentenced to death in 1927 for his involvement in the murders, and his sentence was commuted to life imprisonment only at the last minute in February 1928 by President von Hindenburg.[56] While in prison, Schulz established contact with various right-wing politicians, including several high-ranking National Socialists, one of whom was Strasser.[57] At the first meeting of the newly elected twelve-man NSDAP Reichstag faction in May 1928 it was agreed to make the campaign for Schulz's release a primary concern,[58] and in June of the following year an NSDAP motion for all convicted *Feme* prisoners to be granted amnesty was rejected by the Reichstag.[59] As a result of a political amnesty in October 1930, which owed more to the efforts of nationalist lawyer Professor Friedrich Grimm than to anyone else,[60] Schulz gained his freedom and immediately joined the NSDAP at Strasser's instigation.

Schulz was attracted to the NSDAP on account of its extreme nationalism, anti-Marxism and apparent preparedness to defend conservative middle-class values.[61] He had no sympathy for 'socialism' and set out with the backing of his numerous contacts with the army, civil service and industry to promote a more decidedly anti-socialist direction in the party,[62] and at the same time to eliminate or neutralise the influence of radical figures, among whom he counted Goebbels, Himmler and Röhm. Schulz quickly perceived his role as strengthening those within the NSDAP who favoured a moderate conservative-nationalist course, and after 1930 Strasser came very much into the reckoning as the most important anti-radical voice in the party, his demagogic style notwithstanding. Highly capable in his own right, as shown by his successful clean-up operation in the Berlin party organisation and effective rallying of SA morale in eastern Germany following the Stennes revolt in spring 1931,[63] and by his instrumental role as leader of the Arbeitsdienstpflicht department in the Reich Organisation Leadership II (October 1931–June 1932) in setting up the NSDAP's prototype labour service system,[64] Schulz very soon established a warm personal friendship and sound political understanding with Strasser. He became, in effect, his indispensable intermediary to influential people outside the NSDAP, including Schleicher and Brüning.[65] The nature and extent of Schulz's impact, facilitated as it was by inherent changes already taking place in the Organisation Leader's political conceptions, were poignantly revealed in early 1931 when what was tantamount to a volte-face in Strasser's relations with big business took place.

When the NSDAP began to attract the serious interest of some parts of industry after the September 1930 elections, it might have been expected that this growing but still limited *rapprochement* would have provoked vehement opposition from the 'socialist' Strasser. On the contrary, he now displayed a striking propensity to co-operation which completely belied his reputation for radicalism. For the post-1930 period this reputation rests for the most part on a serious misinterpretation of his major pronouncements and speeches, particularly his 'Work and Bread' Reichstag statement in which he dramatically referred to the 'anti-capitalist yearnings' of the majority of the German people.

Strasser's growing stature in sections of public opinion after 1930 was not based on impassioned appeals for socialism. His main concern in public pronouncements was to denounce the Republic, its parliamentary system and its representatives from an ultra-nationalistic stance. It was for this activity that he made his name. In a widely noted speech in Stuttgart in December 1931 he not only exhorted a warlike German foreign policy towards France, with whom he believed there could be no reconciliation, but also threatened: 'If we come to power there will no longer be any more Marxist or democratic republicans. Those who owe allegiance to any International, or who perhaps shout "Hail Moscow", will be strung up . . . and if we have to wade up to the knees in blood for Germany's sake, so be it.'[66] Reaction in France to the speech was unfavourable, to say the least, and one irate Frenchman was moved to inform Strasser that in the event of a Franco-German war 'you could be one of the first victims. . . . At this moment when good Frenchmen and good Germans are working for a *rapprochement* between the two nations, your words are either those of a madman or of a criminal.'[67] Strasser was not contrite. Throughout 1931 he had been making similarly outrageous statements, having a few weeks prior to the Stuttgart speech issued murder threats against the SPD leadership – 'When we are in charge we will throw Breitscheid and his comrades into the mud. A number will be hanged, the rest will be imprisoned'[68] – and against the Marxists: 'We know that the Marxists want to hang us, and because we know this we shall hang them first.'[69] At least this pugnacious style of oratory was warmly appreciated by the party faithful[70] but, more to the point, it further diminished Strasser's earlier association with 'socialism'.

If anything, Strasser's few pronouncements about the meaning of 'socialism', or indeed of National Socialism, were even more ill-defined and unsatisfactory than they had been before 1930. The same romantic verbosity was present, only on a larger scale. In June 1932, for example, he defined National Socialism in these bewildering terms:

> National Socialism is an acceptance of the principle of achievement, of manliness, of community ideas . . . of authority, discipline, duty, freedom, honour . . . the key word and programme, however, is Germany, only Germany, and nothing but Germany![71]

In even more obtuse vein, he declared in October 1932 that 'National Socialism is the opposite of what there is today'.[72] In brief, Strasser had by the early 1930s given up any pretensions to being a party ideologue he ever had, and now concentrated on practical policies, which were more appropriate to his talents.

The industrial sector in the Weimar era was far from homogeneous: there was a clear division of interests in important respects between the older heavy industries, which were oriented towards the domestic market and tended towards an ultra-conservative political outlook, and the more modern, less labour-intensive industries, including chemicals and electricals, which were more dependent on exports and identified with a more moderate conservative-nationalist inclination in politics. While figures like Dr Hjalmar Schacht, Fritz Thyssen and Dr Wilhelm Keppler epitomised heavy industry's links to the NSDAP, the chemical giant I. G. Farben emerged as an advocate of a broadly based bourgeois conservative-nationalist solution to the political crisis in 1932, and later was conspicuous in supporting Schleicher's administration.[73] I. G. Farben's liaison men to the NSDAP were Georg von Schnitzler, Dr Gattineau and Max Ilgner, and they channelled a good deal of their effort towards Strasser.[74]

In line with his changing ideological perspectives, Strasser was prepared after 1930 to initiate a serious dialogue with industrialists, especially with regard to the mining and chemical industries in the Ruhr where Schulz had important contacts. Sympathetic industrialists wanted to be certain that their donations to the NSDAP would be controlled by responsible hands, and August Heinrichsbauer, chief editor of the *Rhenisch-Westfälischer Wirtschaftsdienst* in Essen and principal link-man of Ruhr industry to the political right who was on friendly terms with Schulz,[75] states that some businessmen saw their 'responsible' man in Strasser.[76] As a result, he received from spring 1931 a monthly subvention of RM10,000 from the mining industry with the specific objective of strengthening himself and his 'moderate' associates in the party, and of helping them to advance co-operation with other acceptable right-wing circles.[77] Similarly, Strasser almost certainly received the bulk of the RM180,000 industrialist Otto Wolff paid to the NSDAP during 1932 on the advice of Schleicher,[78] and may also have received smaller amounts from Paul Silverberg and a few other magnates. Strasser's 'socialism' was obviously not taken too seriously by these hard-headed businessmen.

One fairly immediate outcome of Strasser's co-operation with industry was the appointment largely at his prompting of Walther Funk, editor of the conservative and pro-business *Berliner Börsenzeitung*, to the NSDAP Economic Department (Wirtschaftspolitische Abteilung) in late 1931 (see below).[79] Strasser wanted him to act as a counter-weight to the radical economic theories being propagated by the likes of Feder which alarmed many industrialists.[80] By this time, Strasser was informing friends of the need to defend the principles of private property.[81] Shortly, Funk, too, began to receive funds from the same industrial sources as Strasser who, by no fluke, incorporated some of the latter's ideas into his major economic policy statements in 1932. In the summer of that year Strasser appointed Funk his chief economic adviser, a position enjoyed until then by Otto Wagener, who had built up a close personal relationship with Strasser since 1930.[82] Wagener's ideas were essentially based on his somewhat idiosyncratic notions of a corporative *Volksgemeinschaft* and corresponded to Strasser's own evolving neo-conservative outlook in 1930–2. Moreover, Wagener's keen interest in bringing the trade unions into governmental responsibility coincided with Strasser's own progressively collaborationist attitude (see below). By mid-1932, however, Wagener's relationship with Strasser cooled markedly and his influence was severely curtailed following the reorganisation of the NSDAP's Economic Department in autumn 1932.[83]

During 1932, Strasser and moderate industrialists shared a deep unease at the growing totalitarian and inflexible character of Hitler's policies, and funds continued to be allotted with the aim of resisting this development. Strasser's prestige in Ruhr industrial circles resulted in he, not Hitler, being the original choice to address the Düsseldorf Industrieklub in

January 1932,[84] and throughout that year he enjoyed good relations, and sometimes financial backing, from leading industrialists, of whom the most noteworthy were Otto Wolff, Paul Silverberg, Hugo Stinnes, Dr Erich Lübbert, Paul Reusch, Albert Vögler and Fritz Springorum.[85] At the end of 1932 many of them actively favoured a Schleicher-Strasser alliance, in stark contrast to the endeavours of extreme right-wing circles of big business to bolster Hitler against what they persisted in wrongly regarding as a radical Strasser element in the party. The really crucial and important point, however, is that his numerous links with industry illustrate how far Strasser had travelled from his earlier 'socialist' and anti-capitalist days. He was in no way a willing tool of industry, but he was clearly enlarging his political and ideological perspectives into areas where before 1928 or even 1930 he would never have dreamed of treading. It is not without ironic significance that, following his rift with Hitler at the end of 1932, Strasser took up a top managerial position in a large industrial chemical combine in Berlin.[86]

Strasser's dealings with industry have to be understood as a part of the larger field of activity within which he promoted increasing opposition to Hitler's doctrinaire course in the party.[87] From at least the autumn of 1931 Strasser was privately encouraging the idea of a broad government front comprising moderate conservative and patriotic elements from the whole spectrum of politics, and including the trade unions, as the best way of tackling Germany's political and economic crisis. He informed his friend Erich Koch that he believed the best way forward for both the NSDAP and the country was to have a broad right-wing coalition administration,[88] and to Dr Schlange, the Gauleiter of Brandenburg, he stressed that the party's most promising way of attaining power was 'through the expedient of a so-called right-wing cabinet'.[89] By early 1932, Strasser was advocating the need for the NSDAP to co-operate more constructively with other parties in the Reichstag, adding that the party 'had to be prepared under reasonable circumstances to enter coalitions'.[90] The theme of coalition also constituted a major proportion of his public statements towards the end of the year and can be said to have provided the rationale behind his whole political activity. It involved him in negotiations, personally or through intermediaries, with a varied assortment of groups and personalities, often without Hitler's full knowledge.[91] Consequently, there arose in the party the first rumours of Strasser's 'betrayal', which his enemies such as Goebbels and Goering enthusiastically encouraged. Occupying a central position and providing in many respects the essential foundation for his open-ended strategy were neo-conservative interests – above all, the Tatkreis.

The neo-conservative élitist conceptions of Hans Zehrer's Tatkreis exerted a powerful influence on many middle-class intellectuals during the early 1930s; but, while it emerged on the one hand as a kind of high-powered debating club, it also became an energetic promoter of ostensibly unlikely political contacts, beginning shortly after the presidential elections in March–April 1932.[92] Strasser had argued strongly against Hitler taking part in the contest, favouring acceptance of Brüning's proposal for a constitutional amendment which would have permitted Hindenburg to remain in office for a further two years without having to go through an election.[93] Strasser had been overridden in the end by Goebbels, Röhm and Goering, but his judgement seemed to have been vindicated when Hitler lost the contest. Zehrer, concluding that the Führer's failure had dealt a shattering blow to his overall prospects of gaining power in the state,[94] began vigorously to propagate the idea of a 'revolution from above' which he hoped would clear the way for the emergence of a new ruling authoritarian élite representing a vague amalgam of conservative and social ideals. Zehrer's revolution was to be carried through by a so-called 'Third Front' headed by the army under Schleicher, with the co-operation of the trade unions and Strasser who, in a much noticed article in the journal *Die Tat* in April 1932,[95] fully endorsed the notion of a broad political front (*Querfront*), the vital objective of the Tatkreis. From this point on, Zehrer's connections with Strasser intensified.

Strasser's gravitation into the neo-conservative orbit reflected a point of view which was intrinsically concerned with the interests of the bourgeoisie, and flowed consistently from his earlier association with such ideas in the mid-1920s, and then, more decisively, from the changing nature of his outlook after 1930. His continuing friendship with personalities of a broadly neo-conservative orientation helped accelerate this development. Besides his friendship with Spengler, he was interested in reading the works of neo-conservative writers and maintained personal contact with several of them. August Winnig, whom Strasser had unsuccessfully tried to bring into the NSDAP in the mid-1920s, was another acquaintance. His concept during the late Weimar era of a corporativist Christian *Volksgemeinschaft* brought Winnig into closer personal and ideological *rapport* with Strasser.[96] Within the Tatkreis itself, the role of Dr Hellmuth Elbrechter in winning Strasser over to the idea of broad political collaboration was of crucial importance in 1932, complementing as it did the endeavours of Paul Schulz in the same direction. A former *Bezirksführer* of the party in the Ruhr during the mid-1920s and a member of the Arbeitsgemeinschaft Nord-West at that time, Elbrechter had been friendly with Strasser for years. Having later moved to Berlin, where he had a fashionable dental practice patronised by many leading political and social personalities, Elbrechter became a persuasive and eloquent advocate of Zehrer's ideas, as shown by his articles in *Die Tat* and later in the *Tägliche Rundschau*.[97] Building upon his friendly relations with Strasser, he quickly made a considerable impression on the NSDAP leader. Even Schulz saw him as a powerful influence on Strasser.[98] Furthermore, Elbrechter became next to Friedrich Wilhelm von Oertzen the Tatkreis's most useful contact man to the army, and it was he who brought Schleicher and Strasser together for the first time at Zehrer's Berlin home in summer 1932.[99] At the same time, he was an important promoter of a liaison between Strasser and Brüning, both of whom were his patients.[100]

Hitler's unsuccessful interview with Hindenburg on 13 August when he was denied the chancellorship gave a new impetus to Zehrer's efforts, and he immediately let it be known that his primary objective was to bring about not only a Schleicher–Strasser understanding, but also, more dramatically perhaps, a Strasser–trade union alignment.[101] Both courses of action had Schleicher's approval since the General was now convinced that Hitler's chances of the chancellorship were negligible, and that his best strategy was to win Strasser for his plans.[102] Strasser's interest in the trade union movement was already well known within the NSDAP, particularly with regard to the NSBO, and the Deutschnationaler Handlungsgehilfen-Verband (DHV), which had had informal ideological and personnel ties with the party since the 1920s.[103] Gauleiters Albert Krebs, Wilhelm Murr and Albert Forster, as well as Reinhold Muchow (NSBO) and Franz Stöhr (Reichstag deputy) were former DHV officials. The connection with the NSDAP had been broken off by 1931, however, because of the DHV's rejection of Hitler's radicalism, and its subsequent involvement with moderate conservative organisations like the Volkskonservative Vereinigung (VKV) and the Konservative Volkspartei (KVP).[104] After both of these political initiatives had ended in failure the DHV, in search of a new political home, was drawn heavily into the network of developments emanating from the Tatkreis, and Elbrechter, helped by Krebs and Stöhr, made it his business in early 1932 to bring Strasser into a serious dialogue with the organisation. These efforts were reciprocated most notably from the DHV side by Max Habermann, a leading member of its directorate and a former KVP member, who soon became a close associate not only of Strasser but also of Brüning.

Habermann firmly believed that Strasser represented the most constructive and amenable part of National Socialism, and it was his aim to contribute to the forging of a working relationship between Strasser and moderate, conservative Christian-social groups, among which he counted the DHV, the Christian trade unions and, most conspicuously, the Centre Party. The concept of a corporative order of society, partly inspired by vaguely *völkisch* influences, attracted him. He was prompted to make his first move in that direction by the formation of the Harzburg Front in autumn 1931 which Habermann feared would result in a permanent coalition between the NSDAP and the forces of political reaction.[105] On 25 October 1931 he published a leading article in the *Deutsche Handels-*

Wacht entitled 'Brüning and Hitler' in which he argued for the establishment of a government embracing all socially progressive forces from the NSDAP stretching to the Centre Party.[106] Strasser wrote a positive reply in an article of the same title in the *Völkischer Beobachter* on 31 October, suggesting that the NSDAP would negotiate even with the devil if it would help the German people: he was prepared to work with anyone who was interested in securing Germany's freedom. Habermann was delighted, and declared his readiness to open contacts, and a meeting was held in Munich on 6 November involving Habermann and Hans Bechly of the DHV, and Hitler, Hess and Strasser. The meeting amounted to little more than a tentative exchange of views, which was as far as Hitler wanted to take matters anyway, but Strasser was eager to have further exchanges, and in a subsequent article entitled 'Sozialkreation?' he underlined the NSDAP's attachment to socially progressive ideas.[107] The article curiously met with Hitler's warm approval – 'the best you have ever written', he told Strasser[108] – and Habermann was now encouraged to pursue his plans openly, at least until the presidential elections in spring 1932 when the DHV's support for Hindenburg inevitably led to official connections with the NSDAP being severed. Links were maintained on a private and personal level between Strasser and Habermann, however, especially after the Schleicher initiative got under way in the early autumn of 1932. Habermann played a useful supportive role in the discussions between the General and Strasser, who was now keen to include the DHV in any broadly based government that might evolve.

Against the background of Strasser's increasingly complex links with neo-conservative circles and Schleicher, one vital calculation emerged which was a major key to making the notion of a wide government front a feasible proposition: the blue-collar trade unions had to be involved. By the early summer of 1932 it had become a paramount aim of Strasser's to reach an understanding with the unions. His relationship with them formed in many respects the most significant and vexatious component of his whole coalition strategy of 1931–2, while providing the critical basis for his negotiations with Schleicher. The fact that at the same time Strasser had contacts with certain industrial parties, as we have noted, did not involve a contradiction in relation to his own terms of reference, for it was his concern to attract the support of all 'moderates', whatever their genesis and regardless of their narrow spheres of professional or occupational interest, so long as they were prepared to work for the national good. It is from this perspective that his relationship with the trade union movement in 1931–2 is to be seen.

In his 'Sozialreaktion?' article in November 1931, Strasser had taken care to indicate his interest in the possibility of NSDAP co-operation with the unions. Shortly afterwards, informal and secret talks took place on this subject between Strasser and representatives of the Christian trade union newspaper *Der Deutsche* which continued intermittently over the next six months. At the end of this period both sides had indicated willingness to establish a basis for co-operation.[109] It was also known that Theodor Leipart, President of the General German Trade Union Federation (ADGB), was alarmed by the danger posed by extremism on the far right and left to the Republic, and was prepared for this reason to talk to people like Strasser (whom he came personally to dislike),[110] who by early 1932 could be seen to be pursuing a co-operative course within the NSDAP. The critical breakthrough came with Strasser's 'Work and Bread' speech in May 1932 in which, much to Hitler's annoyance, he clearly held out the hand of reconciliation to the unions. They, in turn, responded in a positive fashion. The critical point of contact at this juncture was the agreement of both sides that urgent measures were necessary to deal with the twin problems of unemployment and work creation which by then had understandably become among the most important political issues in Germany. It would, therefore, be appropriate here to analyse Strasser's economic ideas not only as ends in themselves but also for the way in which they help further illuminate his political conceptions during this time.

Despite the establishment in December 1929 of a party commission to study economic ideas under Feder's chairmanship,[111] nothing concrete emerged, and Strasser's growing disquiet at the NSDAP's lack of a definite economic programme was heightened by the nationwide exposure of the party following the Reichstag election in September 1930. It was to remedy this failure, which was being underlined more and more as the depression deepened, that Strasser brought Otto Wagener into the newly established Wirtschaftspolitische Abteilung (WPA) in the Reich Organisation Leadership in January 1931. A number of leading party stalwarts, similarly aware in a period of catastrophic unemployment of the need to produce a clear economic statement for the electorate, warmly welcomed Strasser's initiative.[112] Hitler, who was basically uninterested in economic matters, adopted a more reserved attitude, though his influence is perceptible to some degree in a draft programme entitled 'Wirtschaftspolitische Grundanschauungen und Ziele der NSDAP' ('Basic Economic-Political Views and Aims of the NSDAP') for which the WPA was responsible in March 1931.[113] The general tenor of the Draft was anti-big business and, probably owing to pressure from that quarter, it remained unpublished.[114] As a stopgap measure, the party unofficially adopted the economic ideas put forward in his book by Hans Reupke,[115] a former member of the secretariat of the Reichsverband der deutschen Industrie, who had joined the NSDAP in June 1930 and then the WPA when it was created.[116] Not until Strasser's Reichstag speech in May 1932 did the party's view on the economy become known on a wide basis.

In this speech Strasser presented a comprehensive party statement on measures needed to combat unemployment and create work.[117] Criticising the government's deflationary economic policy and expressing the 'great anti-capitalist yearning' of the masses who, he said, were being betrayed by a false system, he intimated a number of areas where jobs could be made. The most controversial part of the speech dealt with the financing of his proposals which involved raising capital from a variety of sources, including unemployment benefit money, unemployment insurance contributions, higher taxes, subsidies from the beneficiaries of work creation projects (small farmers, for example), and finally what he called 'productive credit creation'. But, unfortunately, he failed to discuss the last proposal in any detail – a crucial omission which was not rectified until his speech to the NSBO in Berlin in October 1932.[118]

The important points about the speech are twofold: it was drawn up partly with an eye on the next Reichstag election, which was expected very soon, and, of course, it did take place at the end of July. More strikingly, there was nothing really original about Strasser's ideas, including the state-controlled credit scheme presented. Strasser was not an original thinker; he simply was not capable of formulating a programme of such detail and relative sophistication. In fact, his ideas represented a synthesis of work-creation theories already widely debated and published by a variety of unorthodox and conservative-minded reformist economists in the 1920s and early 1930s. As with the alternative Draft party programme in 1925–6, only to a greater extent in this 1932 programme, Strasser was merely the figurehead spokesman for the ideas of others.[119] Despite his failure to acknowledge his sources, and even his implication that the plan was of his own making,[120] it is fairly easy to identify in broad terms the genesis of his ideas.

By the early 1930s there was a network of basically neo-conservative, reformist economic circles expressing unconventional ideas about the depression-hit German economy. The influence of the 'free money' economist and former Finance Minister in the Munich Soviet Republic in 1919, Silvio Gesell, on Strasser's plan is unmistakable,[121] as is the work of the Jewish industrialist Robert Friedländer-Prechtl,[122] and the Lübeck factory-owner Dr Heinrich Dräger. One of the leading lights of the broad reformist school of thought, Dräger had set up with Wilhelm Grotkopp in November 1931 in Berlin the Studiengesellschaft für Geld- und Kreditwirtschaft, with which other prominent reformists, Professor Ernst Wagemann, head of the Statistisches Reichsamt and the Institut für Konjunkturforschung, and Wilhelm Lautenbach, a top-ranking civil servant in the Reich Economics Ministry, became closely associated. At the beginning of 1932 Wagemann published an economic plan which Strasser obviously used as a model for his own, and Dräger's publication of an economic treatise in March of the same year also became immediately known to Strasser, who used it extensively.[123] Indeed, into Dräger's circle, which discussed the problem of work creation intensively, came several of

Strasser's junior colleagues in the Reich Organisation Leadership, notably Fritz Reinhardt and Werner Daitz. The latter wrote in 1932 a booklet entitled *Die Grenzen der produktiven Kapitalbeschaffung*, which may also have been available to Strasser. Into the network of reformist economic circles were drawn Walther Funk, and the ADGB's work-creation experts, Wladimir Woytinski, and Fritz Tarnow, who produced with Fritz Baade in January 1932 their own 'WTB-Plan', which closely resembled Strasser's.[124] The so-called 'Gereke Circle', built around Dr Günther Gereke, Reichstag deputy of the Christliche Bauern- und Landvolkpartei and President of the Landgemeindetag, was another group in close contact with the reformers as well as Schleicher.[125] In 1932 the 'Gereke Circle' published its own work-creation plan which was similar in many respects to the Strasser plan.[126]

All these groups and individuals had established by early 1932 a bewildering maze of connections and cross-links, but they were united in their quest for a fresh approach to the serious problems of work creation and economic recovery. Strasser had, therefore, an abundance of ideas and published material to assimilate into his own NSDAP programme. He had personal contact with several of the reformers, notably Dräger,[127] though usually dealt with them through his middleman in this instance, Reinhold Cordemann. He had joined the NSDAP in 1930 at the express wish of his friend Schleicher and became the General's confidant and additional link-man to Strasser and the party. Cordemann, who in late 1931 headed the Berlin office of the WPA, also played a useful role in strengthening contacts between Strasser and both the Tatkreis and the 'Gereke Circle', of which he was a member.[128]

Finally, the ultimate drafting of his plan was undertaken not by Strasser himself, but by Dr Adrian von Renteln, Reichsführer of the HJ (1931–2) and Leader of the sub-department for Currency, Finance and Production in the Reich Organisation Leadership.[129] The claims to authorship that have been made by or on behalf of Feder, Funk,[130] Bernhard Köhler[131] and Elbrechter are spurious.[132] In July 1932 a shortened version of Strasser's plan was published for use by the party during the Reichstag election campaign,[133] and Strasser also broadcast a résumé on radio later the same month,[134] though, if Hanfstaengl is to be believed, he convinced the American journalist Knickerbocker in an interview in October that he hardly understood the plan![135] Strasser's concern, however, was more to do with the reaction of the trade unions.

With the exception of how his scheme should be financed, the unions gave their approval to it. From this time onwards, contact between Strasser and the unions increased significantly and soon involved a host of intermediaries, including Schulz, Elbrechter, Otto Wolff, Dr Erich Lübbert, Cordemann, Franz Josef Fürtwangler (ADGB), the Tatkreis, Dräger, Daitz and Gereke, whose common aim was to promote a Schleicher–

Strasser–trade union alliance on the principles of a moderate social conservatism.[136] Strasser's subsequent attitudes heavily underlined his desire to bring the unions into governmental partnership. In a speech in Dresden on 4 September he called for the formation of a 'Front of Work Creation, the great broad front of social work, the front of creative people',[137] while on 9 September he joined with Otto Wagener, Schleicher, some government and civil service leaders, and trade unionists Peter Grassmann and Wilhelm Eggert (a specialist in work creation) in detailed discussion about what form a broad coalition government should take.[138] Strasser and Wagener, well aware of the growing estrangement at this time between the ADGB and SPD over a number of issues, including work creation and contacts with Strasser and his intermediaries,[139] urged the union leaders to assume their share of responsibility in government. Strasser in particular stressed the urgent necessity of former political enemies coming into a working partnership. But nothing definite was agreed to by either side. The unions had to move cautiously for obvious political reasons, of course, but Strasser was encouraged to intensify his efforts to win them over. Heinrich Imbusch of the Catholic miners' union now strode forward as a firm supporter of a broad front which also included the Centre Party, and Leipart indicated the ADGB's willingness in a speech on 14 October in Bernau to do its duty for the Fatherland. In full reciprocation, Strasser made further conciliatory remarks about the unions, praising the sound common sense of their job-creation ideas, in his address to the NSBO in Berlin on 20 October. In addition, he extended his call for co-operation beyond the unions to groups as far to the right as the DNVP – an appeal not lost on moderate industrial circles.[140] 'Our line is clear,' said Strasser, 'national freedom and social justice. . . . Whoever wants to go along with us is welcome', and he pledged 'to work together with anyone who believes in Germany and who wants to save Germany'. Anyone who believed after this declaration that Strasser was not working directly against the uncompromising *Machtpolitik* of Hitler was guilty of a fundamental misreading of how Weimar politics was developing in late 1932. Strasser clearly wanted participation in government by conservative-minded but socially responsible elements drawn from a wide range of political organisations apart from the NSDAP.

Strasser's political development was naturally viewed with bitter distrust by Hitler and the extremists in the party, especially Goebbels.[141] The NSDAP could ill afford a public disagreement, however, because of the delicate political situation it was in during the summer of 1932. Although the party had made substantial gains at the July Reichstag elections, as Strasser had confidently predicted,[142] a parliamentary majority still eluded it. Despite being the strongest faction, the NSDAP appeared as far from power as ever, and there was a growing feeling that it had exhausted its electoral potential.[143] Hindenburg's rejection of Hitler for the chancellorship on 13 August brought a hint of desperation into the NSDAP ranks, and part of the immediate response, especially from those around Strasser who favoured a more flexible approach to the task of coming to power, was to press in August and September for an accommodation with the rightward-swinging Centre Party. These negotiations, which Strasser not unexpectedly pursued more enthusiastically than any other NSDAP leader, constituted a further dimension of his alignment strategy, and were helped also by his personal friendship with Brüning. The Chancellor later referred to 'my lasting secret association with the Strasser wing [sic] of the NSDAP'.[144]

The starting-point of this relationship was Habermann's article in October 1931 calling on the Brüning government and NSDAP to work together; and, helped considerably by Schulz, who 'had the closest connections' with the Chancellor,[145] the DHV leader arranged a meeting between Strasser and Brüning on 1 and 2 December 1931 at the Freiburg home of Centre Party Reichstag deputy, Dr Föhr – thus at approximately the same time, as we have seen, that Strasser was urging collaboration with non-NSDAP political interests. As this meeting, agreement was reached on the basis of a Centre–NSDAP government coalition, but Hitler vetoed the arrangement. Political and personal links were maintained, sometimes with elaborate secrecy, between Brüning and Strasser none the less and, significantly, Strasser was strongly advocating NSDAP toleration of the Brüning government as early as January 1932.[146] For his part, the Chancellor expressed firm reservations about imposing a ban on the SA in spring 1932 for fear that there would be unfavourable repercussions on Strasser's standing in the party at a time when both men were conducting secret talks on the question of forming a coalition in Prussia.[147] The relationship was further strengthened by Brüning's warm approval of Strasser's major Reichstag speech in May, particularly those sections dealing directly with work creation (excluding the proposals for financing it) and his conciliatory remarks about the Chancellor's leadership of government. Speaking in parliament the following day, Brüning stated his cabinet's 'extraordinary interest' in the NSDAP leader's speech,[148] but his abrupt dismissal from office at the end of that month thwarted this phase of his coalition discussions with Strasser until these were revived following the débâcle of 13 August. Still, once again, Strasser had impressed an important Weimar politician: Brüning thought he was 'a great mind' and 'a great organiser', and felt increasingly close to him personally and politically.[149]

With the trials and tribulations that lay in store for him in the near future, Strasser was going to need these qualities, and more, if he were to carry the political ideas and relationships he had been assiduously cultivating since 1931 to some sort of definite end. The last, agonising phase in the history of the Republic beckoned for all.

6 *The Resignation Crisis, 1932–3*

During the last six months of 1932 the NSDAP was faced by a major dilemma over political tactics which became crystallised in what is usually referred to as the uncompromising 'all or nothing' school of thought around Hitler, and the more flexible 'pro-coalition' collaborationist outlook associated with Strasser. Hitler demanded the chancellorship and nothing else, and spurned talk of coalition. Strasser's pliable pragmatism, which was tantamount to a revisionist strategy in the party, thus presented the NSDAP with two distinctive conceptions of political approach, and produced a period of violently fluctuating moods among its leaders and rank-and-file followers. The profound economic and political crisis in Germany, with unemployment at a peak and changes of government involving Brüning, Papen and Schleicher in fairly quick succession, injected its own destabilising currents into the NSDAP's problem. The party's uncertainty over tactics was thrown into the sharpest possible relief and took Hitler and Strasser on to a collision course.

Strasser was now being urged by some of his friends and supporters to assert his opinions more decisively within the party, even if it meant confrontation with Hitler. Reventlow, for instance, who had been stressing his agreement with Strasser for some time,[1] warned him that unless something were done soon Hitler's hard-line attitude would bring catastrophe for the party.[2] Others argued that Strasser's position had been considerably boosted by the important organisational changes in the party that summer, and that the time for bold action could not be more propitious. Accordingly, he arranged further meetings with Brüning during August at the last of which, on 30 August, other NSDAP leaders, but not Hitler, were present.[3] The Führer, it soon became apparent, was not seriously interested in these talks because he felt that any kind of coalition would bring unbearable constraints on his aims, and by early September the whole scheme had floundered on his intransigence.[4] But the estrangement between Hitler and Strasser continued more markedly than ever before as the latter grew in conviction that the party should play a constructive rather than a negatively oppositional role in Weimar politics without further delay. Hitler sought to counter Strasser's threat by making it appear that his activities and ideas were untypical of general sentiment in the movement. Hence, in September he dissolved the NSDAP's WPA which, of course, was Strasser's brainchild, replacing it with a Hauptabteilung IVA (Staatswirtschaft) under Feder and a Hauptabteilung IVB (Privatwirtschaft) under Funk, forbade further distribution of the emergency economic programme *Sofortprogramm* (partly in response to pressure from heavy industrial circles headed by Schacht), and in October refused to endorse Strasser's speech to the NSBO in Berlin.[5] The critical showdown between Hitler and Strasser, however, came immediately after the November Reichstag election.

The considerable setback sustained by the NSDAP at the election came as no surprise to Strasser, who had in early October predicted a loss of at least forty seats.[6] The result set the seal on his conviction that Hitler's inflexible tactics were leading the party into a political cul-de-sac from which extrication would be virtually impossible. While Hitler deluded himself into believing that Strasser's alleged 'socialist' views had alienated middle-class voters at the election,[7] Strasser was more disposed than ever to falling in with the coalition plans being promoted by Schleicher and other interested parties. He resolved to throw his considerable organisational and political ability behind the idea of a broadly based coalition front involving what support he could muster within the NSDAP. Strasser was simply not prepared to have all his sacrifices and work for National Socialism destroyed by what he regarded as Hitler's unjustifiable political recalcitrance; he sincerely believed that he had as much right as anyone to determine the party's future. His course of action between September and December 1932, including the act of resignation, followed on from the policies and attitudes which had determined his political behaviour from 1930 onwards. Strasser was offering, though not publicly, or even explicitly, an alternative strategy for the NSDAP, and also, in a qualified sense, a different brand of National Socialism from that presented by Hitler. Though accepting the main constituents of the Hitlerian *Weltanschauung*, including racism and anti-semitism, the Strasserite understanding – it was never a defined conception – of National Socialism was altogether less rigid and moderate. It was not without good reason, therefore, that the Gereke Circle could inform Colonel von Bredow, Chief of the *Ministeramt* at the Reichswehr Ministry, on 23 November (the same day as Hitler once again unsuccessfully demanded the chancellorship), that Strasser 'was ready to throw himself personally into the breach'. Cordemann also informed Schleicher at the same time that in the party 'an extraordinarily powerful element was on hand which would "regret" if the party once again lapsed into "fruitless opposition"', adding that 'a considerable part' of the NSDAP would be prepared to secede if this happened.[8] Subsequent political developments in November and December clearly seemed to vindicate Strasser's analysis of the NSDAP's situation, and to reassure him that, if he failed to bring Hitler round to his way of thinking, he would be confronted by two alternatives: to cease playing a major political role in the NSDAP, or to try to seize the initiative by leading a revolt of his friends and general sympathisers. His view that 'politics is now a rough business, especially in a strongly activist-oriented movement like ours', was never more true than at this juncture.[9]

The November election result had produced a drastic decline in morale and cohesion in the NSDAP, leading Strasser to believe in the possibility of the party disintegrating.[10] As Reich Organisation Leader he was in daily touch with grassroots opinion and could readily perceive the widespread disenchantment with Hitler's negative opposition to the government of Papen. In industrial areas, a worryingly high percentage of members were resigning and going over to the KPD, subscriptions to party newspapers were dropping off, secessions were occurring at a local level, serious rumblings of discontent were surfacing in the SA and, most of all, the financial position of the party was hopeless, with debts reputedly totalling 12 million Reichsmarks.[11] Uschla was progressively tightened in an attempt to stifle frustration and tension in the movement, but to little avail.[12] Political opponents freely predicted the rapid decline of National Socialism, especially in view of the shattering losses sustained by the party in a series of local elections during November in Saxony, Lübeck and Bremen-Land. Consequently, Strasser had every reason to believe that, if another general election were called in the immediate future, which was not unlikely, the party would be irrevocably destroyed.

Hitler still would not seriously listen to Strasser's arguments, brushing them aside as indicative of defeatism. The more empirical evidence that appeared to corroborate Strasser's views, the more violently stubborn Hitler became. The Führer was a politician of feeling and intuition. For him, politics was a game of chance and opportunity, not of rational development, and he was determined to adhere doggedly to his inflexibility because he was, in essence, as a man and political leader, incapable of taking any other course. From his standpoint, it could only be total victory or total defeat. He identified himself entirely with the NSDAP, indeed, as the NSDAP. Strasser's transcending loyalty in late 1932, on the other hand, was to Germany – not Hitler, and certainly not the party. This crucial difference in the outlook of the two men goes a long way to explaining why, given the political circumstances of the time, their head-on clash was unavoidable. In a major speech entitled 'Das Gebot der Stunde' on 14 November, Strasser reiterated his policy of doing everything possible 'to introduce the extraordinary strong, constructive , sacrificial and energetic powers of National Socialism into government'.[13] By now he was in deep despair over what he thought had become of the NSDAP under Hitler. Not only the sterile oppositional tactics, but also the increasing violence of the SA which Hitler encouraged (the Bloody Sunday incident in Altona and the notorious Potempa murder[14] were only two examples) repelled him,[15] as did the widely publicised exploits of the homosexual circle around Röhm. There was also Strasser's unease at Hitler's increasingly close association with reactionary elements of heavy industry and landed wealth. The Harzburg Front, which in 1931 Strasser had agreed to as a necessary tactical step,[16] now seemed in late 1932 to be being unofficially resurrected in a more intense form than before. He wanted nothing to do with 'Die Reaktion'. An important part of Strasser's anti-Hitler psychosis in November–December was, therefore, his genuine fear of the calamitous implications for the future of Germany which National Socialism under the Führer signified.

At this time in November, Strasser was convinced that his personal position directly *vis-à-vis* Hitler was becoming distinctly less favourable. Since the election he had been excluded more and more from Hitler's inner circle of advisers, while the influence of rivals and enemies such as Goebbels and Goering was increasing, and although he continued to issue public declarations of loyalty to the Führer right up to virtually the last minute[17] he often expressed quite the opposite in private. For instance, he remarked to party lawyer Hans Frank: 'It seems to me that Hitler is completely in the hands of his Himmler and Himmlers. . . . Goering is a brutal egotist, Goebbels is a lame devil . . . Röhm a filthy creature. That is the Führer's guard. It is terrible!'[18] Strasser continued to stress that the leader and idea of the National Socialist movement were separate and distinct, and, if necessary, the latter should have pre-eminence; Hitler, he believed, could never be unconditionally identified with National Socialism – a standpoint in stark contrast to the widely accepted wisdom in the party at this time. Strasser still regarded himself, as before, as Hitler's colleague, not as his subordinate follower. He joked about the 'Heil Hitler' greeting, even though he had used it as early as the mid-1920s, and often used instead the Bavarian 'Grüss Gott' or, in letters, 'With German Greetings'. Addressing Hitler himself, he did not use the salutation 'Mein Führer', preferring 'Mein Chef'.[19] Hence, Strasser did not openly or publicly acknowledge the Führer myth, and his natural independence of mind had always set him apart from the vast majority of sycophantic party leaders. When he had misgivings about Hitler's policies he was not afraid of voicing them, though by being a continuous thorn in Hitler's side their personal relations always had an essential element of unease and tension which was exacerbated by the Führer's apparent jealousy of the highy capable Bavarian.[20] Moments of closeness or of friendship were rare and transient. Strasser's anxious comforting of Hitler following the suicide of his niece, Geli Raubal, in the autumn of 1931, when he allegedly talked the Führer out of his own suicidal tendencies, is one noteworthy example.[21] By December 1932, Strasser's alienation from Hitler had reached a critical juncture, and was accentuated during the first week of that month when Goering replaced him as Hitler's nominee for the post of Prussian Minister of the Interior. By then, Strasser had no further illusions concerning his standing with the Führer: the gap was 'unbridgeable', as Schulz affirmed.[22]

Not to be dismissed in this situation is the question of Strasser's personal ambition, an indefinable, elusive but real factor which perhaps has been too readily discounted by most historians of this period. Only a handful of contemporary observers like Goebbels, Ludecke, Heiden and Hans Frank noted the ambitious streak in Strasser's political make-up.[23] Frank goes so far as to state even that Strasser was ultimately a 'victim of his own ambition'.[24] He had been to the fore so frequently and over so many important issues during his party career, and taken so many fundamental initiatives, that it seems only reasonable to pinpoint ambition – an ambition which stretched to the highest level of the party – as a primary motive force behind his rise to the political limelight. Coupled with his vital disagreements with Hitler by the end of 1932, it would appear more likely than not that he would not have been averse to taking over the leadership of the NSDAP.[25] After all, Strasser had always been a natural leader of men, as shown by his distinguished army war record, his prominence in the Bavarian paramilitary and SA organisations just after 1918, his outstanding contribution to the reconstruction of the NSDAP in northern Germany during the mid-1920s, and his subsequent role as party propagandist, organiser and public figure. In any case, by December 1932, convinced as he was of the NSDAP's imminent decline, Strasser had every reason to take seriously Schleicher's offer of governmental participation. The prospect of cabinet office appealed not only to his political wisdom, but also to his personal ambition.

The key to the success of Schleicher's plans to construct an administration based on the army but composed of disparate socially progressive, nationalist elements was Strasser and what the General estimated to be his sizeable body of support in the NSDAP. In this way, Schleicher hoped for the kind of popular backing for his administration which his predecessor, Papen, so obviously lacked. Strasser had informed Schleicher of his willingness to act independently if Hitler continued to refuse co-operation,[26] while the General was heartened by the encouragement given to his plan by various leaders of the modern and moderate industrial sector.[27] At a top-level party meeting in Weimar on 30 November, Hitler did reaffirm his negative attitude to the idea of a Schleicher cabinet. On hearing of this, Schleicher dispatched Oberstleutant Eugen Ott, chief of the Wehrmachtsabteilung, to Hitler on 1 December ostensibly to make the Führer a last offer of cabinet posts,[28] but in fact to use his intransigence, which Schleicher could have no reason to believe would be modified at this late hour, as final and conclusive evidence to show Strasser and Hindenburg that the only way out of the political crisis was to entrust him with the chancellorship from where he could implement his strategy of splitting the NSDAP. This hypothesis is supported by the fact that, on the very same day as Ott's visit to Hitler, Schleicher was doing his utmost to convince Hindenburg and Papen of the soundness of the plan, and he finally succeeded. Hindenburg agreed to appoint the General Chancellor largely on the understanding that Strasser could be brought into the cabinet as a stabilising factor.[29] Despite warnings from Papen, Schacht and Otto Braun that his quest to split the NSDAP had no hope of success,[30] Schleicher was undeterred and went ahead with a formal offer to Strasser of the Vice-Chancellorship and the Minister-Presidency of Prussia at a secret meeting in Berlin on 3 December. At the same time, Schleicher opened negotiations with the trade unions.[31]

The offer to Strasser was not conditional in any formal sense, but Schleicher made it in the expectation that Strasser, in agreeing to it, would bring into coalition with him a putative element of support from the NSDAP. Strasser, for his part, did not give Schleicher a specific undertaking that if the offer of the Vice-Chancellorship were made he would automatically accept it, nor did he make specific promises of carrying elements in the party with him. Schleicher's offer was made on the basis of his appraisal of Strasser and the state of the NSDAP at this time. Strasser's eagerness to accept the offer could only have been sharpened when on the following day in local elections (*Gemeindewahlen*) in Thuringia, long regarded as a leading bastion of the NSDAP, the party suffered a shattering reverse: losses of up to 40 per cent on the recent Reichstag election in November were recorded.[32] Strasser's pessimism about the party's future once again appeared fully justified. More important, at this point in time, Schleicher's aims coincided exactly with Strasser's. There can be no question of the General deviously using Strasser for his own selfish ends, or using him specifically as an indirect threat to bring Hitler round to a compromise position.[33] Besides, Schleicher's high regard, even 'infatuation', for Strasser personally[34] would have ruled out any impropriety of this sort, while suggestions that these sentiments were not exactly reciprocated by the National Socialist leader lack evidence:[35] Strasser was aware, of course, of the General's reputation for intrigue and clever manipulation, but there is no record of him expressing his personal hostility towards him. Both men realised that the decisive moment for governmental co-operation had arrived. For Strasser, this was the logical climax to all he had been striving for during the last few years. He and Schleicher knew what they wanted from each other, both were aware what was involved, and both were equally sensitive to the consequences of failure.[36]

At a specially convened meeting of party leaders in Berlin's Kaiserhof Hotel on 5 December, Hitler, who probably did not yet know of Schleicher's specific offer to Strasser, brusquely reaffirmed his all-or-nothing policy, and forbade Strasser from having any further talks with the General on behalf of the party.[37] The meeting, therefore, brought into lucid perspective the nature of the Hitler–Strasser conflict and the contrasting alternatives over policy and tactics being pursued by both. Strasser now had to decide what his future course of action should be. There were a number of possibilities. First, he could accept Hitler's policy, sever his connections with Schleicher and other pro-coalitionist elements outside the NSDAP, and repudiate, therefore, all that he had been working for since 1930–1; secondly, he could publicly demonstrate his disapproval of Hitler by leading a party revolt against him; lastly, he could adhere to his principles but avoid an open confrontation with Hitler by withdrawing from the NSDAP hierarchy and from active politics altogether.

The first course was inconceivable. Strasser had gone too far in his opposition to attempt a humiliating volte-face against his better judgement. The second alternative was much more problematical. Strasser would have to decide whether he had the necessary support in the movement to lead a successful palace revolution. This raises once again the important debate about whether a Strasserite faction, 'Strasser Wing' or 'Nazi Left', under his leadership, actually existed. It has been argued already (see Chapter 3) that there was no such entity in the NSDAP in an organisational, ideological or personal sense. An analysis of the situation in the NSDAP in late 1932 provides final and conclusive evidence in support of this argument.

There can be little doubt that by 1932 Strasser had made such a favourable impression on a relatively significant number of party members that they might be legitimately regarded as Strasser sympathisers. But, apart from his closest advisers such as Schulz, Alexander Glaser, his Chief of Staff in the Reich Organisation Leadership, and Rudolf Vollmuth, his private secretary/adjutant, and close relative, Strasser faced the difficulty of not knowing with absolute certainty how far this sympathy stretched, whether in fact his supporters would be prepared actively to follow him against Hitler – if that had been his intention. In December 1932, he was still widely but unjustifiably regarded as the leader of what was in effect a non-existent entity, a 'socialist' wing of the NSDAP.[38] His anti-capitalist radicalism of the mid-1920s had given him a reputation as a revolutionary which was hard to lose in the popular mind. Prominent among his supporters in this category were the former DVFP members Franz Stöhr, Wilhelm Kube[39] and Count Ernst zu Reventlow, who had joined the NSDAP in 1927 because they were attracted by the Strasserite concept of a nationalist, anti-capitalist socialism. At least until 1933 there existed a basic distrust, even antipathy, between these three and Hitler. In particular, Reventlow with his radically inclined *Reichswart* publication was a constant source of irritation to the Führer as he sought capitalist and right-wing backing in the early 1930s. Reventlow's closeness to Strasser on a personal as well as a political level must also have been known to Hitler.[40]

The general public and the vast majority of party members could hardly have perceived how fundamentally Strasser's ideological attitudes had been changing as he became less and less a 'socialist' and more of what might be termed a populist social or neo-conservative. For this reason, his stock in 1932 remained high among both working-class NSDAP voters and sections of the movement which had a pro-worker orientation, such as the HJ and NSBO. Leading NSBO officials Reinhold Muchow, Walter Schuhmann, Ludwig Brückner and Otto Krüger were Strasser men,[41] and by December 1932 their support could have been especially valuable in view of the organisation's increase in size, and its strengthened position following Strasser's organisational reforms in mid-1932. The NSBO was allowed direct access to party funds for the first time, and its enhanced status was reflected in the presence of eleven of its officials in the 230-strong NSDAP Reichstag faction after the election in July 1932.[42] Robert Ley later exaggerated when he said that Strasser had specifically built up the NSBO as his personal army (*Hausmacht*),[43] but it is clear in which direction its propensities lay.

Although the 'proletarian' SA was showing unmistakable signs of deep unrest at the end of 1932, including outright revolt in some areas like Franconia,[44] the main cause was traditional SA–NSDAP antagonism and local personal rivalries. Hence, any serious SA support for Strasser is extremely doubtful, even in industrial areas such as the Ruhr. The SA, after all, had always been loath to become involved in intra-party disputes and, furthermore, there was the long-standing personal and political enmity between Strasser and Röhm. In December 1932, therefore, the SA remained a factor of support for Hitler.

Within the NSDAP itself, pockets of reliable and potential support for Strasser are ascertainable. His position as Reich Organisation Leader enabled him, as we have seen, to build up an organisation and leadership much to his own liking. He took on personnel whom he believed could be trusted by him, and there is no doubt that a large number of leaders in the organisational structure identified with him, including Konstantin Hierl. Strasser also enjoyed wide support and recognition among many Gauleiters, though not in an anti-Hitler sense, especially those with whom he had been associated in northern Germany. These included Karl Kaufmann, Josef Wagner (Westphalia South), Alfred Meyer (Westphalia North), Bernhard Rust, Carl Röver, Erich Koch, Hinrich Lohse, Helmut Brückner (Silesia), Wilhelm Murr (Württemberg), Josef Bürckel (Rheinpfalz), Rudolf Jordan (Halle-Merseburg), Friedrich Hildebrandt, and Dr Ernst Schlange (Brandenburg).[45] Martin Mutschmann and Josef Terboven were less definitely sympathetic. Strasser was on friendly (and often 'Du') terms with all of them. Indeed, it is suggested that he arranged a meeting of Gauleiters in Stuttgart in autumn 1932 at which Bürckel and other south German leaders declared their support for his pro-coalition outlook.[46] Also to be regarded as pro-Strasser are most of the inspectorate appointed by him in mid-1932, including Heinrich Haake, Jacob Sprenger and Wilhelm Loeper.

Strasser's principal source of support lay, however, in the NSDAP Reichstag faction where as many as one-third of the deputies may have inclined to his position.[47] At a specially convened meeting on 7 December, these sixty to seventy deputies affirmed their belief in the pro-coalition strategy and agreed to follow Strasser if he gave the appropriate signal. Otto Strasser writes: 'They waited on Gregor. He had their trust. He had never let them down. They had decided to follow him. . . .'[48] This may also have applied to a small number of top party leaders who had individually declared backing for Strasser's strategy: Wilhelm Frick, his close friend, who had been involved in some of Strasser's discussions with non-NSDAP groups during 1931–2, and who was held in considerable esteem by the Reich Organisation Leader;[49] Feder, who endorsed Strasser's view of the party's gloomy future,[50] as did, incidentally, Alfred Rosenberg and Walter Buch.[51]

It would be quite wrong to argue that the aforementioned sources constituted a Strasserite faction within the National Socialist movement. These elements were too varied and diverse, ranging from self-styled, insincere 'socialists' to woolly-minded and uninfluential intellectuals and theorists, to be described as anything other than a loose assortment of support. Furthermore, they can in no way be seen as constituting a 'Nazi Left'. This term is even more devoid of meaning than it already was in the mid-1920s. There was neither a 'Nazi Left' nor a 'Strasser Wing' to come to his aid at this moment of fundamental personal and political crisis because they simply did not exist. Consequently, although the extremely serious and unstable position of the NSDAP in December 1932 is not to be underestimated, the unorganised and incohesive nature of Strasser's friends and sympathisers removed any real possibility of his being able to split the party had he so desired. The threat to the NSDAP at this time was admittedly more concrete and of a different kind than during previous party crises in 1924, 1926 or 1930 in view of Strasser's reasoned and honest rejection of Hitler's course, but it could be ultimately and safely contained within the structure of a totalitarian party based on the *Führerprinzip* and Hitler's charismatic leadership.[52] On the mundane practical level, the Führer's control of the party's press and propaganda network, the SA and SS, and the solid backing of leading and powerful figures such as Goebbels, Goering and Röhm militated decisively against a successful Strasser initiative. In addition, it was virtually impossible, given the party's overall organisational character, that an anti-Hitler opposition group could emerge with any prospects of success. Despite the complex administrative apparatus constructed by Strasser and his good relations with most Gauleiters, this élite leadership corps of the party owed their allegiance in the final analysis to Hitler, the Führer. They were aware of their status as his personal envoys in the field of political conflict; they derived their power, status, prestige and legitimacy from him, not from Strasser who, as Reich Organisation Leader, had the authority of a managing director but not of a chairman. The intimate personal relationship between the

Gauleiters and Hitler transcended all other considerations, bureaucratic and political, and functioned independently on the basis of the Führer's supreme authority. In December 1932, this unique bond broke the Gauleiters' ties to Strasser – only Brückner and Schlange came out openly and briefly in support of their friend[53] – and without this indispensable source of support Strasser was doomed to isolation and failure. It still remained to be seen, however, what steps of protest, if any, Strasser would take following his final and acrimonious confrontation with Hitler in the Kaiserhof Hotel on 7 December. The Führer, who by this time had become fully informed of Strasser's dealings with Schleicher, was totally unshaken in his determination to pursue his quest for the chancellorship and nothing less. A break of some kind between the two men became inevitable. But would Strasser on a point of principle take his long-standing opposition to Hitler to its logical conclusion by calling on his alleged supporters to leave the NSDAP with him, or would he merely accept Schleicher's offer of cabinet responsibility as an individual and leave the party without rallying support? In the event, this unpredictable and often imponderable man did neither.

Based on a careful scrutiny of what lay before him, especially the power situation in the party, Strasser was constrained to sacrifice principle and defy the logic of the political crisis his activities since 1930–1 had produced. Apparently disappointed by the failure of his friends in the party openly to give him the support they had pledged in private,[54] he made no declaration to them, no dramatic statement to the press, and no appeal to Hitler. Emphasising the personal nature of his decision, which was undoubtedly influenced by advice from Schulz,[55] Strasser simply withdrew to his room at the Hotel Exzelsior in Berlin where he wrote out his celebrated letter of resignation which was delivered to Hitler at his hotel at noon on 8 December. A few hours previously, Strasser had called a brief meeting of the Landesinspekteure in his Reichstag office at which he intimated his decision.[56] He referred to there being 'reasons of an objective as well as a personnel and personal nature' behind his resignation, and went on to outline the substance of his disagreement with Hitler's policies and methods which, he believed, were confusing and incapable of bringing the party to power on the Führer's terms. Further, Strasser affirmed that Hitler's inflexibility was imposing a severe strain on the unity of the movement whose ideals and aims no longer complemented one another. Finally, he criticised the 'game of intrigue' in Hitler's entourage which Strasser complained had excluded him from important decision-making. In his letter of resignation Strasser expanded slightly on this account; the content was as follows:

Gregor Strasser 8 December 1932

Mr Adolf Hitler,
at present, Berlin,
Hotel Kaiserhof.

Dear Mr Hitler,

I would ask you to take note with this letter that I am resigning my post as Reich Organisation Leader of the party, and at the same time declaring my resignation of my parliamentary seat.

As for the reasons behind this step, which I have taken only after painful inner conflict, I would state as follows:

In a period when, as a result of the political situation and the internal condition of the movement, the strictest authoritative leadership is absolutely necessary, it is impossible for me to carry out organisational work when the Leader of the movement curtails and sabotages regulations, which he himself has signed, concerning those few Gauleiters who are empowered to undertake additional supervisory responsibilities. These belong in any event to the worst administrators of their office and are thereby provoked into outright mutiny. According to my soldiery way of thinking, that is insupportable. Since you have also described the reorganisation of the party carried out by me as mistaken in principle to third parties, my organisational task has become unresolvable, and I am drawing the necessary conclusions from this. I believe that no other party spokesman, except yourself, has pressed the ideological questions of National Socialism into the foreground as strongly as I have.

I have, therefore, the right to say that, in my opinion, the NSDAP is not only an ideological movement which is developing into a religion, but also a fighting movement which must strive for power in the state at every opportunity so as to enable the state to fulfil its National Socialist tasks and to realise German Socialism in all its facets.

The brutal confrontation with Marxism cannot and may not – left to individuals – stand at the centre of the internal political task; rather, I see the great problem of this age as the creation of a great broad front of constructive people and their integration into the new-styled state. The single-minded hope that chaos will produce the party's hour of destiny is, I believe, erroneous, dangerous, and not in the interests of Germany as a whole. In all of these matters your fundamental view is different from mine, and hence my political task as a member of parliament and party spokesman is rendered untenable, and I am drawing the necessary conclusions from this.

During my life I have been nothing other than a National Socialist and will never be anything else; I am therefore returning – without regard for my personal interests and without personal rancour – to the ranks of ordinary party members, thus making room for the advisers who are at present in a position of being able to counsel you.

This decision of mine is the most difficult of my life; after all, I have loyally served the movement and yourself for eleven years.

As I refuse under all circumstances to become the focal point of oppositional endeavours or conflicts of such kind, I am leaving Berlin today and subsequently leaving Germany for a considerable period.

In accordance with my duty, I nominate the former Head of Organisation Department II, Colonel Hierl, as my successor.

Only you are receiving a copy of this letter. I shall make no statement of any kind to the press about my decision.

With German Greeting,
Constantly yours truly,
GREGOR STRASSER[57]

Despite Goebbels urging Hitler immediately to expel Strasser from the party,[58] he did remain an ordinary member, though contrary to what he says in this letter he did not resign his seat in parliament, retaining it until the end of the session in March 1933. Otherwise, the letter tells only in part, and then only in bare outline, why Strasser was resigning his party posts – or some of them, to be more correct. The letter does not even refer to his extensive dealings with other non-NSDAP political groups and personalities during the previous few years which lay at the very heart of his disillusionment with Hitler, nor does he indicate the somewhat different, more moderate interpretation of National Socialism he had come to accept. Instead, Strasser intimates in a tone of hurt pride and self-justification his inability to accept an intolerable degree of organisational disarray in movement, particularly regarding the attitude of certain Gauleiters – probably including those not involved in the inspectorate system – and Hitler himself to his organisational methods. More important, Strasser criticises the party's selfish approach to winning power which he saw as not being in the wider interests of Germany, and reiterates *en passant* his basic theme of bringing together creative and constructive people regardless of political affiliation in one broad front for the purpose of governing the country. Strasser ought to have been much more explicit and forthcoming about this most fundamental of elements in his political vision at this time. His protestation that he remained and would always remain a National Socialist is ironic, to say the least, in view of his emphatic if undeclared repudiation of Hitlerian National Socialism, and of his own intrinsic development in the early 1930s into a rather moderate, neo-conservative nationalist. Finally, Strasser's allusion to Hitler's present advisers – meaning Goebbels, Goering, Röhm and a few others – underlined his feeling of alienation in the top ranks of the party. Hurt and resentful, he no longer felt wanted. As he later confided to Otto Strasser when they met in May 1933: 'I did not feel like being placed after Goering, Goebbels, Röhm. . . . I regard that as a snub, as a humilitation of my person, which I have not deserved. . . . I have reached the end of my strength and nerves. . . .[59]

Strasser added a little to his explanation in later correspondence with his friend and former NSDAP member, Dr Curt Horn of Hamburg:

> You can be assured that I took my decision only after mature deliberation and with a full sense of responsibility once my endeavours to carry through a necessary cleaning-up operation [*Reinigungsaktion*] in the party had failed, and also once my view that we had to participate in the running of the state and to appeal to the people with deeds rather than words had been utterly rejected. . . . I want to promote the coming together of all constructive-minded people, no matter where they come from, on the basis of new ideas in government, the economy and the cultural sphere. I am convinced that the time of agitation and of parties is fast disappearing and that the immediate future calls for men who are prepared to come into government with courage and a sense of responsibility who, amidst the most difficult personal and objective circumstances, attempt finally to draw conclusions from an understanding of the present time, and achieve results.[60]

Strasser obviously had himself and his broadly based contacts outside the NSDAP in mind here, and his steadfastness in the belief that his decision was correct is rather striking. In objective political terms, there is an argument that his decision was a serious mistake, and Otto Strasser later claimed that this brother realised this.[61] But this cannot be squared with the fact that, from his personal ideological and political viewpoint, Strasser had taken the only logical road open to him in withdrawing from the party leadership. He had been increasingly superseded in terms of contact and influence with Hitler by his enemies and, more tellingly, he had lost confidence and conviction in what the NSDAP, and hence National Socialism, had become under the Führer. Strasser's protest may have been politically wrong, but it was, from a personal standpoint, sincere, honest and imperative.

Notably absent from Strasser's thoughts on the crisis was any emphasis on 'socialism' as a motive for his decision, and the evidence presented in this study is consistent with that. In December 1932 the crisis was not about a last stand by the party's 'socialists' against Hitler's pro-big business and ultra-nationalist course, and it is misleading to interpret it as representing the final victory of the reactionary, anti-semitic Munich wing over the 'socialist' wing.[62] 'Socialism' had been politically extinguished in the NSDAP for some time, and in December 1932 there was no 'Nazi Left' or 'left wing' for Strasser, or anyone else, to lead.

Having dropped his bombshell on 8 December, Strasser left Berlin by train early the next morning for Munich, picked up a few odds and ends at his home, and drove off in his recently purchased new car via Austria to Italy on holiday, thus effectively withdrawing from active politics for good, and leaving behind a party which frantically tried to grasp the implications of his action.

Strasser's insistence on making his resignation a purely personal matter followed on, as we have observed, from his realistic and correct assessment of the power situation in the NSDAP. But it is also possible to supplement this fundamental explanation with reference to a number of political and character weaknesses which at the critical moment let him down. It was not that he was too idealistic, honest or good-natured.[63] He did possess these positive qualities, but alongside them were others which exercised a tempering effect: determination, independence of mind, energy and even ruthlessness. Nor is it fair or accurate to suggest that Strasser was a poor politician who weighed matters up badly in 1932, because his whole comprehension of Weimar politics during the early 1930s, was founded on a considerable and sensitive skill. But unlike Hitler, essentially a politician of instinct and intuition who was not afraid of a gamble,[64] Strasser was to his own detriment too much of a *Realpolitiker* who could not move very far in any direction without having thought and calculated hard about what might lie ahead. He certainly lacked that essential Machiavellian touch for success. In addition, and very necessary to an understanding of Strasser the man in December 1932, was his complex and tortuous relationship with Hitler. Despite the profound differences in their respective political outlooks by 1932, Strasser continued to harbour underneath his scathing criticisms of the Führer a perverse personal loyalty of sorts to him which may only be intrinsically explicable by what Karl Paetel has called Strasser's 'curious Paladin complex' (*merkwürdige Paladin-Komplex*).[65] It froze Strasser against his better judgement into submission at Bamberg in 1926, and contributed psychologically to his inability to make the final challenge at the end of 1932. The irony is that, while Strasser had consistently and overtly repudiated the quasi-mystical Führer cult, it would appear that for all his bluff assertiveness the innately sensitive Strasser really was captivated by Hitler's charismatic personality. He thus became the most unsuspecting victim of the Führer myth.

Strasser's resignation caused a major sensation in Weimar politics. The reaction of astonishment, even incredulity, inside and outside the party bore ample testimony to his substantial reputation.[66] But the manner in which he made his resignation meant that the crisis in the NSDAP effectively ended almost as soon as it had come publicly to a head. An editorial by Hans Zehrer in the *Tägliche Rundschau* on 11 December tried to project Strasser as about to take over the party, but this clearly was a rather clumsy piece of speculative optimism.[67] Elbrechter praised him as the representative of 'true' National Socialism, which Strasser undoubtedly felt was a fair point.[68] Quite unappreciated by him, however, were Otto Strasser's efforts to exploit the affair for his own political ends. For his pains, he received a sharply worded letter from his elder brother, the first contact they had had since the summer of 1930:

> I am unable to meet you. You are highly dangerous for your friends and a tonic for your enemies. Your articles have harmed me enormously and served Hitler exceptionally well. Everything which I had brought up for discussion in respectable circles fell largely on deaf ears because you, quite wrongly, gave the impression that I was in touch undercover with you. Moreover, your figures were mostly incorrect and of the thirty-five Reichstag deputies hardly one stood up. So leave off. The methods of the Black Front will never weaken the NSDAP, even if a couple of Berlin intellectuals tell you the opposite . . . keep me out of your game in 1933![69]

Strasser's complaints against his brother were seen as totally justified by some of his friends who were also irritated by Otto's negative antics.[70]

More relevant was that, with Strasser out of the way and his varied collection of followers without guidance, it was relatively easy for Hitler to regain his composure and turn the situation to his advantage by rallying support from all sections of the movement. He did so with that consummate blend of pathos, cunning and unscrupulousness which had served him so admirably in previous times of party crisis. He started off on the very day the crisis broke by holding an emotional meeting of the party's organisational inspectorate at which he expressed his incomprehension of Strasser's action and demanded loyalty. Still shaken, Hitler allowed Rust to make immediate contact with Strasser in the hope of promoting a reconciliation, but the former Reich Organisation Leader brushed off the approach.[71] Hitler's response was to buy time by having an announcement made in the party press that with his permission Strasser had gone on three weeks' holiday leave. At meetings over the following few weeks every branch of the movement declared their unconditional loyalty to the Führer, while Hitler himself conferred with party officials all over Germany, especially in areas such as the Ruhr and Saxony where Strasser's influence was thought to have been strong.[72] Many of Strasser's 'friends' were among those joining the ritual, including Frick, Stöhr, Hierl and Koch.[73]

Hitler moved quickly on to the offensive. Strasser's major creation, the organisational apparatus, was roundly condemned for being mechanical and ineffective, and then thoroughly remodelled under new management.[74] Suspected Strasserites were purged, including personnel throughout the party and its ancillary groups who were regarded as being 'left wing'. Close colleagues such as Schulz, Glaser,[75] Vollmuth and Albert Dressler (Strasser's second adjutant) were the first to go, while the position of those seen as his protégés, such as Elsbeth Zander of the NSF and Dr Hans Nieland of the Foreign Department, came under intense pressure which frequently resulted in eventual dismissal.[76] At the same time, the numbers seceding or resigning from the movement in sympathy with Strasser were insignificant.[77] Consequently, his enemies had no difficulty in denouncing him as a traitor to the party, a stigma which made Strasser a compromising figure in NSDAP circles until his murder.[78] Associates like August Heinrichsbauer and close personal friends like the Württemberg industrialist and NSDAP Reichstag deputy, Fritz Kiehn, went to frantic lengths with party leaders to denounce Strasser and stress their loyalty to Hitler, particularly after the party had come to power.[79] More immediately, Strasser became the popular scapegoat for all the failures sustained by the party during the preceding months.[80]

The net result of the assault on Strasser's organisational structure in the aftermath of the resignation crisis was severely to reduce its coherence and all-round effectiveness. The NSDAP soon discovered when in power that it did not have the organisational structure needed to administer the Third Reich. In the absence of a strong controlling force at the centre, the party organisation had little co-ordination, and began in fact to disintegrate into its component parts. Accordingly, not only did the NSDAP conspicuously fail to dominate the state machinery after 1933, but it was also forced to rely on the traditional bureaucracy and the social élite associated with it for support. It was a heavy price to pay for demolishing Strasser's impressive achievements in this sphere.

With Strasser's departure from the scene, Schleicher's political plans, which were pinned on the aim of splitting the NSDAP, were dealt a mortal blow, though the General still optimistically believed the former NSDAP leader could be brought into government. It was rumoured that he was to promote a Strasser-led 'Soziale Nationalpartei' to contest the next general election,[81] but this was an altogether fanciful notion. The tide of political events was turning inexorably against Schleicher, though it took him a few more weeks to realise it. In the meantime, the return of Strasser from holiday just before Christmas provided a brief sparkle of hope for Schleicher, and contributed to a renewed burst of political momentum which carried on until the middle of January 1933. Strasser, described at this point by his brother as 'a broken man',[82] did not show a great deal of appetite for politics. It is true that during the Christmas vacation he spent a few days at the home of his friend Fritz Kiehn in Trossingen where he conferred with a number of political colleagues, including Brüning[83] and Gauleiter Murr,[84] but he failed to take any clear decision about his future. Strasser was a man caught in a desolate political wilderness, rejected by his party and not yet welcomed by the government. Rumours of meetings, or intended meetings, of reconciliation with Hitler proliferated but were groundless.[85] Meetings that did take place in early January between an increasingly tired and disillusioned Strasser and Schleicher, and Strasser and Hindenburg, had an air of unreality about them, and must be seen as little more than a tawdry epilogue to the December crisis in the NSDAP. The expanding vacuum in government which ensued allowed Papen gradually to seize the political initiative from Schleicher and bring Hitler into contact with heavy industrial, banking and large agrarian interests.[86] They had watched the Schleicher–Strasser dialogue with deep alarm and were encouraged by the latter's resignation from the NSDAP that 'socialism' had been finally eliminated from Hitler's movement, and thus began to feel more confident about lending support to the conservative-nationalist–NSDAP coalition government now being mooted and worked for by Papen and other similar interested figures.

Events by mid-January 1933 were moving decisively against Schleicher and in favour of those around Papen. The failure of the trade unions positively to commit themselves to the General's overtures – largely through their innate distrust of him and also through pressure from the SPD – was another damaging blow. Even worse was the resurgence of the NSDAP that was evident at the Lippe-Detmold state election on 15 January 1933.[87] The final nails in Schleicher's attempt to keep Hitler from power were ready to be driven in. At a meeting of Gauleiters in Weimar on 16 January, Hitler demonstrated that his old confidence had returned and that, although the party still had serious problems,[88] the recent crisis had been fully overcome.[89] Strasser had been permanently expunged from the NSDAP's consciousness; he was, in the chilling words of Goebbels, a politically 'dead man': 'now he sinks into the void whence he came'.[90] Paradoxically, at a cabinet meeting, also on 16 January, Schleicher unconsciously captured the futility of his government's situation when he persisted in formulating further grandiose plans for a broadly based front, comprising this time Strasser, Hugenberg, Seldte (Stahlhelm) and Stegerwald (Christian trade unions).[91] The General's days as Chancellor could only be numbered by the time the Reichstag reassembled on 24 January.

The Strasser crisis, paradoxically, made an indispensable contribution to solving the NSDAP's strategic *impasse*; for, having set out to prevent Hitler and his brand of National Socialism from coming to power, Strasser's actions and involvement with Schleicher merely succeeded in accelerating the chain of events that led to the Führer's appointment as Chancellor. Despite showing signs in late 1932 of having passed its peak, the NSDAP was finally brought into government thanks to the last-minute interventionist power politics of industrial and agrarian élitist groups representing conservative-nationalist, propertied and Protestant Germany. By the turn of the year 1933, reactionary forces controlling heavy industry and organisations like the Reichslandbund in agriculture saw their man in Hitler. A series of events had brought about this new situation. The Führer's decision in autumn 1932 to back the economic interests of big business as opposed to those of the lower *Mittelstand*, which was clearly underlined by the nature of the changes he made in the Party's Economic Department, was a useful starting-point. The removal of the 'radical' Strasser, the alarmingly 'social' policies of Chancellor Schleicher, the attractions of the NSDAP's economic concept of *Grossraumwirtschaft* (offering the prospect of huge profits from rearmament and new markets in south-east Europe), and Hitler's overall expansionist aims in foreign policy finally convinced the conservative élites of the path they needed to take in order to defend their entrenched privileges and power. With Papen their figurehead and Hindenburg their stooge, they solved Hitler's problem of how to rescue his party from the political dead-end into which his intransigence had led it.[92] In January 1933, therefore, the Führer consummated that alliance with the traditional Right which he had inaugurated immediately following the 1928 Reichstag election. The vagaries of the Weimar power game rather than Hitler's teleological comprehension of political strategy brought the NSDAP into office: its negative, anti-modernist, counter-revolutionary ideology, which was supported by broad sections of the middle and upper classes with the aim of destroying the liberal-democratic value-system of the Weimar Republic and replacing it with the restorative ethos of the past, at last found the political leverage it lacked by itself. Hitler and the NSDAP had won; Strasser and, more importantly, Germany had decisively lost.[93] Brüning put it rather well some time later when he wrote to Strasser's brother, Father Bernhard: 'your brother Gregor was the only person in the NSDAP who could have one day eliminated Hitler and similar figures, and prepared a party evolution which might have spared Germany and Europe all that has occurred'.[94]

Epilogue

There is no record of Gregor Strasser's reaction to Hitler's appointment as Chancellor, but he must have viewed this momentous event with mixed feelings. Had he remained in the party in December 1932, despite everything, he would certainly have been appointed to a leading position in the state, probably to the Interior Ministry or the Economics Ministry. The influence and prestige he would have enjoyed would have been particularly gratifying to an ambitious man who had laboured so much and for so long to bring the NSDAP into office. Yet Strasser was more aware than most in Germany in 1933 of the depressingly low calibre of the country's new leadership, their inordinate capacity for intrigue and criminality, and of this he had had his fill. He wanted no further active part in the party, though was not averse to encouraging others to stand up against the corrupting influence of the new masters. For instance, Walter Rohland, technical director of the Deutsche Edelstahlwerke at Krefeld, later explained how he came to join the NSDAP in 1933:[1]

> In March of that year, Gregor Strasser appealed to me, saying: 'This is the beginning of the end. Criminals have gained control of the Party. You and people like you will be responsible for the inevitable débâcle if you don't join up now and help remove the praetorians. Are we to stand idly by and let ourselves be overrun? It is your duty to join.'

Having made his official exit from politics on renouncing his Reichstag seat in March 1933, Strasser's most pressing problem was finding employment and means of support for his family. His friend Hans Reupke had been on the lookout for a suitable position or small chemist's business in Berlin for him, but without success.[2] Strasser, therefore, spent a few anxious months before being informed in May that Hitler had given his consent to his taking up a well-paid directorship in the large chemical–pharmaceutical company of Schering-Kahlbaum, a Berlin subsidiary of I. G. Farben.[3] The chemical giant's support for the Schleicher–Strasser political initiative, Strasser's own personal contacts with its leading officials, and his professional background as a chemist obviously explain this development. Before being finally allowed to proceed with his new career, however, Strasser had to give a written undertaking to both his employers and the NSDAP that he would remain outside politics altogether.[4] The many rumours and the press speculation about his future, which had been circulating freely since the beginning of the year, were thus brought to an end, at least for the time being. He had been variously named as the next 'Reichskommissar' for Work,[5] 'General Secretary' of the party, Reich Minister of Labour, the head of a new fascist-style 'Corporations Ministry' with responsibility for trade unions, employment and employers, or simply as Reich Minister for Trade Union Affairs.[6]

Strasser retained his party membership, but now concentrated on making a success of his business opportunities from his new apartment home in Berlin to which he had moved from Munich at Easter.[7] By all accounts he did precisely that. In July 1933, he was appointed to the three-man management committee of the National Association of the German Pharmacology Industry and shortly thereafter became its chairman.[8] Towards the end of the year he gave up this post when appointed to the prestigious position of chairman of the so-called Reichsfachschaft of the Pharmaceutical Industry.[9] He found his work interesting and stimulating, and very demanding on his time.[10] Strasser was seen frequently at business conferences and seminars, at which he occassionally came across friends from his political past.[11] How some of them must have marvelled at the change in his circumstances. The former rabid anti-capitalist demagogue who used to demand the destruction of the free-enterprise system was now enjoying to the full the comfortable life of a top industrial executive! What price 'German socialism' now, Herr Strasser? his one-time followers might have asked. Strasser's new-found contentment and well-being, and his lack of regret at being out of politics, helped to stabilise his private affairs. With the pressures of the *Kampfzeit* no longer a source of some friction and strain at home, marital and family life received a welcome boost.

Strasser was hardly to know that his powerful enemies in the NSDAP were behind the discreet but close surveillance on his activities throughout 1933 and into the following year.[12] Goering is reported to have wanted him murdered in August 1933.[13] Lurking at the back of the minds of Goering, Goebbels, Himmler and a few others was the uneasy feeling that, if anything untoward happened in the party or in the country at large, the door might be opened for a political comeback by Strasser, which could be reasonably expected to result in their own exclusion from power. The deep insecurity of these party leaders would probably have come to nothing in the long term had not serious problems arisen for the regime in 1934.

With the nationalist euphoria which greeted the *Machtergreifung* petering out before the end of the party's first year in power, latent tensions between Hitler and his conservative allies were causing increasing concern, especially where the SA–army relationship was involved. By the early spring of 1934, discontent with the way matters in general were going began to surface despite the tight police and SS control. Papen's Marburg speech was one of the most notable expressions of this trend, and Goebbels was moved to issue warnings against troublemakers, gossip-mongers and suchlike whom, he claimed, were attempting to sabotage the Führer's work of recovery for Germany. An atmosphere of crisis descended on the country, and Strasser fell victim to it. Rumours of his alleged collusion with Schleicher and even with Röhm went round party circles,[14] no doubt inspired by his enemies in high places.[15] Strasser could readily perceive the lurking danger in these stories and went to considerable lengths in private and with officialdom to stress his total non-involvement in politics, which happened to be true.[16] He informed his friend and former colleague, Glaser: 'Politically, I have become as completely disinterested as is possible – often I go a whole week without reading a newspaper'.[17] On another occasion he emphasised: 'I am endeavouring with success to detach myself totally from everything to do with politics . . . and to find satisfaction in my new [business] activity'.[18] Indeed, Strasser developed a certain placid, philosophical outlook on life by this time: 'The comings and goings in the world show very clearly . . . how fleeting everything finally is and how the present life is only a part of a great journey whose beginning and end we know nothing about.'[19]

Contrary to some reports,[20] he had no contact with his brother's Black Front or with any other political organisation or figure,[21] and had no knowledge, for example, of a list of ministers for an alternative government, in which he was designated Economics Minister, alleged to have emanated in spring 1934 from Schleicher.[22] Strasser had positively shunned meeting friends and former political associates, with the exception of Reupke and Elbrechter, since the beginning of 1933. Social invitations to his home were few. Even his former right-hand man, Schulz, who, following his departure from the party leadership, had taken up a managerial post in his friend Dr Erich Lübbert's Allgemeine Baugesellschaft Lenz in Berlin,[23] was only in spasmodic contact with him, and any dealings Strasser had with Glaser were by letter. In short, he had done everything humanly possible to convince the party – and Hitler in particular, of course – of his good faith and complete renunciation of political interests. Unfortunately for him, it was not enough.

The smouldering crisis of confidence and identity in the National Socialist regime broke out in the Röhm Purge in June 1934, resulting in the murder of an unknown but substantial number of SA leaders, dissident politicians, and personal enemies of the party leadership. Strasser succumbed on 30 June to the nefarious machinations of Goering and Himmler, above all, who seized the opportunity to get rid of a persistent and worrying problem. They conveniently used Strasser's *Verrat* of December 1932 as a pretext for having him murdered. Their disquiet about his possible political future had been heightened a few weeks earlier, on 13 June, when he had had an unexpected meeting with Hitler at which he had been offered the post of Economics Minister in succession to the struggling Kurt Schmitt. Strasser was apparently ready to accept, provided at least two of his bitter adversaries, Goering and Goebbels, were removed from office.[24] Hitler rejected this condition, but for his enemies

Strasser was getting too close for comfort.[25] They decided on drastic preventive action.

Just after midday on 30 June, Strasser's lunch at home with his family was disrupted by the sudden appearance of five Gestapo officials at the door of his apartment. They informed a surprised Strasser that they wanted to search his company office and insisted that he accompany them at once. He tried to assure his anxious wife and children that nothing was amiss and then left with the police. It was the last they saw of him. On arrival at Schering-Kahlbaum, Strasser was handed over to a waiting SS unit who escorted him by car to Columbia House, the Gestapo headquarters in Prinz-Albrecht-Strasse. There he joined other arrested SA men before being taken to his own cell, ostensibly to await interrogation. Instead, after a brief period, he was shot several times by an SS captain.[26] Strasser's end was no more and no less sordid than that.[27] His body was cremated, and on 7 July an urn containing his ashes and inscribed simply, 'Gregor Strasser, born 30.5.92 in Geisenfeld, died 30.6.34 Gestapo Berlin', was delivered to his widow. The authorities warned her not to make any kind of public show or acknowledgement of her husband's death. Officially, he was declared to have committed suicide. The ashes were never buried. Else Strasser created a small memorial shrine in Gregor's study at the centre of which was placed the urn:[28] it has remained in the family's possession ever since.

In his address to the Reichstag on 13 July about the shootings, Hitler's only reference to Strasser came when he curtly remarked that he had been 'pulled into' a conspiracy by others against the state. A week or so previously, Hitler had during a ministerial meeting accused Strasser of having been directly involved in a Schleicher–Röhm plot.[29] Like so much more in the Third Reich these were abominable lies. Whether Hitler directly ordered Strasser's murder or not is unknown, but he displayed no regret or remorse at the brutal elimination of his former principal lieutenant. During the war the Führer denounced Strasser as a 'great traitor' who 'had met his just punishment'.[30]

Several of Strasser's friends and close associates from his days in politics were also murdered in June 1934. Alexander Glaser, who had gone into legal practice in Munich after a short period in the NSBO, was shot.[31] Strasser's lawyer, Dr Alexander Voss, was shot in his Berlin office after refusing to hand over Strasser's private papers to the Gestapo men sent to seize them; his safe was broken into, the papers taken and presumably destroyed, for they allegedly contained material highly damaging to Goering, among others.[32] Paul Schulz was more fortunate. After being taken by a group of Gestapo officials to Berlin's Grünewald for execution, he managed to make a miraculous escape, despite suffering several bullet wounds. He subsequently left Germany for Switzerland at Hitler's express command.[33] Schulz took up his business career which led him during the war to Hungary where he then became heavily involved in the work of the International Red Cross. After 1945 he returned to West Germany and resumed his career in business.[34] Some other figures who had been very close to Strasser, like Erich Koch, managed to come through the purge without too much difficulty, while lesser-known colleagues were often dismissed from the party and its affiliates.[35] No Strasser ghost was to be allowed to linger in National Socialism.

A final macabre note was added to Strasser's murder when his widow was awarded a state pension in recompense. A law of December 1934 made provision for the immediate relatives of those murdered in June 1934 to claim a pension, and supported by the Interior Ministry the SS took on the major supervisory role.[36] Consequently, among those given a pension were the mother of SA leader and Police President in Breslau, Edmund Heines, the widow of Edgar Jung, and Else Strasser. In April 1936 she was informed by Interior Minister Frick, a former intimate friend of the family, that because of the 'death of her husband, the Director Gregor Strasser' (!), she was to be paid from 1 May 1936 a monthly allowance of RM500. This was composed of RM300 for herself and RM100 for each of her two sons. She was to have this award for life, while the payment to her sons would be discontinued when they reached the age of 25 years.[37] Before attaining that age, however, both Günter and Helmut were killed in action in July 1941 and May 1942 respectively, and the pension was accordingly reduced.

The massacres of June 1934 constituted an important turning-point in the history of the Third Reich. The Conservative–National Socialist alliance which had made possible the *Machtergreifung* in the first place, and which appeared to have been further strengthened by the political emasculation of the SA, began in reality to disintegrate before very long. Henceforth, the rising influence of the SS, the increasing emphasis on racism and anti-semitism as instruments of state policy, extensive rearmament and foreign-policy adventurism shaped the 'new' Germany. Gregor Strasser, had he lived, would not have approved of these developments, or of the terroristic repression and brutality which they produced against the German people themselves. It was the unfolding of the nightmare which he had perceived in embryonic form during 1931–2, and he had ultimately intimated his clear abhorrence of it. Strasser had fought for a rather different kind of Germany, strong, respected, proud, but never fanatical, destructive, intolerant. His overall contribution to the success of the NSDAP was fundamental and substantial, and surpassed only by that of the Führer himself. Yet Strasser realised too late perhaps how his many and varied talents had been abused, so that by the end of 1932 his vision of a resurrected Fatherland owed more to a neo-conservative patriotism than to a thoroughgoing Hitlerian National Socialism. The tragedy of his life embraced more than a mere personal dimension, for Strasser, with all his abilities and weaknesses, personified to some degree the martyrdom of a whole generation cruelly misled and finally annihilated by National Socialism.

Strasser was neither a consummate politician nor an outstanding statesman, but he was a man of considerable personal and political substance. Historical analogies can often serve to obfuscate rather than enlighten, but perhaps in the final analysis he may be compared with Trotsky in the Soviet Communist Party: both offered important challenges to their respective political masters, both had to die for their unorthodox conduct. The 'Trotsky of the Nazi Party' might be, therefore, an appropriate final epitaph for Gregor Strasser.

Notes

Introduction

1 The most recent overall appraisals worth noting are Karl Dietrich Erdmann and Hagen Schulze (eds), *Weimar. Selbstpreisgabe einer Demokratie. Eine Bilanz heute* (Düsseldorf, 1980); Michael Stürmer (ed.), *Die Weimarer Republik. Belagerte Civitas* (Königstein/Ts, 1980).
2 A new study offers a useful overview: Pierre Ayçoberry, *The Nazi Question: An Essay on the Interpretations of National Socialism (1922–1975)* (London, 1981).
3 'Macht Platz, ihr Alten, eure Zeit ist abgelaufen . . .', speech by Gregor Strasser of 8 May 1927, reprinted in Gregor Strasser, *Hammer und Schwert. Ausgewählte Reden und Schriften eines Nationalsozialisten*, Teil II, *Kampf* (Berlin, 1928), pp. 62–4.
4 Konrad Heiden, *Geschichte des Nationalsozialismus. Die Karriere einer Idee* (Berlin, 1932), p. 180.
5 The following are examples: Karl Dietrich Bracher, *Die Auflösung der Weimarer Republik. Eine Studie zum Problem des Machtverfalls in der Demokratie* (Stuttgart, 1957), pp. 108–16, 362 ff., 376 ff., 507 ff., 663–705; Wolfgang Horn, *Führerideologie und Parteiorganisation in der NSDAP (1919–1933)* (Düsseldorf, 1972), pp. 330 ff., 358–60, 367–74; Dietrich Orlow, *The History of the Nazi Party, 1919–1933* (Pittsburgh, Pa, 1969), pp. 254–60, 268–75, 279–98; Gerhard Schulz, *Aufstieg des Nationalsozialismus. Krise und Revolution in Deutschland* (Berlin, 1975), pp. 387–9, 731 ff.; Albrecht Tyrell, *Führer befiehl . . . Selbstzeugnisse aus der 'Kampfzeit' der NSDAP . . .* (Düsseldorf, 1969), pp. 312–17, 323–6, 329–33, 342–9; Thilo Vogelsang, *Reichswehr, Staat und NSDAP. Beiträge zur deutschen Geschichte 1930–1932* (Stuttgart, 1962), pp. 269–76, 340–2.
6 See below for details.
7 Rohan D. O. Butler, *The Roots of National Socialism 1783–1933* (London, 1941), p. 271, says he had 'sincere socialist convictions'. In agreement with this observation are, for example: Konrad Heiden, *Geburt des dritten Reiches. Geschichte des Nationalsozialismus bis Herbst 1933* (Zurich, 1934), p. 88; Wilhelm Hoegener, *Flucht vor Hitler. Erinnerungen an die Kapitulation der ersten deutschen Republik 1933* (Munich, 1977), p. 39; Heinrich Brüning, *Memoiren 1918–1934* (Stuttgart, 1972), p. 488. The view has been endorsed by: Karl Dietrich Bracher, *The German Dictatorship: The Origins, Structure and Effects of National Socialism* (London, 1973), p. 348; Arthur Rosenberg, *Entstehung und Geschichte der Weimarer Republik* (Frankfurt, 1955), pp 472, 476; and Martin Broszat, *Der Staat Hitlers. Grundlegung und Entwicklung seiner inneren Verfassung* (Stuttgart, 1971), p. 64. More recently, the West German weekly magazine *Der Spiegel* (29 October 1979) referred to Strasser as 'this last brown socialist' (p. 34).
8 Ernst Rüdiger Starhemberg, *Between Hitler and Mussolini* (London, 1941), p. 37. Starhemberg was the leader in the early 1930s of the Austrian Heimwehr, and the impression recorded here is based on an interview he had with Strasser in autumn 1930.
9 *Documents on British Foreign Policy*, 2nd ser. Vol. IV, p. 28. Ambassador Rumbold's remark on 13 August 1932.
10 Henry R. Knickerbocker, *Kommt Europa wieder hoch?* (Berlin, 1932), p. 204.
11 Anton M. Koktanek, 'Spenglers Verhältnis zum Nationalsozialismus in Geschichtlicher Entwicklung', *Zeitschrift für Politik*, vol. 13 (1966), pp. 49–50.
12 Wilhelm Hoegener, *Die Verratene Republik. Geschichte der deutschen Gegenrevolution* (Munich, 1958), p. 123.
13 Otto Meissner, *Staatssekretär unter Ebert-Hindenburg-Hitler. Der Schicksalsweg des deutschen Volkes von 1918–1945* (Hamburg, 1950), pp. 251 ff.

14 Rudolf Jordan, *Erlebt und Erlitten. Weg eines Gauleiters von München bis Moskau* (Leoni am Starnberger See, 1971), p. 69. Jordan was Gauleiter of Halle-Merseburg 1931–7 and then of Magdeburg-Anhalt until 1945.

15 A term used by Helmut Heiber, *Die Republik von Weimar* (Munich, 1971), p. 266, and by Reinhard Kühnl, *Deutschland zwischen Demokratie und Faschismus* (Munich, 1969), p. 55.

16 Heinz Pol in *Die Tat*, 15 April 1930, pp. 563 ff.

17 Hermann Rauschning, *Gespräche mit Hitler* (Vienna, 1973), p. 153.

18 Serge Lang and Ernst von Schenck (eds), *Porträt eines Menschheitsverbrechers. Nach den hinterlassenen Memoiren des ehemaligen Reichsministers Alfred Rosenberg* (St Gallen, 1947), p. 158. In *Letzte Aufzeichnungen. Ideale und Idole der nationalsozialistischen Revolution*, ed. H. Härtle (Göttingen, 1955), Rosenberg remarks (p. 111) on 'the human tragedy that was Gregor Strasser'. Douglas Reed in *Nemesis? The Story of Otto Strasser and the Black Front* (London, 1940), p. 58, goes one further in describing Gregor as 'the living embodiment of the German tragedy'.

19 cf. Paul Schulz, *Meine Erschiessung am 30. Juni 1934*, written in 1948 and available in the Bundesarchiv Library, B.I.P. Paul Schulz, No. 1. This forty-page pamphlet has little information on his close association with Strasser during the early 1930s. A second booklet by Schulz, *Rettungen und Hilfeleistungen an Verfolgten 1933–1945 durch Oberleutnant a.D. Paul Schulz*, also available in the Bundesarchiv Library, B.I.P. Paul Schulz, No. 2, deposited in 1969, is similarly disappointing on Strasser's role.

20 My application to the East German authorities for permission to consult archives in Potsdam and Merseburg was unsuccessful. I am reliably informed, however, that there are few, if any, important documents on Strasser at these centres.

21 Hans Diebow, *Gregor Strasser und der Nationalsozialismus* (Berlin, 1932), amounting to sixty-five pages; and Michael Geismaier (a pseudonym for Otto Strasser!), *Gregor Strasser* (Leipzig, 1933), ninety-five pages long.

22 The ones to note in this regard are: *30 Juni. Vorgeschichte, Verlauf, Folgen* (Prague, 1934), pp. 4 ff.; *Die deutsche Bartholomäusnacht* (Zurich, 1935), pp. 32–44, 59–62; *Hitler and I* (London, 1940), pp. 131–3, 149 ff.; *History in My Time* (London, 1941), pp. 239–43; *Exil* (Munich, 1958), pp. 63–6, 72–4; *Mein Kampf. Eine politische Autobiographie* (Frankfurt, 1969), pp. 38–9, 75–82, 90–2.

23 *Die deutsche Bartholomäusnacht*, p. 32.

24 Gregor Strasser, *Freiheit und Brot. Ausgewählte Reden und Schriften eines Nationalsozialisten*, Teil I, *Idee* (Berlin, 1928); *Hammer und Schwert*; *Kampf um Deutschland. Reden und Aufsätze eines Nationalsozialisten* (Munich, 1932).

25 Pater Bernhard Strasser, *Gregor und Otto Strasser. Kurze Darstellung ihrer Persönlichkeit und ihres Wollens*, 2nd edn (Munich, 1965).

26 Gerhard Schildt, 'Die Arbeitsgemeinschaft Nord-West. Untersuchungen zur Geschichte der NSDAP, 1925–26', doctoral dissertation, University of Freiburg i.B., 1964; Werner Jochmann (ed.), *Nationalsozialismus und Revolution. Ursprung und Geschichte der NSDAP in Hamburg 1922–1933. Dokumente* (Frankfurt, 1963); Georg Franz-Willing, *Putsch und Verbotszeit der Hitlerbewegung, November 1923–Februar 1925* (Preussisch Oldendorf, 1977); Joseph Nyomarkay, *Charisma and Factionalism in the Nazi Party* (Minneapolis, Minn., 1967); Bradley F. Smith, 'Hitler and the Strasser challenge', thesis, University of California, 1957; Jeremy Noakes, 'Conflict and development in the NSDAP 1924–1927', *Journal of Contemporary History*, vol. 1, no. 4 (1966), pp. 3–36; Reinhard Kühnl, 'Zur Programmatik der Nationalsozialistischen Linken: Das Strasser–Programm von 1925/26', *Vierteljahrshefte für Zeitgeschichte (VFZG)*, vol 14 (1966), pp. 317–33.

27 Max H. Kele, *Nazis and Workers: National Socialist Appeals to German Labor, 1919–1933* (Chapel Hill, NC, 1972); Reinhard Kühnl, *Die Nationalsozialistische Linke 1925–1930* (Meisenheim, 1966).

28 In connection with this crisis see the memorandum by Gauleiter Hinrich Lohse, 'Der

Fall Strasser' in Institut für Zeitgeschichte: Zeugenschrift 265. His analysis is clearly deficient. The value of Lohse's work lies exclusively in its detailed description of the events immediately preceding 8 December 1932, the day Strasser resigned.

29 Joseph Murdoch Dixon, 'Gregor Strasser and the organisation of the Nazi Party, 1925–32', doctoral dissertation, Stanford University, Calif., 1966; Ulrich Wörtz, 'Programmatik und Führerprinzip. Das Problem des Strasser-Kreises in der NSDAP', doctoral dissertation, University of Erlangen, 1966; Udo Kissenkoetter, *Gregor Strasser und die NSDAP* (Stuttgart, 1978).

Chapter 1

1 Details in a feature article on Strasser in *Der Angriff*, 2 June 1932: copy in BA: NS26 (Hauptarchiv der NSDAP)/1370; see also Otto Strasser, *Exil*, p. 9.

2 Bernhard Strasser, *Gregor und Otto Strasser*, p. 1.

3 He fled Germany, allegedly to escape prosecution for homosexual offences: see report of 23 November 1939 in BA: Sammlung Schumacher: 278. By his own account (*Gregor und Otto Strasser*, p. 1), he left Germany in 1935 for the United States where he eventually took out American citizenship.

4 Otto fought in the First World War, was promoted to lieutenant and was highly decorated for bravery. After the war, he completed his studies in national economy and law at the universities of Berlin, Munich and Würzburg, leaving with his doctorate in 1921 (ibid., pp. 4 ff.).

5 She was still living in Munich in the mid-1970s and had at no time been politically active.

6 See letter of condolence of 6 June 1946 from Heinrich Brüning, the former German Chancellor, to Father Bernhard (Institut für Zeitgeschichte (IfZG)): ED-118, Band 2, Bernhard und Otto Strasser.

7 *Reichstags-Handbuch*, Vol. III, *Wahlperiode 1924*, ed. Bureau des Reichstags (Berlin, 1924), p. 377.

8 Jochmann, *Nationalsozialismus und Revolution*, pp. 256–7, description of an NSDAP meeting in Hamburg on 4 November 1926. Strasser's bitter enemy in the late 1920s, Artur Dinter, formerly an NSDAP leader in Thuringia, wrote that Strasser was widely known in the party as a Jesuit (*Das Geistchristentum*, Heft 16 (1929), p. 182, in BA: Zeitgeschichtlicher Sammlung (ZSg) 103: 783).

9 James M. Rhodes, *The Hitler Movement: A Modern Millenarian Revolution* (Stanford, Calif., 1980), pp. 135–6, for author's interview with Otto Strasser, dated 1967.

10 Helmut Heiber, *Goebbels* (London, 1972), p. 41.

11 Paul Wegr, *Das neue Wesen. Betrachtungen und Ausblicke* (Kempten, 1912). Otto Strasser, *Exil*, p. 10, wrongly gives the date of publication as 1896, as does Wörtz, *Programmatik und Führerprinzip*, p. 36; both also give the pseudonym as 'Weger', which is incorrect.

12 Bernhard Strasser, *Gregor und Otto Strasser*, p. 1.

13 Gregor Strasser, *Freiheit und Brot.*

14 Diebow, *Gregor Strasser*, p. 16.

15 Speech of 18 May 1932, 'Vom Marxismus zum Sozialismus', in BA: Reichskulturkammer R56I/71.

16 Bayerisches Hauptstaatsarchiv (Bay. HSA): Kriegsarchiv: Akten des König. Kriegsministeriums: Offizier-Personal: OP 49979 (Gregor Strasser).

17 See his letter of 17 December 1931 to Gauleiter Carl Röver, in: BA: NS 22 (Reichsorganisationsleiter der NSDAP)/1074.

18 Testimonial of 10 January 1919 by Hauptmann Fürholzer, in: Bay. HSA: Kriegsarchiv: Akten des König. Kriegsministeriums: OP 49979 (Strasser).

19 Strasser in the *Berliner Arbeiter-Zeitung*, 7 October 1928.

20 Strasser speech of 18 May 1932, in: BA: R56I/71.

21 Strasser speech of 23 July 1932 in Ostragehege (near Dresden), in BA: NS26/58.

22 Strasser, 'Von der Revolte zur Revolution!', *Berliner Arbeiter-Zeitung*, 6 November 1927.

23 Strasser, 'Nationalsozialismus und Geschichte', *NS-Jahrbuch* (Munich, 1928), pp. 190–9; also published in Strasser, *Kampf um Deutschland*, pp. 225–8.

24 See his 'Es lebe die Revolution', *Völkischer Beobachter* (*VB*), 9 November 1926.

25 Strasser, 'Von der Revolte zur Revolution!'

26 Strasser, '"Ihr habt es so gewollt!" Zehn Jahre Versailles', speech of 23 June 1929, in *Kampf um Deutschland*, pp. 229–33.

27 Speech in the Reichstag of 17 October 1930, 'Das Wesen und Ziel der Nationalsozialistisches Idee', in BA: NS26/1209.

28 Strasser, 'Frontsoldaten', *VB*, 24–5 April 1927; and his 'Eine sehr notwendige Feststellung', *VB*, 12 February 1932.

29 Strasser speech of August 1930 in Teterow (Mecklenburg), in BA: ZSg 2/195.

30 Strasser speech of 23 July 1932 in Ostragehege, in BA: NS 26/58.

31 Strasser, 'Gedanken über Aufgaben der Zukunft', in *NS-Briefe*, 15 June 1926.

32 Strasser in *Berliner Arbeiter-Zeitung*, 7 October 1928. See also his article, 'Quo Vadis Reichswehr', in *VB*, 16 March 1928.

33 Gerhard Schulz *et al.* (eds), *Staat und NSDAP 1930–1932. Quellen zur Ära Brüning* (Düsseldorf, 1977), p. 53, speech of April 1929 in Breslau.

34 Strasser, 'Gedanken über Aufgaben der Zukunft'.

35 Strasser's decrees of 4 July 1932 (BA: NS26/549), and of 20 February 1932 (BA: NS22/340). The NSDAP made a point of stressing the large number of former soldiers in its ranks and leadership. On 6 January 1931, for example, the party's Reichstag faction, responding to taunts from the SPD, published a statement which claimed that 68 per cent of its 107 deputies, compared with only 20 per cent of SPD deputies, had taken part in the war (BA: ZSg: NS-Drucksachen (NSD) 5 (Reichstagsfraktion der NSDAP)/5).

36 Albert Krebs, *Tendenzen und Gestalten der NSDAP. Erinnerungen an die Frühzeit der Partei* (Stuttgart, 1959), pp. 183 ff.

37 Diebow, *Gregor Strasser*, p. 20.

38 Otto Strasser, *Exil*, p. 23, and *Die deutsche Bartholomäusnacht*, p. 33. For details of Otto's political activity in the early 1920s, see BA: Munziger-Archiv: Otto Strasser and IfZG: ED-118, Band 25: Otto Strasser.

39 One must be extremely sceptical of the suggestion of Ralph M. Engelmann, 'Dietrich Eckart and the genesis of Nazism', doctoral dissertation, University of Washington, DC, 1971, fo. 106, that in 1919 Eckart, Father Bernhard Stempfle (who later edited *Mein Kampf*, and was murdered in the Röhm Purge) and Gregor Strasser formed a three-man delegation which unsuccessfully proposed to Gustav von Kahr of the Bavarian People's Party (BVP) a merger of that party and the Deutsch-sozialistische Partei (DSP) into a Christian-Social Party. Engelmann's source for this information is a letter sent to him on 19 December 1969 from Georg Grassinger, who was apparently chairman of the DSP in Munich in 1919. I have found no other source or reference which would indicate Strasser's involvement in this episode. Stempfle, like Strasser, was subsequently active in the Bavarian Einwohnerwehr: he was an editor of that organisation's publication *Heimatland* – see Hans Fenske, *Konservativismus und Rechtsradikalismus in Bayern nach 1918* (Bad Homburg, 1969), p. 87.

40 Curt Rosten, *Geschichte der nationalsozialistischen Revolution* (Berlin, 1933), p. 17.

41 Bruno Thoss, *Der Ludendorff-Kreis 1919–1923* (Munich, 1978), p. 140; Robert G. L. Waite, *Vanguard of Nazism: The Free Corps Movement in Postwar Germany 1918–1923* (New York, 1969), pp. 202–3.

42 Description used in a Bavarian police report of 14 November 1922, in Bay. HSA: Allgemeines Staatsarchiv (ASA): Staatsministeriums des Innern: 73685.

43 Bernhard Strasser, *Gregor und Otto Strasser*, pp. 3 ff.; Dixon, 'Gregor Strasser', fo. 9, nn. 20 and 21.

44 James M. Diehl, *Paramilitary Politics in Weimar Germany* (Bloomington, Ind., 1977), esp. pp. 55, 66 ff., 70 ff.

45 The best study of the Bavarian EW in David Clay Large, *The Politics of Law and Order: A History of the Bavarian Einwohnerwehr 1918–1921* (Philadelphia, Pa, 1980), pp. 16–77.

46 An EW unit had been set up in Landshut in 1919 with about a thousand members. Strasser took about the same number with him into the organisation (Bay. HSA: Kriegsarchiv: Gruppen kommando 4: Bund 33: Akt 5).

47 Personal details on Strasser in BA: R2 (Reichsfinanzministerium): 11905.

48 Henry A. Turner (ed.), *Hitler aus nächster Nähe. Aufzeichnungen eines Vertrauten 1929–1932* (Frankfurt, 1978), p. 125. This is Otto Wagener's description.

49 BA: R2/11905. Personal details on Strasser. Both sons were later killed in action serving with the Wehrmacht on the Russian front.

50 Hellmuth Auerbach, 'Hitlers politische Lehrjahre und die Münchener Gesellschaft 1919–1923', *VfZG*, vol. 25 (1977), pp. 19–20.

51 Uwe Lohalm, *Völkischer Radikalismus. Die Geschichte des deutschvölkischen Schutz-und Trutz Bundes 1919–1923* (Hamburg, 1970), pp. 61 ff., 88 ff., 176 ff., 283 ff., 301 ff.

52 Reginald H. Phelps, 'Hitlers "Grundlegende" Rede über den Antisemitismus', *VfZG*, vol. 16 (1968), pp. 390–420.

53 Albrecht Tyrell, *Vom 'Trommler' zum 'Führer'. Der Wandel von Hitlers Selbstverständnis zwischen 1919 und 1924 und die Entwicklung der NSDAP* (Munich, 1975), pp. 155–66, 272 n. 125.

54 Michael H. Kater, 'Zur Soziographie der Frühen NSDAP', *VfZG*, vol. 19 (1971), pp. 124–59, esp. pp. 138 ff., 149 ff., 153 ff.; Donald M. Douglas, 'The parent cell: some computer notes on the composition of the first Nazi Party group in Munich 1919–21', *Central European History*, vol. 10 (1977), pp. 55–72, esp. pp. 60 ff., 67 ff.

55 Michael H. Kater, 'Sozialer Wandel in der NSDAP im Zuge der nationalsozialistischen Machtergreifung', in Wolfgang Schieder (ed.), *Faschismus als Soziale Bewegung. Deutschland und Italien im Vergleich* (Hamburg, 1976), p. 26.

56 *Reichstags-Handbuch*, Vol. III, p. 377, or Vol. IV (Berlin, 1928), pp. 448–9, Vol. V (Berlin, 1930), p. 489, Vol. VI (Berlin, 1932), p. 232, or Vol. VII (Berlin, 1932), p. 421.

57 Strasser to NSDAP Reichsleitung, 3 November 1931, in BA: NS22/348.

58 Strasser to Schwarz, 4 April 1931, in BA: NS1 (Reichsschatzmeister)/258.

59 'Die Braunhemden im Reichstag', Munich 1933, copy in BA: NSD70/111.

60 Edgar von Schmidt-Pauli, *Die Männer um Hitler* (Berlin, 1932), p. 118.

61 Diebow, *Gregor Strasser*, pp. 22–4. The assertion of Mühlberger that Strasser was campaigning for the party in Rhineland-Westphalia in 1920 is plainly erroneous. Not surprisingly, no source is quoted (Detlef W. Mühlberger, 'The Rise of National Socialism in Westphalia 1920–1933', doctoral dissertation, University of London, 1975, fo. 202).

62 *Hitler und Ich*, pp. 17–18. See also Otto's letter of 8 November 1948 to B. Schwertfeger, author of *Rätsel um Deutschland* (1948), complaining that the meeting did not take place in Deggendorf, as Schwertfeger wrote (p. 555), in BA: Nachlass Schwertfeger: No. 258.

63 Otto Strasser, *Die deutsche Bartholomäusnacht*, p. 34; see also Geismaier, *Gregor Strasser*, p. 29.

64 Alan Bullock, *Hitler: A Study in Tyranny* (London, 1965), p. 135; Wörtz, *Programmatik und Führerprinzip*, p. 37. On the other hand, Kissenkoetter, *Gregor Strasser*, ignores the controversy altogether (cf. pp. 14–15).

65 Tyrell, *'Trommler'*, p. 224, n. 391. Into the same dubious category comes Otto's

assertion that Hitler was godfather to Gregor's twin sons (*Die deutsche Bartholomäusnacht*, p. 44). Gregor could not possibly have been on sufficiently intimate terms with Hitler at the end of 1920 or early 1921, when the christening would have taken place according to traditional Catholic practice, to give him this honour. As a family-conscious person, moreover, Gregor would scarcely have entertained the idea of allowing an outsider, even if he were a Catholic, to assume the role of godfather.

66 Donald M. Douglas, 'The early Ortsgruppen: the development of National Socialist local groups 1919–1923', doctoral dissertation, University of Kansas, 1968, fos 100–4.

67 As indicated by the correspondence of the Landshut NSDAP from March–August 1921, in BA: NS26/134.

68 On 28 February he spoke on the theme 'Der Weltkrieg und seine Macher', and on 21 March on 'Staatsmänner oder Staatsverbrecher'. Details in Eberhard Jäckel and Axel Kuhn (eds), *Hitler. Sämtliche Aufzeichnungen 1905–1924* (Stuttgart, 1980), pp. 327–9, document 202, and p. 355, document 215.

69 Mitgliederverzeichnis der DAP/NSDAP seit den 2.2.20, in BA: NS26/230.

70 Mitgliederverzeichnis der NSDAP Landshut, den 20.9.22, in BA: NS26/215.

71 The list is dated October 1923, in Bay. HSA: Staatsarchiv München (SAM): Polizeidirektion München: 6697; and, also in the same archive, Staatsanwaltschaft München I: 3103.

72 Strasser to Reichsleitung, 14 November 1922, in BDC: Personal File Gregor Strasser.

73 From Mitgliederverzeichnis seit den 2.2.20, in BA: NS26/230. Gottfried Feder claimed Strasser had not been in the party in 1920 or 1921: see his letter of 2 May 1926 to the Reichsleitung, given in Tyrell, *Führer befiehl*, p. 126.

74 There were no Gauleiters in the pre-1923 party. Leaders of the Landshut NSDAP changed frequently in 1921–2, from Konrad Meier, to Anton Brandl, to Franz Zirngibl (see miscellaneous correspondence of the branch in BA: NS26/134). In May 1923, Karl Vielweib was elected branch chairman. After 1933 he became mayor of the town, having rejoined the NSDAP in August 1925 (BDC: Personal File Karl Vielweib).

75 BA: NS26/100, report of 14 March 1940 to the Hauptarchiv der NSDAP.

76 The SA recruited quite heavily from former EW members (Large, *Politics of Law and Order*, p. 40, n. 99).

77 Heinrich Bennecke, *Hitler und die SA* (Munich, 1962), p. 50.

78 *VB*, 22 March 1923.

79 The Landshut NSDAP had already entered a period of relative stagnation in mid-1922, which accelerated in 1923. Membership, which stood at 215 in September 1922, rose very slowly thereafter (see letter of 25 July 1922 from Paul Albrecht, secretary of the party in Landshut, to the Reichsleitung, in BA: Sammlung Schumacher: 199).

80 Strasser's report of 18 July 1923 to SA Headquarters in Munich, in BA: NS26/296.

81 BA: NS26/514, memorandum by SA man Carl Dittmar of Landshut; BA: NS26/296, Strasser report of 26 March 1923.

82 BA: NS26/296, Strasser's report of 27 July 1923 to SA Chief of Staff concerning Franz Schrafstetter, a former leader of the SA in Landshut.

83 In February 1923 the SA joined the newly created Arbeitsgemeinschaft der vaterländischen Kampfverbände, and in September of that year the Deutsche Kampfbund (see Werner Maser, *Der Sturm auf die Republik. Frühgeschichte der NSDAP* (Stuttgart, 1973), pp. 377 ff.).

84 BA: NS26/296, Strasser report of 24 June 1923 concerning the SA's participation in a Schlageter festival; BA: NS23 (Sturmabteilungen-SA)/494, report on his attendance at a rally of Austrian National Socialists in Salzburg, autumn 1923.

85 BA: NS26/100, report of 14 March 1940 to the Hauptarchiv der NSDAP.

86 BA: NS26/296, letter of 7 August 1923 from SA Chief of Staff to NSDAP Reichsleitung.

87 BA: NS22/1044, Strasser's account dated July 1930, also John J. Cahill, 'The NSDAP

and May Day, 1923: confrontation and aftermath, 1923–1927', doctoral dissertation, University of Cincinnati, 1973, fos 174–81, 188 ff., 219–21.

88 BA: ZSg 103/783, report in *Volkswille* of 21 October 1930; Peter Kritzer, *Wilhelm Hoegener. Politische Biographie eines bayerischen Sozialdemokraten* (Munich, 1979), p. 65; Wilhelm Hoegener, *Der Schwierige Aussenseiter* (Munich, 1959), p. 59.

89 BA: NS22/1044, Strasser letter to Wagner of 28 November 1930.

90 Hauptstaatsarchiv Stuttgart: E 131: Akten der Pressestelle des Württ. Staatsministeriums: Büschel 166.

91 Bennecke, *SA*, p. 63.

92 Bay. HSA: SAM: Polizeidirektion München: 6706, Strasser's affidavit of May 1923 to police.

93 Harold J. Gordon, *Hitler and the Beer Hall Putsch* (Princeton, NJ, 1972), pp. 185 ff., 270 ff., 313 ff.

94 Bay. HSA: ASA: Sonderabgabe I: Polizeidirektion München: Vernehmung Gregor Strassers am 25.11.1923; Harold J. Gordon (ed.), *The Hitler Trial before the People's Court in Munich*, 3 vols (Arlington, Va, 1976), Vol. One, pp. 402–4, Strasser testimony on 4 March 1924.

95 BA: NS26/114I, Statements at Hitler's trial 1924; see also letter intimating Strasser's unawareness of a *Putsch* from the Stadtkommissar Landshut to the Stadtrat Landshut of 3 December 1923, in BA: NS26/118.

96 BA: NS26: Nachlass Streicher, AL94, report of November 1923.

97 BA: NS22/1049, Strasser to Reichsleitung of 5 November 1931. Also Strasser outlined his role on 9 November in an article entitled 'Der 9. November 1923. Erlebnisse eines Mitkämpfer', published in Ernst Niekisch (ed.), *Der Kampf um das Reich* (Essen, 1931), pp. 281–6.

98 BA: NS26/100, report to Hauptarchiv der NSDAP of 6 April 1940.

99 Bay. HSA: ASA: Sonderabgabe I: 1771, Strasser in Bavarian Landtag on 1 August 1924.

100 Bay. HSA: SAM: Polizeidirektion München: 6724, Die Regierung von Niederbayern an das Staatsministerium des Innerns, Landshut 6 February 1924.

101 BA: NS26: Nachlass Streicher: AL94.

Chapter 2

1 Bay. HSA: ASA: Sonderabgabe I: 1771, speech of 1 August 1924 in Bavarian Landtag.

2 Peter D. Stachura, 'The political strategy of the Nazi Party, 1919–1933', *German Studies Review*, vol. III (1980), pp. 267 ff.

3 There were signs that the Führer cult was developing in embryonic form shortly before the *Putsch*. See Ian Kershaw, *Der Hitler-Mythos. Volksmeinung und Propaganda im Dritten Reich* (Stuttgart, 1980), pp. 28–9.

4 Bay. HSA: ASA: Sonderabgabe I: 1771, speech of 1 August 1924 in Bavarian Landtag.

5 Strasser, 'Nationaler Sozialismus, "Was heisst das: Vaterland?"', article of 4 September 1925 in *Kampf um Deutschland*, pp. 72–7.

6 Strasser, 'Wie wird man Nationalsozialist?', speech of 19 December 1927 in the Hofbräuhaus, published in *VB*, 21 December 1927.

7 Krebs, *Tendenzen*, pp. 183 ff.

8 Kurt G. W. Ludecke, *I Knew Hitler: The Story of a Nazi Who Escaped the Blood Purge* (London, 1938), p. 226.

9 Strasser regrouped his Landshut SA in a cover organisation, the Schützenbund Tell, in late November 1923 (BA: NS26/100, report of 14 March 1940 to Hauptarchiv der NSDAP).

10 BDC: Personal File: Gregor Strasser, memorandum of NSDAP Reichsleitung 15 May 1931.

11 BA: R43 (Reichskanzlei) I/2219, list of Landtag deputies, 1924 (Bavaria).
12 BA: NS26/869 for examples of election poster.
13 Thomas Childers, 'The social bases of the National Socialist vote', *Journal of Contemporary History*, vol. 11 (1976), pp. 20–1, 24–5.
14 Falk Wiesemann, *Die Vorgeschichte der nationalsozialistischen Machtübernahme in Bayern 1932/33* (Berlin, 1975), pp. 77–8.
15 Larry E. Jones, 'Inflation, revaluation, and the crisis of middle-class politics: a study in the dissolution of the German party system, 1923–28', *Central European History*, vol. XII (1979), p. 153.
16 BA: NS26/1370, Gregor Strasser personal details, 1932. The sentence was formally quashed by a Bavarian government pardon on 21 December 1925.
17 Bay. HSA: ASA: Sonderabgabe I: 1809, report on Landtag session of 19 November 1924.
18 Bay. HSA: SAM: Polizeidirektion München: 6674, report of 20 November 1924 on Landtag proceedings.
19 Bay. HSA: ASA: Sonderabgabe I: 1809, from the *Völkischer Kurier* of 20 November 1924.
20 Strasser, *Kampf um Deutschland*, pp. 11–35.
21 Bay. HSA: ASA: Sonderabgabe I: 1771, speech of 1 August 1924 in Bavarian Landtag.
22 The number of *völkisch* deputies fell from thirty-two to fourteen, reflecting a virtual halving of their popular vote. Three other NSDAP members were elected alongside Strasser: Gottfried Feder, Wilhelm Frick and Hans Dietrich (Hans-Adolf Jacobsen and Werner Jochmann (eds), *Ausgewählte Dokumente zur Geschichte des Nationalsozialismus, 1933–1945* (Bielefeld, 1961), p. 28).
23 BA: R43I/1004, list of Reichstag members, 1924.
24 He spoke, for example, in Essen in December on the theme 'Der Nationalsozialismus und der Wiederaufbau Deutschlands' (Herbert Kühr, *Parteien und Wahlen im Stadt- und Landkreis Essen in der Zeit der Weimarer Republik* (Düsseldorf, 1973), p. 236).
25 BA: R43I/1004, statement by Strasser of November 1924.
26 Strasser, 'Wahlbeteiligung oder nicht', *NS-Briefe*, 1 December 1925.
27 Jochmann (ed.): *NS und Revolution*, Fobke–Volck correspondence, document 28, fo. 94. See also BA: NS26/899, Rundschreiben 32, supplement to *Völkischer Kurier* of 19 August 1924.
28 Jochmann (ed.), *NS und Revolution*: Fobke to Volck of 18 July 1924, document 28, fo. 94.
29 ibid., Fobke to Volck of 29 July 1924, document 33, fos 122–4.
30 ibid., Volck to Fobke of 1 August 1924, document 34, fo. 125.
31 ibid., document 30, fos 98–102: 'Dr Adalbert Volck: Vertraulicher Bericht über die nationalsozialistische Vertretertagung in Weimar am 20. Juli 1924'; and Sunkel's report of the meeting in BA: NS26/894.
32 BA: NS26/1504, report in *Völkischer Kurier* of 28 October 1924. See also the unity appeal of the NSFB on 27 October 1924.
33 *Rüstzeug der Nationalsozialistischen Freiheitsbewegung Gross-Deutschlands* (Berlin: Arbeitszentrale für völkische Aufklärung, 1924). Copy in BA: NSD70/16.
34 cf. reports of his speeches in Kassel and Fulda in *VB* of 25 August and 5 September 1924 respectively.
35 Donald R. Tracey, 'The development of the National Socialist Party in Thuringia, 1924–30' *Central European History*, vol. VIII (1975), p. 31.
36 Bay. HSA: SAM: Polizeidirektion München: 6777, Strasser criticism of Dinter in *Völkischer Kurier* of 20 November 1924.
37 BA: R43I/1004, report of Regierung München of 27 October 1924. See also letter of 29 July 1924 from Karl Kaufmann to Strasser, quoted in Franz-Willing, *Putsch und Verbotszeit*, p. 411.
38 BA: Nachlass Streicher: AL13, statement about Streicher issued by Strasser and Dr Alexander Glaser on 17 July 1924.

39 BA: NS26/1504, see statements in *Völkischer Kurier* of 26–7 and 28 October 1924.
40 Bradley F. Smith, *Heinrich Himmler: A Nazi in the Making, 1900–1920* (Stanford, Calif., 1971), p. 152.
41 Otto Strasser, *Die deutsche Bartholomäusnacht*, p. 120.
42 Konrad Heiden, *Der Führer: Hitler's Rise to Power* (London, 1967), p. 227.
43 On hearing that Hitler was to be freed, Strasser and Captain von Pfeffer travelled together to Landsberg to escort him back to Munich, but Esser and Streicher got there first (Schildt, *Die Arbeitsgemeinschaft*, p. 26).
44 BA: NS1/41C, Strasser letter to Duisburg lawyer, Borries, of January 1925.
45 Weigand von Miltenberg (pseud. Herbert Blank), *Adolf Hitler, Wilhelm III* (Berlin, 1931), p. 53.
46 Kissenkoetter, *Gregor Strasser*, p. 20, is convinced that this is the date, citing a schedule of Strasser's meetings in 1925 (copy in BA: Sammlung Schumacher: 382). This indicates a meeting Strasser addressed in Munich on 17 February, and a few other meetings he attended prior to the Hamm meeting of 22 February. Kissenkoetter omits to say that Graefe founded his DVFB on 17 February, which may have convinced Strasser that his only option was to follow Hitler. The meeting addressed by Strasser in Munich on 17 February, incidentally, was of the just-dissolved NSFB (undated Munich police report in BA: NS26/1504). Historians differ widely on the date given for Hitler's commissioning of Strasser to reconstruct the party in northern Germany: 2 February, which is too early, is quoted by Schildt, *Die Arbeitsgemeinschaft*, pp. 28 ff., Peter Hüttenberger, *Die Gauleiter. Studie Zum Wandel des Machtgefüges in der NSDAP* (Stuttgart, 1969), p. 11, and Wilfried Böhnke, *Die NSDAP im Ruhrgebiet 1920–1933* (Bonn–Bad Godesberg, 1974), p. 86; 11 March, which, in view of the Hamm meeting when Strasser was acting already as Hitler's plenipotentiary, is too late, is quoted by Kühnl, *Die NS Linke*, pp. 8 ff; 21 February, which is a possibility, is quoted by Wörtz, *Programmatik und Führerprinzip*, p. 73, and Noakes, 'Conflict and development', p. 13.
47 Heiden, *Geschichte des NS*, p. 195.
48 Strasser and his three National Socialist colleagues in the Reichstag continued to co-operate uneasily with Graefe's DVFB within a *Völkische Arbeitsgemeinschaft* until 15 March 1927, when they withdrew to form a separate NS faction along with three defectors from the DVFB – Reventlow, Stöhr and Kube (Wilhelm Frick (ed.), *Die Nationalsozialisten im Reichstag 1924–1931* (Munich, 1932), pp. 4 ff.).
49 BDC: Personal File: Gregor Strasser.

Chapter 3

1 From the end of 1926 until October 1928 it was Gau Lower Bavaria-Oberpfalz.
2 See letter from Reichsleitung to Strasser of 8 July 1925 (BA: Sammlung Schumacher: 199), and letter from Bouhler to Gau Lower Bavaria of 29 September 1925 (ibid.).
3 BA: NS26/134, Strasser circular of 25 August 1925. He was present at Gau meetings on 2 May and 12 September 1926 (BA: Sammlung Schumacher: 199).
4 BA: NS 1 (Reichsschatzmeister)/341, letter from NSDAP branch Bochum to Goebbels of 1 August 1925.
5 Strasser was pessimistic about Ludendorff's chances even before the election: report of Reichstag meeting of party leaders on 13 March 1925, BA: NS26/895.
6 Strasser letter to northern Gauleiters of 20 October 1925, BA: NS26/57.
7 BA: Sammlung Schumacher: 382, for full list, dated end of 1925.
8 Hauptstaatsarchiv Düsseldorf: RW23-NS Stellen: Gauleitung Ruhr, Circular of Gau Westphalia, dated 20 July 1925.
9 *Das Tagebuch von Joseph Goebbels, 1925–26. Mit weiteren Dokumenten*, ed. Helmut

Heiber (Stuttgart, 1961): 'A splendid fellow . . . with a wonderful sense of humour' (entry for 21 August 1925); 'I have come very close to him' (entry for 2 October 1925); 'Strasser is a real man' (entry for 6 March 1926); appreciation of Strasser's radicalism in entry for 30 September 1925.

10 For example, see letter from Kaufmann to Strasser of 4 November 1927, BA: NS 18 (Reichspropagandaleitung)/579; and Koch to Hitler of 6 December 1927, Hauptstaatsarchiv Düsseldorf: RW 23: Gauleitung Ruhr.

11 BA: Sammlung Schumacher: 199, Report of October 1925 confirms Peter Strasser and Vollmuth as party members in Deggendorf, Lower Bavaria. Peter Strasser remained in the party until his death in January 1928 (BA: NS18/574). For Vollmuth's background see BDC: Personal File Rudolf Vollmuth, and for his later career see BA: NS22/317, description of Reich Organisation Leadership of June 1932. Otto Strasser joined the party on 20 November 1925 (BDC: Personal File Otto Strasser). See his correspondence with the NSDAP Reichsleitung in November 1925 in BA: Sammlung Schumacher: 199.

12 For instance, Strasser maintained contact with Ludendorff's Tannenbergbund and others until Hitler prohibited such contact on 15 September 1925 (BA: NS26/185) and again on 5 February 1927 (BA: NS26/187).

13 Speech of 13 September 1925 entitled 'Das Versailles der deutschen Volkswirtschaft' in Strasser, *Hammer und Schwert*, pp. 27 ff.

14 Speech in Reichstag on 25 November 1925 in ibid., pp. 6–18.

15 Strasser, 'Fur einen Bund der unterdrückten Völker! Nieder mit Stresemann!', *VB*, 12–13 July 1925; 'Nationale Aussenpolitik. Der Bund der unterdrückten Völker', in Strasser, *Freiheit und Brot* (1928), pp. 46 ff.; 'Russland und wir', *VB*, 22 October 1925; 'Abrechnung', *VB*, 23 May 1925. See also Klaus Hildebrand, *Von Reich zum Weltreich. Hitler, NSDAP und die koloniale Frage 1919–1945* (Munich, 1969), pp. 60–1, 237–47.

16 Strasser, 'Mehr Aussenpolitik', *NS-Briefe*, 15 November 1926. None the less, sympathy for the Soviet Union was maintained in some Kampfverlag circles – see *NS-Briefe* of 15 October and 15 December 1927.

17 Strasser, 'Wir und die anderen' of 20 July 1925, in *Kampf um Deutschland*, pp. 62–71.

18 Reichstag speech of 25 November 1925, in Strasser, *Hammer und Schwert*, pp. 6–18.

19 BA: NS26/274, Strasser bill of 10 August 1925.

20 'Noch ein Rückblick und Ausblick, 1925–1926', in *VB*, 5 January 1926.

21 Strasser, 'Wir und die anderen', in *Kampf um Deutschland*, pp. 62–71.

22 Strasser, 'Nationaler Sozialismus. "Was heisst das: Vaterland?"' of 4 September 1925, in *Kampf um Deutschland*, pp. 72–7.

23 Strasser, 'Nationale Wirtschaft. Zum Abschluss des internationalen Eisenkartells', of 12 June 1925, in *Kampf um Deutschland*, pp. 43–9.

24 Another attempt to define what he meant by the concept, but which was similarly unclear, was: 'Autarkie! Grundsätzliches und Taktisches über unser Wirtschaftsprogramm', in April 1930, copy in BA: ZSg 103/809. But see report from Martin Blank to industrialist Paul Reusch of 29 December 1930, quoted in David Abraham, *The Collapse of the Weimar Republic: Political Economy and Crisis* (Princeton, NJ, 1981), pp. 164–5, and unjustifiably favourable comment in Barbara Miller Lane and Leila J. Rupp (eds), *Nazi Ideology before 1933: A Documentation* (Austin, Texas, 1978), p. xviii.

25 Strasser, 'Wir und die Agrarzölle', *VB*, 28–9 June 1925.

26 A completely opposite view which sees Otto as Gregor's disciple is unconvincingly presented by Miller Lane and Rupp (eds), *Nazi Ideology*, introduction.

27 This is underlined by his article, 'Der Tod des Mittelstandes', *VB*, 5 January 1926.

28 The claim that Gottfried Feder was a major and enduring influence on Strasser's ideas is quite unfounded (Miller Lane and Rupp (eds), *Nazi Ideology*, introduction). A suitable corrective to standard interpretations of Feder's role in the party as a whole is

given in Albrecht Tyrell's excellent 'Gottfried Feder und die NSDAP', in Peter D. Stachura (ed.), *The Shaping of the Nazi State* (London, 1978), pp. 48–87.

29 Anton M. Koktanek (ed.), *Oswald Spengler. Briefe 1913–1936* (Munich, 1963), pp. 391–3, letter of 2 June 1925.

30 Koktanek, 'Spenglers Verhältnis, pp. 48–50.

31 Koktanek (ed.), *Oswald Spengler*, pp. 397–401, letter of 8 July 1925.

32 Bay. HSA: ASA: Sonderabgabe I: 1809, report of 12 August 1925. He suffered from severe throat infection, high temperature, and other complications.

33 Lohse, *Der Fall Strasser*, pp. 4–5, exaggerates the severity of Strasser's depression at this time. Details in BDC: Personal File Gregor Strasser.

34 Goebbels, *Tagebuch*, entry of 21 August 1925; letter from Strasser to Goebbels of 29 August 1925 in BA: NS1/340.

35 He was unable to attend because his mother was seriously ill: Strasser telegram of 9 September to Gau Ruhr, in BA: NS1/340.

36 Full details of the meeting are given in Schildt, *Die Arbeitsgemeinschaft*, pp. 96 ff., 105 ff.; Wörtz, *Programmatik und Führerprinzip*, pp. 79 ff.; Jeremy Noakes, *The Nazi Party in Lower Saxony 1921–1933* (London, 1971), pp. 68 ff. On *NS-Briefe*, see Reichsleitung circular of 11 December 1925 in BA: NS26/185, and report of Hauptarchiv der NSDAP dated 10 October 1936 in BA: NS26/1175.

37 The Statutes are reprinted in Ernst Deuerlein (ed.), *Der Aufstieg der NSDAP in Augenzeugenberichten* (Munich, 1974), pp. 253–4.

38 Bullock, *Hitler*, p. 135, writes that in 1925–6 Strasser 'was threatening to take Hitler's place as the effective leader of the Party'; Lang and Schenck (eds), *Porträt eines Menschheitsverbrechers*, p. 159, suggest he would have split the party provided other Gauleiters supported him; but Schildt ('Die Arbeitsgemeinschaft', fos 111 ff.) Noakes (*Nazi Party*, p. 69) and Orlow (*History of the Nazi Party*, p. 67) all argue against any far-reaching ambitions on Strasser's part. More recently, Kissenkoetter, *Gregor Strasser*, p. 29, supports the latter view, albeit in cursory fashion.

39 Eitel Wolf Dobert, *Convert to Freedom* (New York, 1940), p. 181.

40 BA: NS1/340, Strasser to Goebbels of 11 November 1925.

41 Goebbels, *Tagebuch*, entries of 21 August and 2 October 1925.

42 BA: NS26/900, Fobke to Heinrich Dolle of 26 January 1926.

43 Perhaps a small example of this attitude came when Strasser invited the renegade Anton Drexler to address the Landshut branch of the party on 2 July 1925, and then had the temerity to introduce him as 'the founder of our movement'! The Reichsleitung was not amused; see letter of reprimand from Bouhler to Strasser of 8 July 1925, BA: Sammlung Schumacher: 199.

44 Konrad Heiden, *Adolf Hitler* (Zurich, 1936), pp. 227 ff.

45 According to Nyomarkay, *Charisma and Factionalism*, p. 13, Hitler identified himself with the 'idea' in 1930. Albrecht Tyrell believes it happened in 1930–1; see his 'Führergedanke und Gauleiterwechsel. Die Teilung des Gaues Rheinland der NSDAP 1931', *VfZG*, vol. 23 (1975), pp. 345–7.

46 BA: NS1/340, Strasser to Goebbels of 11 November 1925.

47 ibid., Goebbels to Strasser of 16 November 1925.

48 BA: NS26/86, description used by party member Josef Böger of Münster to Hitler on 8 August 1925.

49 The full title of the Draft was: 'Der nationale Sozialismus. Dispositionsentwurf eines umfassenden Programms des nationalen Sozialismus'. A copy is available in BA: NS26/896, but it has been printed in Kühnl, 'Zur Programmatik der Nationalsozialistischen Linken', pp. 324–33.

50 There are divided opinions among scholars regarding the authorship of the Draft, but most acknowledge Otto's influence to one degree or another: cf. Bradley Smith, *Hitler and the Strasser Challenge*, p. 117; B. Strasser, *Gregor und Otto Strasser*, p. 5; Kühnl, *Die NS-Linke*, p. 19, n. 110; Schulz, *Aufstieg des Nationalsozialismus*, p. 391. Otto

Strasser's own claims are contradictory; compare his *Exil*, p. 40 with *Hitler und Ich*, p. 109.

51 Goebbels criticised the Draft as 'deficient' (Goebbels, *Tagebuch*, entry 18 December 1925). But his correspondence with Otto Strasser over the Draft in December 1925 and January 1926 (BA: NS1/340 and /341) would seem to indicate his involvement. Kele, *Nazis and Workers*, p. 94, unaccountably stresses Goebbels' major influence.

52 BA: NS1/340, Strasser to Goebbels of 11 November 1925; BA: NS1/341, Otto Strasser to Goebbels of 30 December 1925.

53 Feder received a copy from the NSDAP leader in Quedlinburg, a Herr Freyberg, over Christmas. Strasser made a futile attempt to pacify Hitler by sending him a copy on 8 January 1926 with the feeble explanation that he was merely gathering the views of various colleagues for a possible new programme. See Jochmann (ed.), *Nationalsozialismus und Revolution*, Dok. 71, Strasser to Goebbels of 8 January 1926, and Goebbels, *Tagebuch*, entries for 6 January and 6 February 1926.

54 Peter D. Stachura, 'The NSDAP and the German working class, 1925–1933', in Isidor Walliman and Michael Dobkowski (eds), *Towards the Holocaust: Fascism and Anti-Semitism in Weimar Germany* (New York, 1982).

55 BA: NS26/896 for these critiques.

56 BA: NS26/1304 for Harnisch critique.

57 Mühlberger, *Rise of National Socialism in Westphalia*, p. 221.

58 Goebbels, *Tagebuch*, entry for 15 June 1926, for an unflattering description of Strasser's showing at Bamberg. The AG was dissolved in practice in July 1926, with Strasser giving formal notice on 1 October 1926 (*NS-Briefe* of that date). Strasser wrote to AG members on 5 March 1926 requesting return of the Draft (BA: NS26/900).

59 Goebbels, *Tagebuch*, entry for 22 February 1926.

60 BA: Sammlung Schumacher: 203, Strasser letter to Bouhler of 5 March 1926; BA: NS1/341, Strasser letter to Goebbels of 3 October 1925.

61 BA: NS1/340, Strasser to Goebbels of 1 April 1926.

62 *VB*, 11 March 1926; Goebbels, *Tagebuch*, entry for 10 March 1926.

63 BA: NS1/340, Strasser to Goebbels of 29 March 1926.

64 Strasser, 'Gedanken über Aufgaben der Zukunft', *NS-Briefe*, 15 June 1926, also printed in his *Kampf um Deutschland*, pp. 129–39.

65 Strasser, 'Nationaler Sozialismus' of 4 September 1925, in *Kampf um Deutschland*, pp. 72–7.

66 BA: NS26/1370, 'Die Staatsidee des Nationalsozialismus', speech of June 1932.

67 Rosenberg, 'Nationaler Sozialismus?', *VB*, 1 February 1926.

68 Strasser, 'Nationaler Sozialismus!' *NS-Briefe*, 15 February 1927.

69 BA: NS 8 (Kanzlei Rosenberg): 143, Rosenberg letter to Strasser of 24 February 1927.

70 Strasser speech in Reichstag on 10 May 1932 entitled 'Arbeit und Brot', in *Kampf um Deutschland*, pp. 345–78.

71 BA: NS26/1370, speech of June 1932, 'Die Staatsidee des Nationalsozialismus'.

72 Strasser, *NS-Briefe*, 1 July 1927.

73 Strasser, 'Bürger oder Proletarier – wen wollen wir?', in *Kampf um Deutschland*, pp. 162–6.

74 Strasser, *NS-Briefe*, 15 August 1926, 'Deutschvölkische Freiheitspartei und wir'.

75 ibid.; and Strasser, 'Das Ende des Bürgertums', *NS-Briefe*, 1 November 1929.

76 Strasser, 'Rot Front – Falsche Front', of 5 June 1927, in *Hammer und Schwert*, pp. 57 ff.; 'Götzendammerung des Marxismus' of 25 April 1926, in *Kampf um Deutschland*, pp. 117–24; 'Landesverrat als Programm' of 14 August 1927, ibid., pp. 183–8; 'Die Sozialdemokratie. Eine Abrechnung', of 15 November 1927, ibid., pp. 191–7.

77 Strasser in *Berliner Arbeiterzeitung*, 11 March 1928, copy in Staatsarchiv Koblenz: 403 (Oberpräsident der Rheinprovinz): 16742.

78 Strasser, *VB*, 1 February 1931. Similar sentiments are found in his article,

'Nationalsozialismus und Geschichte', of 1 January 1929, in *Kampf um Deutschland*, pp. 225–9; and in his 'Der letzte Abwehrkampf des Systems', 1931, ibid., pp. 317–34.

79 Strasser, 'Noch ein Rückblick und Ausblick', *VB*, 5 January 1926.

80 ibid. For background, see Rhodes, *The Hitler Movement*, pp. 58–66.

81 George L. Mosse, *Germans and Jews: The Right, the Left, and the Search for a 'Third Force' in Pre-Nazi Germany* (New York, 1970), p. 103, and *The Crisis of German Ideology: Intellectual Origins of the Third Reich* (New York, 1964), p. 289.

82 Strasser, *NS-Briefe*, 1 February 1927.

83 ibid., 15 February 1927.

84 Strasser: speech in Bavarian Landtag, 9 July 1924, in *Kampf um Deutschland*, p. 29.

85 Strasser, 'Die Frau und der Nationalsozialismus' of 4 April 1932, in *Kampf um Deutschland*, p. 338.

86 BA: R56I/71, speech of 18 May 1932 entitled 'Vom Marxismus zum Sozialismus'. For further examples of similar sentiments, see his 'Zum 29. August' of 29 August 1926, in *Hammer und Schwert*, pp. 43 ff.; 'Der Sklavenmarkt des Kapitalismus' of 23 August 1926, ibid., pp. 45 ff.; 'Triumph der Börse' of 31 October 1926, in *Kampf um Deutschland*, pp. 152–6.

87 Strasser, *NS-Briefe*, 15 May 1930.

88 BA: ZSg 103/831, Strasser Reichstag speech of 17 October 1930 entitled 'Wesen und Ziel der nationalsozialistischen Idee'. His radio speech of June 1932 carried similar demands (BA: NS26/1370).

89 Bay. HSA: ASA: Staatsministeriums des Innern: 73707, speech in Berlin Sportpalast of 23 October 1931.

90 BA: ZSg 103/771, report on Reichstag sitting of 15 June 1929.

91 BA: NS26/58, Strasser speech of 23 July 1932; and also in speech in Stuttgart on 20 December 1931, BA: NS26/1370.

92 Strasser, 'Götzendammerung des Marxismus' of 25 April 1926, in *Kampf um Deutschland*, p. 120.

93 Strasser, *VB*, 5 December 1928.

94 Donald L. Niewyk, *The Jews in Weimar Germany* (London, 1980), p. 88; Arnold Paucker, *Der jüdische Abwehrkampf gegen Anti-Semitismus und Nationalsozialismus in den letzten Jahren der Weimarer Republik* (Hamburg, 1968), pp. 81–2.

95 Goebbels, *Tagebuch*, entries for 21 and 25 August and 23 September 1926, indicate the beginnings of a rift. See also Helmut Heiber, *Goebbels* (London, 1972), pp. 48 ff.

96 Koch, 'Folgen der Rassenvermischung', in *Der Nationale Sozialist* of 23 April 1927 and in other Kampfverlag newspapers. In *Exil*, p. 42, Otto confirms Goebbels was the target.

97 Ernest K. Bramsted, *Goebbels und die nationalsozialistische Propaganda 1925–1945*(Frankfurt, 1971), p. 47.

98 IfZG: FA-114, Gregor Strasser to Hess of 15 June 1927; and BA: NSD5/4, report on Reichstag sitting of 16 December 1930.

99 BA: Sammlung Schumacher: 260, Strasser letter to Reichsleitung of 14 October 1927 stresses the point about competition.

100 IfZG: FA-114, Goebbels letter to Hitler of 5 June 1927, Gregor Strasser to Hess of 15 and 18 June 1927. Further documentation in Goebbels, *Tagebuch*, appendix.

101 BA: NS26/1175, reports of 30 October 1936.

102 BA: NS26/487, Strasser letter of 8 October 1928 to all party members, asking them to sign a declaration in support of the leadership's stand against Dinter. Ignoring Hitler's direct summons, Dinter had failed to appear at the party's conference in Munich, August/early September 1928: details in BA: Sammlung Schumacher: 373. See also Tyrell, *Führer befiehl*, pp. 149, 202–5, 210–11.

103 *Das Geistchristentum*, Heft 16 (1929), 182; copy in BA: ZSg 103/771.

104 BA: NS18/592, letter of 10 July 1929 from Himmler to NSDAP Gau Silesia, which dismisses Dinter's accusations as 'not worth a reply'.

105 *Der Jungdeutsche* of 27 August 1930 (copy in BA: ZSg 103/783) reported Dinter's continuing anti-Strasser campaign in 1930.
106 Strasser in Bavarian Landtag, 9 July 1924, in *Kampf um Deutschland*, p. 24.
107 BA: ZSg 103/831, speech of 17 October 1930, 'Wesen und Ziel der nationalsozialistischen Idee'.
108 In his radio speech of June 1932, 'Die Staatsidee des Nationalsozialismus', BA: NS26/1370.
109 BA: Sammlung Schumacher: 319, Strasser letter of 5 June 1931 to NSDAP Reichstag deputy Jürgen von dem Knesebeck. As a matter of incidental interest, twenty-five of the 107 NSDAP deputies elected to the Reichstag in September 1930 were Catholics (BA: ZSg 103/776).
110 Rudolf Jordan, appointed Gauleiter of Halle-Merseburg on 19 January 1931.
111 Strasser, *NS-Briefe*, 1 March 1928.
112 Strasser, *Der Faust*, 15 July 1929.
113 ibid., 2 February 1929, 13 November 1929.
114 Strasser, *VB*, 3–4 May 1931 as one example.
115 Strasser, 'Das Wesen des Zentrums' of 1 January 1928, in *Kampf um Deutschland*, pp. 198–206.
116 Strasser, *NS-Briefe*, 15 May 1930.
117 Otto Braun, the Prussian SPD leader.
118 BA: Nachlass Friedrich Grimm, Band 6, fo. 8. Strasser's remarks of August 1932.
119 Kurt Meier, *Der Evangelische Kirchenkampf*, Band I (Göttingen, 1976), pp. 56–76; Jonathan R. C. Wright, *'Above Parties': The Political Attitudes of the German Protestant Church Leadership 1918–1933* (London, 1974), pp. 148–51, which has details of the 1931 correspondence between Wilhelm Kube and Strasser.
120 BA: ZSg 103/772, Strasser statement of May 1931; BDC: Personal File Gregor Strasser.
121 Jill Stephenson, *The Nazi Organisation of Women* (London, 1981), pp. 14–15, 20, 38–42, 44–52, provides an authoritative discussion of the group's establishment and development.
122 Strasser, 'Die Frau und der Nationalsozialismus' of 4 April 1932, in *Kampf um Deutschland*, pp. 335–41; see also his remarks in brochure entitled *Was hat die deutsche Frau vom Nationalsozialismus zu erwarten?* (Berlin, 1932), p. 26 – copy in BA: ZSg 2/196; and his *Principles of the NS–Frauenschaft* in BA: Sammlung Schumacher: 230.
123 Strasser speech to NS-Frauenschaft meeting, *VB*, 27–8 March 1932.
124 Strasser, 'Gedanken über Aufgaben der Zukunft', *NS-Briefe*, 15 June 1926.
125 NS26/1370, speech of 6 December 1931 to NS-Deutscher Ärztebund (Doctors' League).
126 David Schoenbaum, *Hitler's Social Revolution: Class and Status in Nazi Germany, 1933–39* (London, 1966), pp. 187 ff.
127 Henry A. Turner, 'Hitlers Einstellung zu Wirtschaft und Gesellschaft vor 1933', *Geschichte und Gesellschaft*, vol. 2 (1976), pp. 95–6, 98 ff., 105 ff.; Martin Broszat, *German National Socialism 1919–1945* (Santa Barbara, Calif., 1966), pp. 57–8, 69.
128 Adolf Hitler, *Mein Kampf*, ed. D. Watt (London, 1969), examples on pp. 339, 340–3, 347, 370, 391, 447.
129 The ban on his speaking in public was enforced by many states from 1925 until 1927–9. Details in Adolf Dresler and Fritz Maier-Hauptmann (eds), *Dokumente zur Zeitgeschichte. Dokumente der Sammlung Rehse aus der Kampfzeit* (Munich, 1941), pp. 185–7.
130 BA: R43I/2696, Berlin police report of 1 November 1926.
131 Orlow, *History of the Nazi Party*, pp. 77–126.
132 Hauptstaatsarchiv Stuttgart: E 130 II: Akten des Württ. Staatsministeriums 1813–1943: Büschel 535, report of Strasser meeting in Ulm in June 1927 being dis-

rupted by leftists. See also Bay. HSA: SAM: Polizeidirektion München: 6745 for report of 7 May 1927 on meeting in Magdeburg at which Strasser's head was badly gashed during a fight with KPD members.

133 BA: NS26/1176; Walter Görlitz and Herbert A. Quint, *Adolf Hitler. Eine Biographie* (Stuttgart, 1952), p. 252. Strasser reputedly sold at a considerable loss: see BA: NS26/1370, Berlin police report of 27 March 1931.

134 Otto Strasser, *Hitler und Ich*, p. 91.

135 By 1930 it published three daily newspapers (*Der Nationale Sozialist*, printed in eight or nine regional editions; *Der Märkischer Beobachter;* and *Der Sächsischer Beobachter*) and three weeklies (*Berliner Arbeiterzeitung*; *Rhenisch-Westfälische Arbeiter-Zeitung*; and *Der Faust*). Details in BA: ZSg 2/196 and BA: ZSg 103/782. For speculation on the financial implications, see BA: ZSg 103/777, report by *Volkswille* of 31 December 1930.

136 Klaus F. Schmidt, 'Die "Nationalsozialistischen Briefe" (1925–30)', in *Paul Kluke zum 60. Geburtstag* (Frankfurt, 1968), pp. 111–26, esp. pp. 117 ff.; on 23 April 1927, Hitler decreed that the periodical had no official character (*VB*, 23 April 1927). The party programme had been declared unalterable as early as 1921 when Hitler became leader (Tyrell, *Führer befiehl*, p. 32).

137 BA: NS1/340, Strasser to Goebbels of 22 June 1926; on the same theme Strasser to Kaufmann of 13 July 1926 (BA: NS1/340), and to the Wiesbaden branch of 4 April 1927 (Hessisches Hauptstaatsarchiv: Abteilung 483/2921).

138 BA: ZSg 2/196.

139 Martin Broszat, 'Die Anfänge der NSDAP in Berlin 1926/27', *VfZG*, vol. 8 (1960), p. 91.

140 BA: Sammlung Schumacher: 203, Kaufmann report of January 1927 to Reichsleitung; Noakes, *Nazi Party*, pp. 101 ff.; Johnpeter H. Grill, 'The Nazi Party in Baden, 1920–1945', Vol. I, doctoral dissertation, University of Michigan, 1975, fos 157–8; BA: R43I/2696, Berlin police report of March 1927.

141 Bay. HSA: Geheimes Staatsarchiv: MA 101248, report of 15 October 1927 by Reichskommissar für die Überwachung der öffentl. Ordnung; Heinrich A. Winkler, *Mittelstand, Demokratie und Nationalsozialismus. Die Politische Entwicklung von Handwerk und Kleinhandel in der Weimarer Republik* (Cologne, 1972), pp. 159, 165.

142 Michael H. Kater, 'Der NS-Studentenbund von 1926 bis 1928: Randgruppe zwischen Hitler und Strasser', *VfZG*, vol. 22 (1974), pp. 156 ff., 161–73.

143 Peter D. Stachura, *Nazi Youth in the Weimar Republic* (Santa Barbara, Calif., 1975), pp. 47–62.

144 Conan J. Fischer, 'The occupational background of the SA's rank and file membership during the Depression years, 1929 to mid-1934', in Stachura (ed.), *Shaping of the Nazi State*, pp. 138, 152.

145 BA: NS26/1370, Gregor Strasser personal details.

146 BA: Sammlung Schumacher: 382, Strasser to Reichsleitung of 10 July 1926.

147 Bay. HSA: ASA: Sonderabgabe I: 1768, Strasser statement of 17 September 1926.

148 Bay. HSA: Geheimes Staatsarchiv: MA 101247, Berlin police report of 1 November 1926.

149 BA: R43I/2696, Berlin police report of July 1927.

150 Ibid, Berlin police report of 15 October 1927.

151 Werner Jochmann (ed.), *Im Kampf um die Macht. Hitlers Rede vor dem Hamburger Nationalklub von 1919* (Frankfurt, 1960); Henry A. Turner, 'Hitler's secret pamphlet for industrialists, 1927', *Journal of Modern History*, vol. 40 (1968), pp. 348–74.

152 Henry A. Turner, 'Emil Kirdorf and the Nazi Party', *Central European History*, vol. 1 (1968), pp. 326–31, 334–5; Turner, 'Big business and the rise of Hitler', *American Historical Review*, vol. 75 (1969–70), pp. 60 ff.

153 *Mein Kampf*, pp. 544–53.

154 Kater, 'Sozialer Wandel', pp. 25–8; Kater, 'Ansätze zu einer Soziologie der SA bis zur Röhm-Krise', in Ulrich Engelhardt *et al.* (eds), *Soziale Bewegung und Politische Verfassung* (Stuttgart, 1976), p. 802.

155 Timothy W. Mason, *Sozialpolitik im Dritten Reich. Arbeiterklasse und Volksgemeinschaft* (Opladen, 1977), ch. 2.
156 BA: NS26/1103, Reventlow statement of February 1927.
157 BA: NS18/592, report on Strasser's decision. See also extracts from *Das Deutsche Tageblatt*, BA: ZSg 103/779.
158 BA: NS18/592, reports on Mecklenburg and Thuringian campaigns in 1927.
159 *Statistisches Jahrbuch für das Deutsche Reich, 1927* (Berlin, 1928), p. 501.
160 Strasser, *Berliner Arbeiterzeitung* of 11 March 1928, copy in Staatsarchiv Koblenz: 403/16742.
161 Peter D. Stachura, 'Der kritische Wendepunkt? Die NSDAP und die Reichstagswahlen vom 20. Mai 1928', *VfZG*, vol. 26 (1978), pp. 83 ff.
162 *VB*, 4 January 1928.
163 BA: R43I/2696, Berlin police report of December 1927; Bay. HSA: SAM: Polizeidirektion München: 6759, police report of 25 February 1928.
164 Strasser, *Der Nationale Sozialist für Sachsen*, 9 January 1927.
165 Bay. HSA: SAM: Polizeidirektion München: 6782, Hitler statement of 15 December 1927.
166 ibid., Hitler statement of 8 January 1927.
167 *VB*, 21 December 1927, Strasser, 'Wie wird man Nationalsozialist?', and Strasser statement of 19 December 1927, BA: NS18/595.
168 Jochmann (ed.), *NS und Revolution*, pp. 243–65, documents 80, 82–5, 87.
169 BA: NS26/1290, Reichsleitung memorandum of 29 March 1927.
170 BA: NS18/577, letter from NSDAP Königsberg to Reichsleitung of 21 January 1928; and Richard Bessel, 'The SA in the eastern regions of Germany, 1925–1934', doctoral dissertation, University of Oxford, 1980, fo. 41.
171 BA: NS26/1524, Munich police report of 20 May 1928.
172 BA: ZSg 2/196, report on his attendance at over 200 public meetings in 1928. Details of his numerous engagements during the election campaign in BA: NS18/574, 573, 577, 537. See also letter of appreciation for Strasser's services from SA members in Regensburg, 25 May 1928, to Reichsleitung, BA: NS18/576.
173 BA: R43I/1005 for full list of names, NSDAP May 1928. Strasser was a candidate in sixteen districts. It might have been seventeen had Gau Rhineland not objected to him; letter to Reichsleitung of 16 April 1928, BA: Sammlung Schumacher: 203.
174 BA: R43I/2696, Berlin police report of July 1928.
175 Stachura, 'Der kritische Wendepunkt?', pp. 84 ff., for full electoral details. In Strasser's home town of Landshut the NSDAP won 12 per cent of the vote, which undoubtedly reflected his popularity there (figures in *Statistik des Deutschen Reiches*, Band 372, II, *Die Wahlen Zum Reichstag am 20. Mai 1928*, Heft II (Berlin, 1930), pp. 55–6. In Lower Bavaria as a whole the BVP and Bauernpartei totally eclipsed the NSDAP (Geoffrey Pridham, *Hitler's Rise to Power: The Nazi Movement in Bavaria, 1923–33* (London, 1973), pp. 83 ff.).

Chapter 4

1 BA: NS26/1509, miscellaneous correspondence of party members. See also the *VB*, 22 and 23 May 1928.
2 ibid., 31 May 1928.
3 ibid., 23 May 1928, for Rosenberg statement; *NS-Jahrbuch* 1929 (Munich, 1930), p. 158, for Frick's remarks.
4 *VB*, 31 May 1928.
5 BA: Sammlung Schumacher: 260, Hitler's letter of 27 June 1928 to all NSDAP editors.
6 BA: NS26/1516 for details of Führertagung 31 August–2 September 1928; see also *VB*, 2–3 September 1928; Orlow, *History of the Nazi Party*, p. 134 ff.

7 Gerhard L. Weinberg (ed.), *Hitlers zweites Buch. Ein Dokument aus dem Jahre 1928* (Stuttgart, 1961), esp. pp. 78 ff.

8 BA: Sammlung Schumacher: 374, Hitler directive of 15 September 1928.

9 BA: NS22/366, Strasser to Bergmann of 11 September 1928; BA: NS22/383, Strasser to T. Müller of 11 February 1929.

10 Among these were, for example: Kaufmann as Gauleiter of Hamburg in April 1929; Franz Stöhr as Deputy Gauleiter of Halle-Merseburg; Friedrich Karl Florian as Gauleiter of Düsseldorf in October 1929; Fritz Reinhardt as Gauleiter of Upper Bavaria in October 1928; Carl Röver as Gauleiter of Weser-Ems in October 1928; Erich Koch as Gauleiter of East Prussia in October 1928; Josef Wagner as Gauleiter of Westphalia South and Alfred Meyer of Westphalia North in January 1931; Rudolf Jordan as Gauleiter of Halle-Merseburg in January 1931. See also the case of Konstantin Hierl later in this chapter.

11 See interesting letter in this respect from Albert Krebs to Otto Strasser of 19 October 1929, BA: Nachlass Krebs, No. 7.

12 Ernst Hanfstaengl, *Hitler: The Missing Years* (London, 1957), p. 161.

13 Anseln Faust, *Der Nationalsozialistische Deutsche Studentenbund. Studenten und Nationalsozialismus in der Weimarer Republik* (Düsseldorf, 1973), pp. 76 ff.

14 Stachura, *Nazi Youth*, pp. 57–66.

15 BA: NS26/82, Hitler directive of 7 May 1928; BA: NS18/579, Himmler to Hans Schemm, November 1928.

16 Richard Breitman, *German Socialism and Weimar Democracy* (Chapel Hill, NC, 1981), pp. 144 ff.

17 BDC: Personal File Gregor Strasser.

18 See letter of 11 November 1929 to Strasser from members in Gau Schleswig-Holstein complaining about Gauleiter Lohse, BA: NS22/1069.

19 BA: NS22/1070, Strasser letter of 16 October 1929 in which he expresses his dissatisfaction with the performance of Gau Württemberg; see also his letter of 21 October 1929 to Fritz Strauss of branch Lindau (Swabia), urging more care in its administration, BA: NS22/1070, and his letter of 15 April 1929 to Gauleiter Josef Wagner of Westphalia, BA: NS22/1076.

20 BA: NS22/1064, Strasser letter of 9 May 1930 to Wilhelm Kube on this theme.

21 BA: Nachlass Krebs: No. 7, Strasser letter to Krebs of 28 January 1929. See also in this file Krebs' letters to Strasser of 6 October and 11 December 1928. Strasser further clarified his position to Franz Stöhr in letter of 8 January 1929, BA: NS22/1049.

22 BA: Nachlass Krebs: No. 5, Krebs letter of 28 August 1929 to Erich Lindner.

23 BA: Sammlung Schumacher: 218, Strasser order of 16 January 1930.

24 The ban on these two groups was repeated on 29 April 1931 (ibid., Strasser directive of 29 April 1931). In June 1932 he estabished a civil service department (Beamtenabteilung) in the Reich Organisation Leadership.

25 BA: NS26/1390, Reich Organisation Leadership document of December 1929.

26 BA: NS22/348, Strasser directive of 9 January 1930.

27 His ideas on general organisational development were outlined in his article, 'Die Bedeutung der Organisation', *Illustrieter Beobachter*, 3 August 1929.

28 Details in *VB*, 12 September 1929.

29 BA: NS26/1352, personal details Hierl. See also Gert Borst, *Die Ludendorff-Bewegung 1919–1961* (Augsburg, 1969), pp. 124–6; Wolfram Mallebrein, *Konstantin Hierl. Schöpfer und Gestalter des Reichsarbeitsdienstes* (Hanover, 1971), pp. 44 ff.

30 BDC: Personal File K. Hierl.

31 Hierl put out his first ideas on long-term planning in a memorandum of 22 October 1929 entitled 'Geistige Vorbereitung des zukünftigen nationalsozialistischen Staatsaufbaues', BA: Sammlung Schumacher: 373.

32 *NS-Briefe*, July 1928 editions, miscellaneous contributions; *Der Angriff* of 16 July 1928.

33 Otto Strasser, 'Gedanken zum Wahlergebnis', *NS-Briefe*, 15 June 1928.
34 BA: NS18/579, Bouhler letter of 14 July 1928 to Strasser; BA: NS18/592, report of October 1928 by NSDAP Reichsleitung.
35 Erich Rosikat, *Die Lehren der Maiwahlen 1928 für die Partei-völkische Bewegung Deutschlands* (Breslau, 1928). He was later associated with Otto Strasser's Black Front organisation (BA: ZSgl/240).
36 Gregor Strasser, *Berliner Arbeiterzeitung*, 27 May 1928, in which he notes the advance of the Left at the election and the NSDAP's success among small farmers because of its nationalism and racism.
37 BA: NS22/348, Strasser memorandum of 22 June 1928.
38 Gregor Strasser, *Das Hitlerbüchlein. Ein Abriss vom Leben und Wirkens des Führers der nationalsozialistischen Freiheitsbewegung Adolf Hitler* (Kampfverlag (sic!), Berlin, 1928), esp. pp. 13–16. A copy is available in BA: NSD70/39; 80,000 copies of the twenty-four page booklet were printed, costing fifty Pfennig each.
39 Kissenkoetter, *Gregor Strasser*, p. 40, n. 63, reproduces a private letter supposedly written by Hitler on 4 January 1929 indicating his hostility to Strasser. Kissenkoetter does not quote a source other than 'private' for this letter. But even if the letter is genuine, which in this author's view is extremely doubtful, Kissenkoetter has grossly exaggerated its significance.
40 BA: NS22/1066, Strasser letter of 20 July 1928 to Dr Repfennig of Pasewalk.
41 BA: NS22/363, Strasser letter to Gau Brandenburg of 5 December 1928.
42 BA: ZSg103/1381, Strasser statement of January 1928.
43 *VB*, 11 May 1929; Kühnl, *Die NS-Linke*, p. 186.
44 See Strasser's 'highly confidential' memorandum to Gauleiter Fritz Reinhardt of 12 August 1929, BA: Sammlung Schumacher: 206.
45 As expressed in Strasser's forty-eight-page pamphlet, '58 Jahre Young-Plan!' of October 1929: copy in BA: NSD70/533. Criticism of his attacks on some of his allies came from several quarters, including Major von Stephani, the Berlin Stahlhelm leader, BA: ZSg2/195. Another of Strasser's anti-capitalist speeches in connection with the Young Plan, on 11 September 1929, is in Bay. HSA: Geheimes Staatsarchiv: MA 101235/3.
46 BA: R58 (Sicherheitspolizei und polit. Nachrichtendienst): 1150, Rundschreiben der Nachrichtensammelstelle im RMI of 13 November 1929.
47 Strasser in *NS-Briefe*, 1 November 1929, and in *Der Nationale Sozialist*, 30 March 1930.
48 For example, his discussion of 'Revolution' in *NS-Briefe*, 15 May 1929, and in a Reichstag speech on 11 June 1929 (BA: ZSg103/812).
49 BA: NS26/1299, Strasser statement of 9 February 1930; BA: R134/90, Reichswehr report of 16 April 1930 on the NSDAP.
50 Strasser article, 'Nie wieder Krieg', in *Berliner Arbeiterzeitung*, 7 October 1928, also in *Kampf um Deutschland*, pp. 217–21.
51 BA: NS26/1370, Strasser speech in Stolp of 13 June 1929; his 'Bemerkungen zur Lage', *NS-Briefe*, 1 October 1929; speech in Breslau in April 1929, BA: R43I/2682; speech in Reichstag on 14 March 1929, BA: NSD5/34, and on 13 December 1929, BA: NSD5/35; article 'Gegen das System' of 17 November 1929, in *Kampf um Deutschland*, pp. 250–2; speech in Düsseldorf on 1 March 1929, SAK: 403/16742, and others.
52 Strasser in *NS-Briefe*, 1 June 1929.
53 BA: NS22/1076, Strasser letter to lawyers in Hamm of 19 November 1929.
54 Details in BA: NS26/1370, personal details Gregor Strasser; BA: ZSg103/781 and /782. On a few occasions he was the injured party and won small damages, for example, from *Vorwärts*, the SPD organ (BA:NS26/968, report of 30 March 1930).
55 *VB*, 15 June 1929; Bay. HSA: SAM: Polizeidirektion München: 6767, report of June 1929.
56 The first occasion concerned a KPD deputy accused of high treason, Bay. HSA: SAM: Polizeidirektion München: 6767, report of June 1929.

57 BA: ZSg2/196.
58 *Der Faust*, February 1929, copy in BA: ZSg103/789.
59 Bay. HSA: SAM: Polizeidirektion München: 6772, various reports. See also the *Central-Verein-Zeitung* of 8 March 1929, BA: ZSg103/782; and *Der Jungdeutsche*, 6 March 1929, BA: ZSg103/789.
60 BA: NS26/391.
61 See an interesting letter on this theme from Graf Heinz Finckenstein of the Silesian SA to Himmler, 10 July 1930, BS: NS18/582.
62 Otto Strasser, *Hitler und Ich*, p. 103; Gregor Strasser to Rudolf Jung of 22 July 1930, BA: Sammlung Schumacher: 313; IfZG: F28 – Private Dokumente Dr Curt Korn, Strasser to Korn of 25 July 1930. Otto's post-1933 statements about the close intimacy of his relationship with Gregor were highly coloured by the circumstances of June 1934 and glossed over any difficulties. In the foreword to his *Die deutsche Bartholomäusnacht*, p. 12, he writes that Gregor was 'the best, the only friend of my life', and in his *30 Juni*... comments that 'my brother was for more than thirty years my best friend'.
63 The book was published in 1929 by a Kampfverlag team which did *not* include Gregor Strasser.
64 His *Aufbau des deutschen Sozialismus* (Leipzig, 1932).
65 BA: NS26/1404, Mücke speech in Stuttgart, 10 March 1931.
66 Hessisches Hauptstaatsarchiv: Abteilung 483 (NSDAP Hessen-Nassau): 2657, H. Friedrich to Theo Habicht of 15 January 1929.
67 Hitler informed Otto Wagener that Strasser had 'too strong a personality' for this post (IfZG: Otto Wagener Tagebuch: ED-60/3. Also given in Turner (ed.), *Hitler aus nächster Nähe*, p. 310.
68 BA: ZSg103/781, report of 20 June 1930 in *Volkswille*.
69 IfZG: Z18: *Deutsche Nationale-Zeitung* of 29 August 1969, p. 12, Strasser letter to Herr Erckmann of 7 August 1930.
70 Bernhard Strasser, *Gregor und Otto Strasser*, pp. 7 ff.
71 BA: NS26/190, meeting of 24 April 1930.
72 *VB*, 29 April 1930.
73 Bay. HSA: ASA: Sonderabgabe I: 1740; BA: NS26/1403, Württemberg police report of 24 April 1930.
74 Contrary to a Berlin police report of 15 June 1930, SAK: 403/16764, Gregor did not attend a founding meeting in Berlin in May 1930 of the 'Gruppe sozialrevolutionärer Nationalisten'.
75 Otto Strasser, *Hitler und Ich*, pp. 137–49; and his *Ministersessel oder Revolution? Eine wahrheitsgemässe Darstellung meiner Trennung von der NSDAP* (Berlin, 1930), pp. 5, 12, 17–25.
76 *Der Faust*, 25 May 1930, copy in BA: NSD5/35.
77 BA: NS26/1176, Strasser declaration of 30 June 1930. Hans Hinkel, who had bought himself into co-ownership of the Kampfverlag with the Strassers, also stayed in the party, but claimed to have lost a lot of money in selling his share of the press to the Eher-Verlag (IfZG: Zeugenschrift 1878: Hans Hinkel). In November 1931, Otto formally wound up the Kampfverlag.
78 Bay. HSA: SAM: Polizeidirektion München: 6791, statement of 3 July 1930.
79 BA: Sammlung Schumacher: 313, Strasser to Jung of 22 July 1930.
80 BA: NS22/1062, Strasser to Bayer of 17 September 1930.
81 IfZG: Z18, letter of 7 August 1930. See also IfZG: F28, Strasser to Dr Korn of 25 July 1930.
82 *Der Angriff*, 3 July 1930.
83 cf. Otto Wagener's and Franz von Pfeffer's high opinion of Strasser, in Turner (ed.), *Hitler aus nächster Nähe*, pp. 17, 97. Rank-and-file appreciation of him at this time is illustrated by a letter to Strasser from party member Ludwig Hassel, Erlangen, 18 June 1930, in BA: NS22/1060.

84 Rosenberg, *Letzte Aufzeichnungen*, p. 112.

85 Wolfgang Schäfer, *NSDAP. Entwicklung und Struktur des Staatspartei des Dritten Reiches* (Hanover, 1957), p. 5.

86 Ernst Niekisch, *Gewagtes Leben. Begegnungen und Begebnisse* (Cologne, 1958), p. 180; Charles Bloch, *Die SA und die Krise des NS-Regimes 1934* (Frankfurt, 1970), p. 16.

87 Otto Strasser, *Aufbau*, p. 120.

88 This is made clear in Gregor's letter to Otto of 31 December 1932, BA: R43II/1194.

89 On these rumours in 1931–2 see BA: NS26/87, report of 29 August 1931; ibid., report of 18 December 1931; BA: R22 (Reichsjustizministerium): 5006, Berlin police report of May 1931; ibid., report in *Münchener Post* of 24 June 1931; BA: NSD5/17, report of 12 January 1932.

90 BA: NS22/1067, Gregor Strasser to Dr Fritsch of Gau Saxony, 1 July 1931.

91 BA: Sammlung Schumacher: 204, Strasser to Loeper, 1 October 1930.

92 BA: R43II/1194, Gestapo report of 8 January 1934; Otto Strasser, *Exil*, p. 72; and *Die deutsche Bartholomäusnacht*, p. 39.

93 BA: NS26/1403, Württemberg police report of June 1930. On the Black Front see Louis Dupeux, *Stratégie communiste et dynamique conservatrice. Essai sur les différents sens de l'expression 'National-Bolchevisme' en Allemagne, sous la République de Weimar, 1919–1933* (Paris, 1979) pp. 366 ff., 493 ff.; Richard Schapke, *Die Schwarze Front. Von den Zielen und Aufgaben und vom Kämpfe der Deutschen Revolution* (Leipzig, 1932).

94 Kühnl, *Die NS-Linke*, pp. 1, 89, 230, 260. But he reaches the correct conclusion for the wrong reasons. For instance, Kühnl believes there was a coherent 'Nazi Left', and is totally unaware of Gregor Strasser's changing outlook before and after 1930.

95 Rumours that Goebbels and Count Reventlow would join Otto Strasser were unfounded, BA: NS26/1363, Berlin police report of 27 March 1931, and 1 May 1931. Gottfried Feder felt it necessary to clear his lines with Hitler by welcoming the exclusion of Otto and his 'Bolshevik ideas' from the Party, IfZG: MA-393, Feder to Hitler, 10 July 1930.

96 As suggested by Otto Strasser, *Mein Kampf*, p. 9, and Bernhard Strasser, *Gregor und Otto Strasser*, p. 8.

Chapter 5

1 BA: NS26/1403, Württemberg police report of 7 May 1930.

2 BA: NS26/392, Strasser memorandum of August 1930.

3 BA: NS18/584, for details of his speeches. See also his article, 'Sammlung der Todfeinde', in *VB*, 9 September 1930.

4 Heinrich A. Winkler, 'Extremismus der Mitte? Sozialgeschichtliche Aspekte der nationalsozialistischen Machtergreifung', *VfZG*, vol. 20 (1972), p. 181.

5 Karl O'Lessker, 'Who voted for Hitler? A new look at the class basis of Nazism', *American Journal of Sociology*, vol. 74 (1968–9), pp. 63–9.

6 Brüning, *Memoiren*, p. 191; Gottfried R. Treviranus, *Das Ende von Weimar. Heinrich Brüning und seine Zeit* (Düsseldorf, 1968), p. 161.

7 Larry E. Jones: '"The dying middle": Weimar Germany and the fragmentation of bourgeois politics', *Central European History*, vol. V (1972), pp. 23–54, esp. pp. 49 ff; also Jones, 'The dissolution of the bourgeois party system in the Weimar Republic', in Richard Bessel and E. J. Feuchtwanger (eds), *Social Change and Political Development in Weimar Germany* (London, 1981), pp. 268–88, esp. pp. 278 ff.

8 There is a substantial and expanding volume of literature on the social composition of the National Socialist movement before 1933. A summary of the principal conclusions to date is given in Peter D. Stachura, 'Who were the Nazis? A socio-political analysis of

the National Socialist *Machtübernahme*', *European Studies Review*, vol. 11 (1981), esp. pp. 299–314.

9 *Reichstags: Handbuch*, Vol. V (Berlin, 1930), p. 489; Vol. VI (Berlin, 1932), p. 232; Vol. VII (Berlin, 1932), p. 421.

10 Speech of 17 October, 'Wesen und Ziel der nationalsozialistischen Idee', in BA: ZSg103/831. The May 1932 speech is discussed later in this chapter.

11 Bay. HSA: SAM: Polizeidirektion München: 6767, police report of October 1930.

12 BA: Sammlung Schumacher: 319, Löbe statement of July 1932.

13 BA: R43I/1018, Strasser reply to Löbe of 13 July 1932.

14 Strasser's nomination for the post was Franz Stöhr (BA: ZSg103/784, press report of 4 September 1932).

15 BA: R43I/2684. The assault had taken place in the Reichstag's restaurant. Strasser was acquitted by the court, but several of his associates in the fracas were given brief prison sentences.

16 See above, note 10.

17 BA: Sammlung Schumacher: 319, Strasser letter to Fritz Reinhardt of 14 April 1931; also a few details in BA: NS22/1076. Strasser had gone off on holiday on Boxing Day 1930.

18 BA: NS20: Kleine Erwerbungen: 67, press report of meeting, 28 April 1931. Arising from this meeting was a false report that Strasser was to be appointed leader of all NSDAP Gaue in Prussia (Lohse, 'Der Fall Strasser', pp. 10–11).

19 BA: NS22/349, Strasser letter to Elsbeth Zander of 11 June 1931.

20 BDC: Personal File Reventlow, letter to Strasser from Reventlow of 18 July 1931.

21 BA: NS26/265, Strasser memorandum as Reich Organisation Leader of 15 October 1932 to all Gauleiters. A similar warning about mechanisation was given by him to his own staff on 18 July 1932, BA: NS22/348.

22 Orlow, *Nazi Party*, pp. 258 ff., for full details.

23 See, for example, his detailed memorandum of 8 July 1932 concerning postage, briefing and other minor matters in the Brown House (BA: NS25: Hauptamt für Kommunalpolitik: 117).

24 See his foreword to the *Dienstvorschrift für die Politische Organisation vom 15. Juli 1932*, BA: ZSg3/1079.

25 Hüttenberger, *Die Gauleiter*, p. 60; Orlow, *Nazi Party*, pp. 259–60.

26 Hans-Adolf Jacobsen, 'Die Gründung der Auslandsabteilung der NSDAP (1931–1933)', in E. Schulin (ed.), *Gedenkschrift Martin Göhring. Studien zur Europäische Geschichte* (Wiesbaden, 1968), pp. 353–68; Donald M. McKale, *The Swastika outside Germany* (Kent, Ohio, 1977), pp. 11, 18 ff., 29, 39 ff.

27 Stachura, *Nazi Youth*, pp. 138 ff., 149 ff. There was little love lost between Baldur von Schirach and Strasser: cf. Schirach, *Ich Glaubte an Hitler* (Hamburg, 1967), p. 91.

28 Bay. HSA: Geheimes Staatsarchiv: MA 101235/3, Strasser statement of January 1930 on the NSBO, and in *VB* of 30 January 1931.

29 Hans-Gerd Schumann, *Nationalsozialismus und Gewerkschaftsbewegung* (Hanover, 1958), pp. 36 ff., 167.

30 BA: NS26/265, Strasser memorandum to all Gauleiters of 21 September 1931.

31 BA: NS20/67, Strasser's list of regulations for the NS-Notwehr (Gefangenhilfe) of 5 March 1931.

32 BA: NS22/340, miscellaneous reports of 1931; BA: NS26/265, Strasser circular as Reich Organisation Leader of 20 August 1932.

33 BA: Sammlung Schumacher: 204, Strasser to Gauleiter Loeper of 17 October 1930.

34 Hans Frank, *Im Angesicht des Galgens* (Munich, 1953), p. 108; August Winnig, *Aus Zwanzig Jahren, 1925 bis 1945* (Hamburg, 1951), pp. 57 ff.

35 Hans-Günther Seraphim (ed.), *Das Politische Tagebuch Alfred Rosenbergs, 1934/35 und 1939/40* (Munich, 1964), p. 47; Jacobsen and Jochmann (eds), *Ausgewählte Dokumente*, letter from Hierl to Hitler of 24 March 1932.

36 Schulz's public denial of the charge in *VB*, 3 May 1932. Major Buch, head of Uschla, did apparently hatch a murder plot against Röhm (Hoegener, *Verratene Republik*, p. 325).

37 BA: NS22/1053, letter to Strasser from some Hessian party members, October 1931, in support of Feder's candidature.

38 IfZG: MA-393, letter of 10 July 1930 from Feder to Hitler.

39 BA: NS22/348, Strasser to Feder and vice-versa, September 1931.

40 BA: NS22/364, Strasser letter to Schlange of 1 July 1931. He wrote in similar vein to Karl Weinrich on 29 February 1932, BA: NS22/1054.

41 Herbert S. Levine, *Hitler's Free City: A History of the Nazi Party in Danzig, 1925–39* (Chicago, Ill., 1973), pp. 25 ff.

42 BA: NS22/1065, Koch to Strasser of 9 November and 21 December 1931; Strasser to Koch of 1 September 1931; Koch to Strasser of 4 August 1931 and Strasser's reply of 7 August 1931. But complaints against Koch from fellow East Prussian National Socialists continued in 1932: details in BA: NS22/352.

Gauleiter Rudolf Jordan of Halle-Merseburg also benefited from Strasser's strong support. See Jordan's expression of gratitude in letter to Strasser of 21 December 1931, BA: NS22/1051.

43 BA: NS22/1045, Strasser letter to Florian of 4 April 1931; BA NS22/1059, Strasser letter to Dr Herbert Albrecht of 8 January 1931.

44 BA: Sammlung Schumacher: 319, Strasser letter to Börger of 30 May 1931.

45 Tyrell, 'Führergedanke und Gauleiterwechsel', pp. 348 ff., 356 ff.

46 BA: NS22/7, Strasser statement on Maierhofer, November 1932.

47 BA: NS26/550, Gauleiter Josef Wagner's letters to Strasser of 6 and 10 June 1932; BA: NS22/1055, Strasser letter to Kube of 25 March 1932; BA: NS26/553, Strasser directive as Reich Organisation Leader of 4 June 1932; BA: NS26/547, letter of 2 July 1932 to Strasser from NSDAP Gau Halle-Merseburg; see also Strasser's correspondence with NSDAP groups in Poland concerning placement on the party's list for the July 1932 election, BA: NS26/546.

48 The view expressed by Krebs, *Tendenzen*, p. 191, that Robert Ley was appointed to the Reichsorganisationsleitung in October 1931 to keep an eye on Strasser is without substance (see Tyrell, 'Führergedanke und Gauleiterwechsel', p. 356, n. 68). Strasser himself suggested the appointment (BA: NS20/67, Hitler's directive of 21 October 1931).

49 BA: NS26/87, press report of 18 December 1931; BA: ZSg103/785, press reports of June 1932. Also see interesting letter from Arno Schickedanz, leader of the *VB*'s Berlin office, to his friend Alfred Rosenberg of 19 April 1932, IfZG: MA-251.

50 Small examples tell their own tale. For example, in September 1932 the new office building of NSDAP Gau Saxony in Dresden was named 'Gregor-Strasser-Haus'. See Strasser's letter about this of 22 October 1931 to NSDAP Dresden, BA: NS22/1067.

51 Parts of this section have been published in preliminary form in my article, '"Der Fall Strasser": Gregor Strasser, Hitler and National Socialism 1930–1932', in Stachura (ed.), *The Shaping of the Nazi State*, pp. 93–102.

52 BA: NS22/348, Memorandum of Organisationsabteilung II of the NSDAP Reichsleitung to Gauleiter of 27 October 1930.

53 BA: Nachlass Zarnow, No. 1 (Fall Schulz), esp. letter of 16 August 1934 from Zarnow to Hans Werner, and letter of 7 August 1934 from Zarnow to Schulz; BA: Nachlass Friedrich Grimm, Band 6 fos 6 ff.; BA: NS26/1375 for correspondence between J. F. Lehmann and Walter Buch on 10 July 1934, and between Schulz and Lehmann, a personal friend, on 12 June 1934. See also Josef Goebbels, *Vom Kaiserhof zur Reichskanzlei. Eine historische Darstellung in Tagebuchblättern (vom 1. Januar 1932 bis zum 1. Mai 1933)*, 24th edn (Munich, 1938), pp. 150, 219, 225.

54 BA: Nachlass Grimm, No. 5; more on Schulz's background in his own account, *Rettungen und Hilfeleistungen* (BA: B. I. P. Paul Schulz, No. 2), pp. 5 ff., 42 ff.; BA:

NS26/1367a, police report of 20 April 1931; Ernst Seidl, *Kampfgenossen des Führers. Hitler und die Männer seiner Bewegung* (Linz, 1933), pp. 31–2.

55 On his Black Reichswehr activities see Schulz's correspondence in BA: Nachlass Zarnow, No. 1; BA: Nachlass Grimm, No. 5; Friedrich Grimm, *Politische Justiz. Die Krankheit unserer Zeit* (Bonn, 1953), pp. 63 ff.

56 BA: Nachlass Grimm, No. 5, Schulz–Grimm correspondence. See also Friedrich Grimm, *Oberleutnant Schulz. Femeprozesse und Schwarze Reichswehr* (Munich, 1929); Friedrich Felgen *et al.*, *Oberleutnant Schulz, ein Opfer der Femeluge* (Berlin, 1929).

57 BA: NS26/1374, Schulz correspondence with Grimm and Buch 1928–30.

58 Bay. HSA: SAM: Polizeidirektion München: 6779, police report of June 1928.

59 BA: Sammlung Schumacher: 381, NSDAP Antrag 16 June 1929.

60 Herbert Grabert (ed.), *Friedrich Grimm. Ein Leben für das Recht* (Tübingen, 1961), p. 13; Howard Stern, 'Political crime and justice in the Weimar Republic', doctoral dissertation, Johns Hopkins University, 1966, fos 443 ff. Grimm had been Schulz's chief defence lawyer and later a personal friend; he joined the NSDAP in May 1933 and became also an NSDAP Reichstag deputy (BDC: Personal File F. Grimm).

61 Schulz, *Rettungen*, pp. 7 ff., 20 ff.

62 BA: Nachlass Grimm, No. 5, Schulz–Grimm correspondence.

63 BA: Nachlass Zarnow, No. 1; Bessel, *The SA*, pp. 149 ff. Schulz was appointed temporary SA Gruppenführer East in April 1931 (BA: NS22/5006).

64 BA: NS22/1046, Strasser directive to Schulz, October 1931; Wolfgang Benz, 'Vom Freiwilligen Arbeitsdienst zur Arbeitsdienstpflicht', *VfZG*, vol. 16 (1968), p. 330.

65 Schulz, *Rettungen*, p. 24, quoting a letter from Brüning to a Dr Leutze of 6 December 1956.

66 BA: NS26/1370, speech of 4 December 1931. A Württemberg police report on it of December 1931 is in BA: NS26/1404.

67 BA: NS22/348, letter of 8 December 1931 to Strasser from a Bordeaux correspondent.

68 BA: R43II/1315, Strasser at meeting of Gau Silesia in Brieg on 29 November 1931.

69 BA: NS26/1370, Strasser speech to the annual rally of the NS-Doctors' League in Leipzig, 5 December 1931. One of his most comprehensive, if colourless, attacks on the Republic came in his speech, 'Der Letzte Abwehrkampf des Systems', published in *VB*, 3–4 May 1931.

70 BA: NS18/589, letter of 2 July 1931 to Strasser from Dr Kurt Klare of Scheidegg; BA: NS18/587, letter to NSDAP Reichsleitung from Gau Saar of 6 January 1931.

71 BA: NS26/1370, radio speech of June 1932.

72 Speech to NSBO in Berlin's Sportpalast, 20 October 1932, text in BA: Nachlass Zarnow: No. 44.

73 Robert Black, *Fascism in Germany* (London, 1979), pp. 374, 880 ff.; Abraham, *Collapse of the Weimar Republic*, pp. 172 ff., 221, 322.

74 Helmut Tammen, *Die I. G. Farbenindustrie Aktiengesellschaft (1925–1933)* (Berlin, 1978), pp. 275–93; Michael Wolffsohn, *Industrie und Handwerk im Konflikt mit staatlicher Wirtschaftspolitik?*... (Berlin, 1977), pp. 285–92.

75 Schulz, *Rettungen*, p. 20, dates their association from 1930; BA: Nachlass Zarnow: No. 1.

76 August Heinrichsbauer, *Schwerindustrie und Politik* (Essen–Kettwig, 1948), p. 40. Heinrichbauer's interest in the NSDAP dates from December 1926 when he heard Hitler address industrialists in Essen (Hauptstaatsarchiv Düsseldorf: RW23, Gauleitung Ruhr, letter of 4 December 1926 from Heinrichsbauer to Hess).

77 Heinrichsbauer, *Schwerindustrie*, pp. 40–1. See also letter of 11 August 1931 from Martin Blank, Berlin representative of the Gütehoffnungshütte, to Paul Reusch which identifies Strasser as a sensible NSDAP leader, and another letter of 27 November 1931 from Blank to Reusch in similar vein, in Ilse Maurer and Udo Wengst (eds), *Politik und Wirtschaft in der Krise, 1930–1932. Quellen zur Ara Brüning*, 2 vols (Düsseldorf, 1980), Vol. II, pp. 881 ff., 1119 ff.

78 Fritz Thyssen, *I Paid Hitler* (London, 1941), p. 134; Eberhard Czichon, *Wer verhalf Hitler zur Macht? Zum Anteil der deutschen Industrie an der Zerstörung der Weimarer Republik* (Cologne, 1972), p. 54, n. 210.

79 *The Trial of German Major War Criminals. Proceedings of the International Military Tribunal at Nuremberg* (London, 1946–51), Pt 13, p. 100.

80 Avraham Barkai, 'Die Wirtschaftsauffassung der NSDAP', *Aus Politik und Zeitgeschichte*, supplement to *Das Parlament*, vol. 25 (1975), pt 9, pp. 5–7.

81 BA: Nachlass Grimm: Band 6, fo. 8.

82 IfZG: Otto Wagener Tagebuch: ED-60/1 and 2.

83 Wagener Tagebuch: ED-60/6, Vol. XXXIII, fos 1958–69, and Vol. XXXIV, fos 2102 ff.

84 Thyssen, *I Paid Hitler*, pp. 132–3.

85 Heinrichsbauer, *Schwerindustrie*, p. 49; Henry A. Turner, 'The Ruhrlade, secret cabinet of heavy industry in the Weimar Republic', *Central European History*, vol. 3 (1970), pp. 221–2.

For Silverberg's support in this regard, see Paul Silverberg, *Reden und Schriften* (Cologne, 1951), p. 82, and the account given by his former private secretary Otto Meynen in *Der Volkswirt*, vol. V, No. 18 (4 May 1951), pp. 9–11.

86 Strasser has been accused as having been a paid agent of I. G. Farben! (Kurt Gossweiler, *Die Rolle des Monopolkapitals bei der Herbeiführung der Röhm-Affäre* (East Berlin, 1963), pp. 287 ff.)

87 The suggestion in Paucker, *Der jüdische Abwehrkampf*, p. 125, that the anti-Nazi Jewish information agency Büro Wilhelmshaven established links with Strasser (through Otto Strasser) in 1932 is totally unfounded.

88 BA: NS22/1065, Strasser letter to Koch of 1 September 1931.

89 BA: NS22/1046, Strasser letter to Schlange of 12 September 1931.

90 BDC: Personal File Ernst zu Reventlow, Strasser letter to Reventlow of 23 March 1932.

91 Krebs, *Tendenzen*, p. 182; Rosenberg, *Letzte Aufzeichnungen*, p. 113; Lang and Schenck (eds), *Porträt eines Menschheitsverbrechers*, p. 161.

92 For discussion of the group's ideas, see Kurt Sontheimer, 'Der Tatkreis' *VfZG*, vol. 7 (1959), pp. 229–60; Walter Struve, 'Hans Zehrer as a neoconservative élite theorist', *American Historical Review*, vol. 70 (1964–5), pp. 1035–57; Klaus Fritzsche, *Politische Romantik und Gegenrevolution. Fluchtwege in der Krise der bürgerlichen Gesellschaft: Das Beispiel des 'Tat'-Kreises* (Frankfurt, 1976), pp. 91 ff., 103 ff.; Hans Hecker, *Die Tat und ihr Osteuropabild 1909–1939* (Cologne, 1974), pp. 140 ff.

93 Strasser's views on the election were given in his articles, 'Die Lehre des 13. März', in *NS-Partei-Korrespondenz* of 15 March 1932, copy in BA: NSD 13/7, and 'Der Sinn des 10. April' of 1 April 1932, ibid. See also various press reports in BA: NS26/1169.

94 IfZG: Zeugenschrift 1723: Hans Zehrer.

95 Strasser, 'Der Ultimo ist das Schicksal', *Die Tat*, vol. XXIV (April 1932), pp. 60–8.

96 See their exchange of correspondence in November–December 1931 in BA: NS22/348, in particular Strasser's letter to Winnig of 17 November 1931.

97 See his 'Wider den Sozialismus in jeder Form?', *Die Tat*, vol. XXIV (July 1932), pp. 310–17. Zehrer took over the *Tägliche Rundschau* in May 1932 with largely army (Schleicher) financial backing (Hans-Otto Meissner and Harry Wilde, *Die Machtergreifung. Ein Bericht über die Technik des Nationalsozialistischen Staatsstreichs* (Stuttgart, 1958), p. 74).

98 BA: NS26/1375, letter of 12 June 1933 from Schulz to J. F. Lehmann.

99 Ebbo Demant, *Von Schleicher zu Springer. Hans Zehrer als politischer Publizist* (Mainz, 1971), p. 69.

100 Treviranus, *Das Ende von Weimar*, p. 345. See postwar correspondence between Brüning and Elbrechter in Heinrich Brüning, *Briefe und Gespräche 1934–1945*, ed. Claire Nix (Stuttgart, 1974), pp. 310, 424, 429.

101 *Die Tat*, vol. 24 (August 1932), Heft 5. A detailed examination of Zehrer's approach to the unions is given in Ursula Hüllbüsch, 'Gewerkschaften und Staat. Ein Beitrag zur Geschichte der Gewerkschaften zu Anfang und zu Ende der Weimarer Republik', doctoral dissertation, University of Heidelberg, 1961, fos 160 ff.

102 Demant, *Von Schleicher zu Springer*, p. 99.

103 BA: Nachlass Krebs: No. 7, Strasser–Krebs correspondence of 28 January 1929.

104 Larry E. Jones, 'Between the fronts: the German National Union of Commercial Employees from 1928 to 1933', *Journal of Modern History*, vol. 48 (1976), pp. 471–2.

105 Iris Hamel, *Völkischer Verband und nationale Gewerkschaft. Der Deutschnationale Handlungsgehilfen-Verband 1893–1933* (Frankfurt, 1967), pp. 248–9.

106 Jochmann (ed.), *NS und Revolution*, reprints the article as document 104, pp. 351–6.

107 *VB*, 15–16 November 1931.

108 BA: Sammlung Schumacher: 319, Strasser letter to Stöhr of 20 November 1931.

109 Hannes Heer, *Burgfrieden oder Klassenkampf? Zur Politik der sozialdemokratischen Gewerkschaften 1930–1933* (Neuwied, 1971), p. 50.

110 Ernst Lemmer, *Manches war doch Anders. Erinnerungen eines deutschen Demokraten* (Frankfurt, 1968), p. 167.

111 BA: Sammlung Schumacher: 373, Circular of the Reich Organisation Leadership, 23 December 1929.

112 BA: NS22/348, letter of 20 July 1931 to Strasser from Wilhelm Kube.

113 Avraham Barkai, 'Wirtschaftliche Grundanschauungen und Ziele der NSDAP (mit einem unveröffentlichten Dokument aus dem Jahre 1931', *Jahrbuch des Instituts für Deutsche Geschichte*, vol. VII (1978), pp. 355–85.

114 Dirk Stegmann, 'Zum Verhältnis von Grossindustrie und Nationalsozialismus 1930–1933. Ein Beitrag zur Geschichte der sog. Machtergreifung', *Archiv für Sozialgeschichte*, vol. XIII (1973), p. 448, n. 240.

115 Hans Reupke, *Der Nationalsozialismus und die Wirtschaft. Erläuterung der wirtschaftlichen Programmpunkte und Ideenlehre der nationalsozialistischen Bewegung* (Berlin, 1931).

116 BDC: Personal File Hans Reupke.

117 Reprinted in Strasser, *Kampf um Deutschland*, pp. 345–78.

118 BA: Nachlass Zarnow: No. 44, for full text of speech of 20 October 1932.

119 A weak contrary view is put forward by Kissenkoetter, *Gregor Strasser*, pp. 82 ff., 94 ff.; also see Miller Lane and Rupp (eds), *Nazi Ideology*, pp. 134 ff., 163 ff.

120 *VB*, 22–3 May 1932 article, 'Gregor Strasser und Wilhelm Dreher über das Arbeitsbeschaffungsprogramm der NSDAP'.

121 Silvio Gesell, *Natürliche Wirtschaftsordnung durch Freiland und Freigeld* (Rehbrücke/Berlin, 1911).

122 Principally his books: *Chronische Arbeitskrise, ihre Ursachen, ihre Bekämpfung* (Berlin, 1926); *Die Wirtschaftswende. Die Ursachen der Arbeitslosenkrise und deren Bekämpfung* (Leipzig, 1931). His influence on Strasser is stressed by Gerhard Kroll, *Von der Weltwirtschaftskrise zur Staatskonjunktur* (Berlin, 1958), pp. 421 ff., 435 ff., 455; Helmut Marcon, *Arbeitsbeschaffungspolitik der Regierungen Papen und Schleicher* (Frankfurt, 1974), pp. 54 ff.

123 Heinrich Dräger, *Arbeitsbeschaffung durch produktive Kreditschöpfung. Ein Beitrag zur Frage der Wirtschaftsbelebung durch das sogenannte Federgeld* (Munich, 1932), which was republished in Düsseldorf, 1954.

124 Wilhelm Grotkopp, *Die Grosse Krise. Lehren aus der Überwindung der Wirtschaftskrise 1929/32* (Düsseldorf, 1954), pp. 66–70, 352 ff.; Michael Schneider, *Das Arbeitsbeschaffungsprogramm des ADGB. Zur gewerkschaftlichen Politik in der Endphase der Weimarer Republik* (Bonn–Bad Godesburg 1975), pp. 140 ff.

125 Günther Gereke, *Ich war königlich-preussischer Landrat* (East Berlin, 1970), pp. 162–74, 195 ff.

126 IfZG; Zeugenschrift 1926: Walther von Etzdorf; Czichon, *Wer verhalf Hitler*, p. 34.

Otto Wagener published his own plan in March 1932 which was based on his concept of 'Sozialwirtschaft' (Barkai, 'Die Wirtschaftsauffassung der NSDAP', pp. 10 ff.).

127 National Archives: FA49, Band 3: NSDAP, T81, Roll 1; Grotkopp, *Die Grosse Krise*, p. 37.

128 IfZG: Zeugenschrift: 1862: Reinhold G. Cordemann; IfZG: Zeugenschrift von Etzdorf, letter written by Etzdorf on 26 December 1963.

129 BA: Nachlass Paul Silverberg: 232, f. 194, letter of 9 September 1932 to him from Dr Herle, secretary of the Reichsverband der deutschen Industrie; BA: NS22/11, letter from Renteln to the Reich Organisation Leadership, 17 February 1932.

130 Gottfried Feder, *Kampf gegen die Hochfinanz* (Munich, 1933), p. 371; at his Nuremberg trial Funk claimed sole authorship (*Trial of Major German War Criminals*, Pt 13, p. 102).

131 Schneider, *Das Arbeitsbeschaffungsprogramm*, p. 153. Köhler was a former chief editor of the *VB*, and then editor of the WPA's publication *Wirtschaftspolitischer Pressedienst*.

132 Hüllbüsch, *Gewerkschaften und Staat*, p. 163; Heer, *Burgfrieden oder Klassenkampf?*, p. 58.

133 Das Wirtschaftliche Sofortprogramm der NSDAP: see Kroll, *Von der Weltwirtschaftskrise*, pp. 426 ff., 432 ff.

134 Entitled 'Das nationalsozialistische Aufbauprogramm', copy in *NS-Partei-Korrespondenz*, 29 July 1932 (BA: NSD13/9). Another version was published in August 1932, 'NSDAP Arbeitsbeschaffungsprogramm'.

135 Hanfstaengl, *Missing Years*, pp. 189–90; and report on the interview in BA: NSD13/11.

136 IfZG: Zeugenschrift Cordemann.

137 BA: ZSg103/776, report in *Hannoverische Landeszeitung* of 6 September 1932.

138 The minutes of the meeting are in BA: R43II/1309, but they are not wholly authentic, as has been convincingly demonstrated by Henryk Skrzypczak, 'Fälscher machen Zeitgeschichte. Ein quellenkritischer Beitrag zur Gewerkschaftspolitik in der Ära Papen und Schleicher', *Internationale Wissenschaftliche Korrespondenz zur Geschichte der deutschen Arbeiterbewegung*, vol. 11 (1975), pp. 452–71; and by Dieter Emig and Rüdiger Zimmermann, 'Das Ende einer Legende: Gewerkschaft, Papen und Schleicher-Gefälschte und echte Protokolle', ibid., vol. 12 (1976), pp. 19–43. But the minutes allow a general reconstruction of the debate at the meeting to be made. In his article, 'Schleicher und die Gewerkschaften 1932. Ein Quellenproblem', *VfZG*, vol. 29 (1981), pp. 189 ff., 193 ff., Heinrich Muth denies that the meeting took place at all. But his evidence is largely circumstantial and, more important, is based on the erroneous belief that Strasser gave up his pro-coalition strategy in early September (pp. 206 ff., 208 ff.). Muth has completely misunderstood the whole underlying motivation behind Strasser's disillusionment with Hitler, and has also ignored critical developments during the last quarter of the year which strengthened his determination to continue his oppositional course.

139 For a bitterly critical assessment of the Strasser–union relationship from an SPD standpoint, see Friedrich Stampfer, *Die Ersten Vierzehn Jahre der Deutschen Republik* (Hamburg, 1952), pp. 656 ff.

140 Werner Müller and Jürgen Stockfisch, 'Die "Veltenbriefe". Eine neue Quelle über die Rolle des Monopolkapitals bei der Zerstörung der Weimarer Republik', *Zeitschrift für Geschichtswissenschaft*, vol. 17 (1969), p. 1588.

141 Goebbels, *Kaiserhof*, entries for 6 January (p. 19); 20 January (p. 27); 14 March (p. 63); 18 March (p. 67); 19 March (p. 68); 10 May (p. 94); 19 May (p. 99).

142 BA: NS26/58, Strasser speech on 23 July 1932 in Ostragehege.

143 BA: NS22/382, letter of 4 August 1932 to Strasser from Gauleiter Josef Wagner lamenting the absence of the old *élan* in the party. See also a NSDAP Reich Propaganda Leadership report of August which officially records gloomy feelings about the party's future prospects, BA: Sammlung Schumacher: 382.

144 Brüning, *Memoiren*, p. 488.
145 Brüning, *Briefe und Gespräche*, p. 319, letter from Brüning to G. L. Warren of 18 September 1940; Schulz, *Rettungen*, p. 7.
146 Bracher, *Auflösung*, p. 448.
147 Brüning, *Memoiren*, p. 600; Brüning, 'Ein Brief', *Deutscher Rundschau*, vol. 70 (July, 1947), p. 9; Herbert Hömig, *Das preussische Zentrum in der Weimarer Republik* (Mainz, 1979), p. 257.
148 Heinrich Brüning, *Reden und Aufsätze eines deutschen Staatsmanns*, ed. Wilhelm Vernekohl (Münster, 1968), pp. 150 ff.
149 IfZG; Otto-Strasser-Sammlung: ED-118, Band 18, Brüning in lecture in Detroit, December 1941.

Chapter 6

1 BDC: Personal File Reventlow, letter from Reventlow to Strasser of 21 December 1931.
2 ibid., letter from Reventlow to Strasser of 15 August 1932; see also, in similar vein, BDC: Personal File Albert Krebs, letter of 25 May 1932 from Krebs to Strasser.
3 Rudolf Morsey, *Der Untergang des politischen Katholizismus. Die Zentrumspartei zwischen christlichem Selbstverständnis und 'Nationaler Erhebung' 1932/33* (Stuttgart, 1977), pp. 51, 56 ff., 61 ff.
4 The talks had been bitterly denounced by many Protestant NSDAP circles in northern Germany (Bay. HSA: Geheimes Staatsarchiv: MA/101235/3). See also on this theme the letter of 20 September 1932 from August Heinrichsbauer to Strasser, IfZG: MA/127–1, fos 3 ff. The only positive result of the talks was an agreement by both parties to support (with the DNVP) Goering's election to the Reichstag presidency on 30 August.
5 On big-business fears of a Strasser–trade union *rapprochement* see Michael Schneider, *Unternehmer und Demokratie. Die freien Gewerkschaften in der unternehmerischen Ideologie der Jahre 1918 bis 1933* (Bonn–Bad Godesberg 1975), pp. 111–12; Helmut Müller, *Die Zentralbank – eine Nebenregierung. Reichsbankpräsident Hjalmar Schacht als Politiker der Weimarar Republik* (Opladen, 1973), p. 110. See also Heinrichsbauer's letter of 20 September 1932 to Strasser, IfZG: MA/127–1, in which he complains about recent 'Marxist-type' agitational methods and accompanying 'socialistic' demands in the party – evidence that Heinrichsbauer misunderstood Strasser's strategy at this time.
6 Bay. HSA: Geheimes Staatsarchiv: MA 101235/3, at a national propaganda meeting of the party in Munich on 5–7 October 1932.
7 Bay. HSA: SAM: Polizeidirektion München: 6781, Munich police report of 30 December 1932. See also Goebbels, *Kaiserhof*, entry of 8 November 1932 (p. 198) on Strasser's 'sabotage work'.
8 IfZG: F41, Band 4: Kurzorientierung des Ministeramtes vom 23 November 1932. See also the recent reappraisal of Schleicher's political aims, especially *vis-à-vis* the NSDAP, in Peter Hayes, '"A question mark with epaulettes"? Kurt von Schleicher and Weimar politics', *Journal of Modern History*, vol. 52 (1980), pp. 35–65, esp. pp. 43 ff., 51 ff. Unfortunately, this analysis is fatally undermined by Hayes' fundamental misconception of Strasser's motives and ideas during the second half of 1932.
9 BA: NS22/1074, Strasser of 10 April 1931 to Consul Bernhard of Bremen.
10 BA: NS26/1511, Reich Organisation Leadership report, November 1932. See also various Gauleiter reports October–November 1932, BA: NS22/347.
11 Hans R. Berndorff, *General zwischen Ost und West. Aus den Geheimnissen der Deutschen Republik* (Hamburg, 1951), p. 212, states that Schleicher let it be known

these debts would be settled from secret army funds if Hitler agreed to Strasser becoming Vice-Chancellor in a cabinet led by himself.

12 Donald M. McKale, *The Nazi Party Courts: Hitler's Management of Conflict in His Movement, 1921–1945* (Lawrence, Kan. 1974), pp. 102–5.

13 BA: NSD 13/11, for text of speech.

14 Despite his disgust at this murder, Strasser had to put on a defiant *public* face: his directive of 27 August 1932 as Reich Organisation Leader ordered all Gaue to establish protest committees against the sentences handed out to the NSDAP culprits, BA: NS26/265.

15 Schulz, *Rettungen*, pp. 9, 22, 43; and Schulz, *Meine Erschiessung*, p. 5, stresses the SA terror campaign as a critical turning-point in the Strasser–Hitler relationship. Schulz affirms that serious quarrels between the two men took place, leading Strasser to tell Hitler that he did not want to be a government minister in a Germany ruled by chaos.

16 BA: Nachlass Krebs: No. 7, Strasser letter to Krebs of 22 October 1931; BA: ZSg 103/811, Strasser statement on the Harzburg Front of 29 October 1931.

17 *VB*, 1–2 January 1932; 25 November 1932. Many historians have taken such statements at face value: Dixon, *Gregor Strasser*, p. 3, says Strasser had 'an excellent relationship' with Hitler; and Nyomarkay, *Charisma and Factionalism*, pp. 107 ff., Orlow, *Nazi Party*, p. 272, and Kissenkoetter, *Gregor Strasser*, pp. 162 ff., agree.

18 Frank, *Im Angesicht des Galgens*, p. 108.

19 BA: NS22/1045 for various examples; Reed, *Nemesis?*, p. 80.

20 Hanfstaengl, *The Missing Years*, pp. 130, 182. Also see Strasser's remarks in Helmut Klotz, *The Berlin Diaries* (London, 1934), p. 219.

21 Otto Strasser, *Hitler und Ich*, pp. 201–2; and *Exil*, p. 59; Otto Dietrich, *12 Jahre mit Hitler* (Munich, 1955), pp. 197–8.

22 Schulz, *Rettungen*, p. 9.

23 Goebbels, *Tagebuch*, entry for 2 October 1925; Ludecke, *I Knew Hitler*, pp. 392–3; Heiden, *Der Führer*, pp. 227–9.

24 Frank, *Im Angesicht des Galgens*, p. 108.

25 Jordan, *Erlebt und Erlitten*, pp. 70–2, records an interesting conversation he had with Strasser on this theme in November 1932.

26 Thilo Vogelsang, 'Zur Politik Schleichers gegenüber der NSDAP, 1932', *VfZG*, vol. 6 (1958), p. 105, n. 44.

27 Abraham, *The Collapse of the Weimar Republic*, pp. 173 ff.; Ulrike Hörster-Philipps, 'Grosskapital, Weimarer Republik und Faschismus', in Reinhard Kühnl and Gerd Hardach (eds), *Die Zerstörung der Weimarer Republik* (Cologne, 1977), pp. 112 ff.

28 Vogelsang, *Reichswehr, Staat und NSDAP*, pp. 340–1. See also IfZG: Zeugenschrift: 279: Eugen Ott.

29 IfZG: MA/1300/2 – Otto Meissner statement.

30 Franz von Papen, *Vom Scheitern einer Demokratie 1930–1933* (Mainz, 1968), p. 362; Hjalmar Schacht, *76 Jahre meines Lebens* (Bad Wörishofen, 1953), p. 375; Otto Braun, *Von Weimar zu Hitler* (Hamburg, 1949), p. 274.

31 Gerard Braunthal, *Socialist Labor and Politics in Weimar Germany. The General Federation of German Trade Unions* (Hamden, Conn., 1978), pp. 55–83.

32 *Frankfurter Zeitung*, 7 December 1932. The resultant atmosphere of profound depression in the movement is amply conveyed by Arno Schröder, *Mit der Partei vorwärts! Zehn Jahre Gau Westfalen-Nord* (Detmold, 1940), p. 24.

33 As unconvincingly suggested by General Hans-Henning von Holzendorf, BA: NS20/242–2. Niederschrift vom 22. June 1946. The relationship is correctly assessed in Lutz Graf Schwerin von Krosigk, *Staatsbankrott. Die Geschichte der Finanzpolitik des Deutschen Reiches von 1920 bis 1945* (Göttingen, 1974), pp. 156–7.

34 Klotz, *The Berlin Diaries*, p. 174.

35 Grotkopp, *Die Grosse Krise*, p. 77, n. 1; Wörtz, *Programmatik und Führerprinzip*, p. 223; Hayes, '"A question mark with epaulettes"?', p. 56.

36 Schulz later claimed to have urged Strasser against joining a Schleicher cabinet and to have disapproved of the whole pro-coalition strategy. The claims are spurious (BA: NS26/1375, Schulz letter to Lehmann of 12 June 1933).

37 Goebbels, *Kaiserhof*, entry 5 December 1932, pp. 216 ff.; Bracher, *Auflösung*, pp. 678 ff. Ernst Hanfstaengl, *Zwischen Weissen und Braunen Haus. Erinnerungen eines politischen Aussenseiters* (Munich, 1970), p. 281, claims to have informed Hitler of the latest Schleicher–Strasser meeting, having been told himself by journalist Sefton Delmer. See also Sefton Delmer, *Trail Sinister: An Autobiography* (London, 1961), pp. 169–70.

The story, originally told by Otto Strasser, *Die deutsche Bartholmäusnacht*, and by Edgar von Schmidt-Pauli, *Hitlers Kampf um die Macht. Der Nationalsozialismus und die Ereignisse des Jahres 1932* (Berlin, 1933), pp. 183–4, of Hitler at first agreeing to Strasser accepting Schleicher's offer is surely apocryphal. It is suggested that Hitler was on his way by train from Munich to Berlin in order to confirm personally his decision when he was persuaded by Goebbels and Goering to leave the train at Weimar, and then to change his mind altogether about Schleicher's offer. Some accounts have him changing trains at Jena, while Kissenkoetter, *Gregor Strasser*, pp. 167 ff., goes one better by referring to not one but two trains! His strong emphasis on the importance of this alleged episode contributes to Kissenkoetter's unconvincing account of Strasser's role in November–December 1932.

38 See letter of 7 May 1932 to Strasser from Wilhelm Zimmerman, a Karlsruhe publisher, who writes: 'you are . . . also still today the honest German socialist . . . an idea which many old party comrades continue to share . . .' (BA: NS22/1044). A Berlin police report of 22 July 1932 (BA: NS26/1370) calls him 'leader of the socialist wing of the NSDAP'. The report may have been influenced by Otto Strasser.

39 BA: NS22/1064, letter of 28 December 1931 from Kube to Strasser stressing his friendship and admiration.

40 BDC: Personal File Reventlow, Reventlow–Strasser correspondence 1931–2. At the end of December 1932, thus after the Strasser crisis, Reventlow published a eulogy of Strasser in *Reichswart*, Bay. HSA: SAM: Polizeidirektion München: 6791, quoting report in *Münchener Post*, 4 January 1933. Also see an unconfirmed report in *Die Schwarze Front* of 8 January 1933 by Otto Strasser that an exchange of letters between Reventlow and Hitler on Gregor played an important part in the political developments which led to the latter's resignation (copy in BA: ZSgl/240). The situation changed in 1933, however, when, with the NSDAP in power, Reventlow attempted a reconciliation with Hitler. See his words of praise for the Führer in his book, *Der Weg zum neuen Deutschland. Der Wiederaufstieg des deutschen Volkes* (Essen, 1933), p. 344.

41 Broszat, *German National Socialism*, p. 198; Schumann, *NS und Gewerkschaftsbewegung*, p. 39; Krebs, *Tendenzen*, pp. 72, 190.

42 Timothy W. Mason (ed.), *Arbeiterklasse und Volksgemeinschaft. Dokumente und Materialien zur deutschen Arbeiterpolitik 1936–1939* (Opladen, 1975), p. 30; BA: NS1/258, NSBO report 1932.

43 Paul Meier-Benneckenstein (ed.), *Dokumente der deutschen Politik* (Berlin, 1938), Vol. 4, p. 367; see also report of NSBO official's meeting in Berlin on 2 February 1932, stressing Strasser's concern to have NSBO support (Bay. HSA: SAM: Polizeidirektion München: 6850); Goebbels, *Kaiserhof*, entries of 9 June 1932 (p. 109) and 27 June 1932 (p. 119).

44 Eric G. Reiche, 'From "spontaneous" to legal terror: SA, police, and the judiciary in Nürnberg, 1933–34', *European Studies Review*, vol. 9 (1979), p. 238.

45 See the correspondence between Strasser and many of these Gauleiters in NS26/1068–76.

46 Krebs, *Tendenzen*, p. 192.

47 IfZG: Zeugenschrift Zehrer.

48 *Exil*, p. 65.

49 BA: NS26/1403, Württemberg police report of 24 April 1930.

50 BA: NS20/22, report by Otto Engelbrecht of his meeting with Feder on 30 December 1932; Tyrell, 'Gottfried Feder', p. 78. Also see Tyrell, *Führer befiehl*, 348–50, Otto Erbersdobler statement of July 1968. Erbersdobler was Gauleiter of Lower Bavaria (1929–32).

51 Robert Cecil, *The Myth of the Master Race: Alfred Rosenberg and Nazi Ideology* (New York, 1972), p. 108; Krebs, *Tendenzen*, p. 199.

52 Scholarly opinion is sharply divided on how seriously the crisis threatened the unity of the NSDAP. Among those who believe Strasser could have split the party are: Horn, *Führerideologie und Parteiorganisation*, p. 373; Wörtz, *Programmatik und Führerprinzip*, p. 4; Bullock, *Hitler*, p. 239. More recently, Kissenkoetter, *Gregor Strasser*, pp. 162 ff., takes a similar line, but like his predecessors fails to base his conclusion on sufficiently adequate evidence. Indeed, if anything, his evidence would seem to show the opposite!

53 *Vorwärts*, 13 December 1932 (report on Brückner); and *Münchener Post*, 17–18 December 1932 (report on Schlange). On Kaufmann's 'odium' for not supporting Strasser, see Görlitz and Quint, *Adolf Hitler*, p. 389, and Roger Manvell and Heinrich Fraenkel, *The Hundred Days to Hitler* (London, 1974), p. 198, n. 29.

54 Otto Strasser, *Exil*, p. 74. Mussolini thought Strasser more able than Hitler and more likely, therefore, to emerge the victor in a trial of strength (Elizabeth Wiskemann, *The Rome–Berlin Axis: A History of Relations between Hitler and Mussolini* (London, 1949), p. 28). Strasser also had support from the former secretary of the Italian Fascist Party, Roberto Farinacci: see report in his newspaper *Il Regime Fascista*, copy in BA: ZSg103/832.

55 BA: NS26/1375, letter from J. F. Lehmann to Walter Buch of 10 July 1934 identifies Schulz's responsibility; BA: Nachlass Zarnow: No. 1, letter from Zarnow to Hans Werner (Magdeburg) of 16 August 1932 and from Zarnow to Schulz of 7 August 1934 stress the importance of Schulz's role in the resignation issue. Schulz's own account is contradictory: in *Meine Erschiessung*, p. 5, he admits his co-responsibility, but in a letter of 12 June 1933 to Lehmann (BA: NS26/1375) he claims not to have been informed of Strasser's decision until the very last minute.

56 Lohse, *Der Fall Strasser*, pp. 23–6.

57 The letter is printed in Schulz, *Rettungen*, pp. 9–11. Kissenkoetter, *Gregor Strasser*, pp. 177 ff., doubts whether this is the full, original version, but does not clearly explain his reasons. The German version is reprinted in Stachura, '"Der Fall Strasser"' pp. 113–15.

58 Wörtz, *Programmatik und Führerprinzip*, p. 237.

59 Otto Strasser, *Die deutsche Bartholomäusnacht*, pp. 40–2.

60 IfZG: F28: Dokumente Dr Horn, Strasser letter of 21 February 1933, in reply to Horn's letter to him of 13 January 1933.

61 Otto Strasser, *30 Juni*, p. 36.

62 As suggested, for example, by Otto-Ernst Schüddekopf, *Linke Leute von Rechts* . . . (Stuttgart, 1960), p. 380. Otto Strasser believed basically the same, adding that the NSDAP now had 'a Pope at the top', in *Die Schwarze Front*, 25 December 1932, copy in BA: ZSgl/240.

63 As suggested by Bullock, *Hitler*, p. 171; Ludecke, *I Knew Hitler*, pp. 226, 550.

64 William Carr, *Hitler: A Study in Personality and Politics* (London, 1978), p. 34.

65 Karl O. Paetel, *Versuchung oder Chance? Zur Geschichte des deutschen Nationalbolschewismus* (Göttingen, 1965), pp. 209–10.

66 See the extensive collection of press comment and reports in BA: Nachlass Zarnow: No. 44.

67 Copy in BA: NS20/102.

68 Rolf Boelke (alias Elbrechter), 'Der Weg des Nationalsozialismus', *Die Tat*, 24 (January 1933), pp. 878 ff.

69 BA: R43II/1194, Gregor Strasser letter of 31 December 1932 to Otto Strasser.
70 IfZG: Otto-Strasser-Sammlung: ED-118, Band 2, letter of 24 January 1949 from Brüning to Father Bernhard.
71 Lohse, *Der Fall Strasser*, pp. 33–4.
72 ibid., pp. 27 ff. See also Württemberg police report of 23 December 1932 (BA: NS26/1405) on a typical meeting in Stuttgart. The Reichstag faction's declaration of 9 December is available in Bay. HSA: SAM: Polizeidirektion München: 6767; the NSBO declaration of 11 December in ibid.: 6850.
73 See their declaration of loyalty in BA: Nachlass Zarnow: No. 44, as reported in *Acht-Uhr-Abendblatt.* In his book, *Die NSDAP. Idee, Führer und Partei. Männer und Mächte* (Leipzig, 1933), Koch none the less referred in his introduction to 'my friend Gregor Strasser'. On Feder's reaction see *Frankfurter Zeitung*, 10 December 1932; and BA: NS22/7, for Ley's critical report on him to Hitler, 13 December 1932.
74 Orlow, *Nazi Party*, pp. 293–6, for full details.
75 Glaser seems to have been employed sometime later, and then only briefly, in the NSBO, for whose major publication, *Das Arbeitertum*, he had written articles (BA: NS1/258; BA: Sammlung Schumacher: 375). His close friendship with Vollmuth, Strasser's brother-in-law, underlines the personal ties binding Strasser's most trusted colleagues in the Reich Organisation Leadership – see BDC: Personal File Glaser, letter of 19 February 1934 from Glaser to Vollmuth.
76 Stephenson, *Nazi Organisation of Women*, pp. 49, 98–9, 119; Hans-Adolf Jacobsen, *Nationalsozialistische Aussenpolitik 1933–1938* (Frankfurt, 1968), pp. 96, 99. Hans Reupke, formerly employed in the WPA, was expelled from the NSDAP in October 1934, partly because of his outspoken opposition to Hitler's policy in December 1932 (BDC: Personal File Reupke). SA Oberführer Andreas von Flotow was expelled from the SA on 19 January 1933 and shot on 29 April 1933 for allegedly belonging to the 'Strasser Wing' (IfZG: Otto-Strasser-Sammlung: ED-118, Band 25).
77 For the HJ, see Stachura, *Nazi Youth*, p. 83; for the NSDStB, Faust, *Der Nationalsozialistische Deutsche Studentenbund*, p. 115. For a report of a revolt in Hitler's SS Bodyguard, John W. Wheeler-Bennett, *The Nemesis of Power: The German Army in Politics 1918–1945* (London, 1953), p. 269. The authorities generally exaggerated the amount of disruption caused in the Party. See Bay. HSA: Geheimes Staatsarchiv: MA 1943: 102157, Halbmonatsbericht vom 19.12.32; Bay. HSA: ASA: Sonderabgabe I: 1774, report of Regierungspräsidium of Lower Franconia, vom 20.12.32.
78 Seraphim (ed.), *Das politische Tagebuch Alfred Rosenbergs*, p. 48. See also a revealing speech by Himmler to a group of SS men on 21 July 1944 in which he compares Strasser's 'betrayal' with the July 1944 Plot (IfZG: MA/315).
79 BDC: Personal File Heinrichsbauer, letter of 5 May 1933 from Heinrichsbauer to Hess; BA: R18: Reichsministeriums des Innern: 5035, Kiehn–Frick and Kiehn–Hess correspondence of September–November 1933. Kiehn had known Strasser since at least 1931 (BA: NS18/589, Kiehn letter to Strasser of 13 June 1931), and Strasser and his wife were frequent guests at Kiehn's home in Trossingen (BA: NS22/1077, letters from Kiehn to Strasser of 28 May 1933 and 15 September 1932). For Kiehn's background and post-1933 business and SS career, BDC: Personal File Kiehn; and BDC: Fritz Kiehn, Sammelliste 59.
80 Bay. HSA; SAM: Polizeidirektion München: 6781, Munich police report, 30 December 1932.
81 IfZG: MA/1300/2; Meissner and Wilde, *Die Machtergreifung*, p. 144.
82 Otto Strasser, *Mein Kampf*, p. 81.
83 At Freudenstadt on 29 December: Brüning, *Memoiren*, pp. 675–6; Brüning, *Briefe und Gespräche*, p. 100; Bay. HSA: Kriegsarchiv: Sammlung Rehse, 3820: Gregor Strasser, report in *Bayerischer Staatszeitung* of 14 January 1933.
84 IfZG: MA/329, Memorandum of 3 December 1940 by the Chief of the SS Hauptamt, SS-Brigadeführer Berger to Reichsführer Himmler. Berger claims that, during his

brief sojourn in Württemberg, Strasser caused considerable disruption among SA and SS men, and that he was forced to order the former party leader to leave the state within seventy-two hours.

85 Bay. HSA: Kriegsarchiv: Sammlung Rehse: 3820 – Gregor Strasser; Volker Hentschel, *Weimars letzte Monate. Hitler und die Untergang der Republik* (Düsseldorf, 1978), pp. 150–6, quotes interesting letters written by General Hörauf, Leader of the NSDAP's Wehramt, December 1932. Jordan, *Erlebt und Erlitten*, p. 90, says Hitler sent Mutschmann to Strasser in early January to prepare a reconciliation, but this claim lacks hard evidence (see Manvell and Fraenkel, *The Hundred Days*, p. 198, n. 36).

86 Papen's puzzled anxiety about Strasser's role in January is brought out in his undated (probably February or March 1933) Abschrift, BA: R53 (Stellvertreter des Reichskanzlers): 77.

87 On 21 May 1942, Hitler remarked that the result was 'a success whose importance it is not possible to over-estimate', Hugh R. Trevor-Roper (ed.), *Hitler's Table Talk 1941–44: His Private Conversations* (London, 1973), p. 496.

88 BA: NS22/2021, confidential circular from the Oberste Leitung of the Pol. Organisation of 12 January 1933, for details.

89 Bay. HSA: SAM: Polizeidirektion München: 6735, report of 17 January 1933; *VB*, 17 January 1933.

90 Goebbels, *Kaiserhof*, entry of 9 December 1932 (p. 223); entry of 16 January 1933 (p. 243). Also BA: Nachless Passarge: No. 7, extract from diary of 10 January 1933 on Strasser.

91 BA: R43I/678, minutes of cabinet meeting, 16 January 1933.

92 Stachura, 'The political strategy of the Nazi Party', pp. 287–8; Hans-Erich Volkmann, 'Das aussenwirtschaftliche Programm der NSDAP 1930–1933', *Archiv für Sozialgeschichte*, vol XVII (1977), pp. 254–5, 274 ff; Hans Mommsen, 'Zur Verschränkung traditioneller und faschistischer Führungsgruppen in Deutschland beim Übergang von der Bewegungs-zur Systemphase', in Schieder (ed.), *Faschismus als soziale Bewegung*, pp. 159 ff., 167 ff.

93 cf. Hans Zehrer's forlorn plea for the failed 'Querfront' strategy in his article, 'Schleicher und Strasser', *Die Tat*, 24, Nr. II (1933), pp. 1067 ff.

94 IfZG: Otto-Strasser-Sammlung: ED-118, Band 2, letter of 24 January 1949 from Brüning to Father Bernhard.

Epilogue

1 Louis P. Lochner, *Tycoons and Tyrants: German Industry from Hitler to Adenauer* (Chicago, Ill., 1954), pp. 217–18.

2 BDC: Personal File Reupke, letter of 28 January 1933 from Reupke to Strasser.

3 BA: Nachlass Grimm, fos 129–30.

4 Heiden, *Der Führer*, pp. 748–9.

5 IfZG: FA199/29, report in the Dresden paper, *Nation. Deutsche Zeitung für Freiheit und Recht*, 30 March 1933.

6 Bay. HSA: Kreigsarchiv: Sammlung Rehse: 3820, Gregor Strasser, reports in *Der Jungdeutsche* of 9 February 1933, *Fränkischer Kurier* of 27 March 1933, *Augsburger Post Zeitung* of 28 March 1933, and *Hamburger Nachrichten* of 10 May 1933.

7 ibid., report in *Neue Freie Press* of 22 July 1933.

8 ibid., reports in *Hamburger Nachrichten* of 22 July 1933; in *Fränkischer Kurier* of 24 July 1933; and in *Rhenisch- Westfälische-Zeitung* of 25 January 1934.

9 BDC: Personal File Alexander Glaser, letter from Strasser to Glaser of 2 March 1934.

10 ibid., letter of 21 February 1934 from Strasser to Glaser.

11 BA; R18/5035, letters of 12 September 1933 and 6 November 1933 from Fritz Kiehn to Hess.
12 Otto Strasser, *Die deutsche Bartholomäusnacht*, p. 39.
13 *Trial of Major German War Criminals*, Pt 12, p. 209.
14 Hermann Mau, 'Die "zweite Revolution" – der 30. Juni 1934', *VfZG*, vol. 1 (1953), quotes remarks to this effect made by former SS Gruppenführer Robert Bergmann.
15 The *Berliner Lokal-Anzeiger* published in early 1934 an anti-Strasser article written by Goering. See BDC: Personal File Alexander Glaser, letter from Strasser to Glaser of 21 February 1934; Glaser's reply of 28 February 1934, and again Strasser letter to Glaser of 2 March 1934.
16 BA: R43II/1196a. Gestapo report of 10 January 1934, which confirms Strasser's point.
17 BDC: Personal File Glaser, letter of 21 February 1934 from Strasser.
18 ibid., Strasser letter of 2 March 1934.
19 ibid., Strasser letter to Glaser of 21 February 1934.
20 BA: Sammlung Schumacher: 278, report of 5 June 1933 by the Hanover Criminal Police.
21 BA: R43II/1196a, Gestapo report of 10 January 1934. The Strasser brothers' meeting in May 1933 was clandestine but had no political connotation (Otto Strasser, *Die deutsche Bartholomäusnacht*, pp. 40–2).
22 Brüning, 'Ein Brief', p. 20; Kurt P. Tauber, *Beyond Eagle and Swastika: German Nationalism since 1945* (Middletown, Conn., 1967), p. 49, writes that Schleicher had earmarked Strasser for the chancellorship in the event of Hitler falling from power.
23 Schulz, *Meine Erschiessung*, p. 6.
24 Otto Strasser, *Hitler und Ich*, pp. 213–14.
25 On 1 February 1934, Strasser was sent the coveted Golden Badge of the NSDAP which as an 'Alte Kämpfer' (Old Fighter) he was fully entitled to wear: BDC: Personal File Gregor Strasser; see also his letter about this subject of 16 January 1934 to the Party Reichsleitung. A photocopy of the official permission for Strasser to wear the Badge is available in IfZG: F600/1.
26 Hans-Bernd Gisevius, *Bis zum bitteren Ende* (Hamburg, 1947), pp. 214 ff; Otto Strasser, *Hitler und Ich*, pp. 197–8.
27 For an insight into how some party circles reacted to news of his murder, see BA: Sammlung Schumacher: 402, letter of 6 July 1934 to Walther Darré from his son-in-law, an SS man; and BA: Nachlass Zarnow, No. 1, letter of 13 September 1934 from Hans Werner to Zarnow.
28 Hans F. K. Günther, *Mein Eindruck von Adolf Hitler* (Bebenberg, 1969), p. 87.
29 BA: R43II/1202, minutes of meeting on 3 July 1934.
30 Walter Schellenberg, *The Schellenberg Memoirs* (London, 1956), pp. 182 ff.
31 He was not involved in any kind of political activity: see BDC: Personal File Glaser, letter of 19 February 1934 from Glaser to Rudolf Vollmuth.
32 IfZG: F86, statement by Freiherr von Teichmann-Logischen of March 1935; BDC: Ordnung 402: Röhm-Putsch, report by *Sozialistische Aktion* of August 1934.
33 BA: Nachlass Traub: No. 67, letter to Traub from Schulz of 19 July 1934; Schulz, *Meine Erschiessung*, pp. 7 ff.
34 BA: Nachlass Zarnow: No. 1, letter from Zarnow to Hans Werner of 16 August 1934 alleging double-dealing and larceny by Schulz. See also Schulz, *Rettungen*, passim, for details of his post-1934 career.
35 Reinhard Kühnl, *Formen bürgerlicher Herrschaft: Liberalismus-Faschismus* (Hamburg, 1979), p. 132.
36 BA: R2 (Reichsfinanzministerium): 11905, Gesetz über den Ausgleich bürgerlichrechtlicher Ansprüche vom 13. Dezember 1934.
37 ibid., Frick to Frau Else Strasser, April 1936. Himmler unsuccessfully tried to have the allowance increased to RM600 per month. See his letter to Interior Ministry of 19 December 1936, and the reply of 24 February 1938.

Bibliography

Unpublished Sources

1 Bundesarchiv Koblenz

(*a*) Hauptarchiv der NSDAP (NS26):
All files consulted

(*b*) Reichsorganisationsleiter der NSDAP (NS22):
Files 1–11, 100, 110, 112–13, 122, 182, 184, 200, 293–4, 309–10, 317, 320, 327, 340, 342, 347–53, 355–7, 359–60, 411–13, 427, 459, 461–2, 558–9, 713–14, 787, 840–1, 844, 846, 903, 1044–77, 2001, 2021, 2028–9

(*c*) Sammlung Schumacher:
Ordner 119, 121–2, 124, 130, 191–2, 199–209, 214, 218–20, 227, 230, 232, 235, 242*a*, 254, 260, 275, 278, 280, 289, 291–2, 317, 319, 330, 373–5, 378–83, 388, 392–3, 402–3.

(*d*) Bestand R43: Reichskanzlei:
R43I/222, 676–9, 703, 912, 1001, 1004–11, 1013–15, 1018–21, 1504, 1889, 2193, 2211, 2217–20, 2227, 2234, 2263, 2279, 2281, 2284, 2290, 2298–9, 2311–12, 2316, 2483, 2527, 2557, 2653–5, 2659, 2679, 2681–4, 2696–7, 2701, 2709, 2714, 2729, 2731–2
R43II/141, 396, 396*a*, 397, 481, 910*a*, 972, 1003, 1134, 1149, 1263–4, 1195–7, 1199*a*, 1202–3, 1207, 1214–15, 1309, 1315, 1323, 1376–8, 1398, 1519, 1540

(*e*) Bestand R53: Stellvertreter des Reichskanzlers:
R53/2, 6, 7, 8, 11, 30, 31, 59, 77, 99–102, 172, 189–90

(*f*) Bestand R134: Reichskommisar für Uberwachung der öffentlichen Ordnung und Nachrichtensammelstelle im RMI:
R134/90, 91

(*g*) Bestand R18: Reichsministerium des Innern:
R18/5004, 5023, 5035–6, 5050, 5063–4, 5103, 5106–7, 5117–18, 5130, 5239–40, 5331, 5353

(*h*) Bestand R58: Sicherheitspolizei und politischer Nachrichtendienst:
R58/267–8, 273, 321–2, 1061, 1093, 1177

(*i*) Stellvertreter des Führers/Parteikanzlei (NS6):
NS6/165, 217, 324

(*j*) Untersuchungs-u. Schlichtungsausschuss (Reichsleitung) ab 1934:
Oberstes Parteigericht der NSDAP (NS36):
NS36/2, 4, 5, 8, 14, 19, 20

(*k*) Kleine Erwerbungen (NS20):
NS20/11, 17, 18, 20, 31, 34, 57, 61, 67, 76, 102, 111, 114, 122, 242–1, 242–2, 242–6, 420, 461–5, 566

(*l*) Reichssippenamt (R39):
R39/5, 27*a*, 27*b*, 28, 32–5, 37, 59, 62, 102*a*, 102*b*, 264, 801

(*m*) Reichsschatzmeister der NSDAP (NS1):
NS1/2, 3, 6, 7, 9, 11, 258, 261, 293, 297, 303, 312–13, 338–42, 388–9, 406, 410, 412, 511, 527, 599, 630, 2258, 2285, 2287, 2298, 2331

(*n*) Reichspropagandaleiter der NSDAP (NS18):
NS18/572–95
(*o*) Persönliche Adjutantur des Führers u. Reichskanzlers (NS10):
NS10/50–1, 85, 93, 143, 152, 154, 185, 230, 396
(*p*) Hauptamt für Kommunalpolitik (NS25):
NS25/110, 112, 115, 117–19, 180, 185–6, 191–2, 294, 296–7, 438
(*q*) Kanzlei Rosenberg (NS8):
NS8/2, 3, 20, 37, 116, 122, 143, 175, 215, 221
(*r*) Sturmabteilungen-SA (NS23):
NS23/8, 9, 475, 493–4
(*s*) Reichskulturkammer (R56):
R56I/70, 71, 77, 100, 114
(*t*) Reichsfinanzministerium (R2):
R2/11905
(*u*) Reichsjustizministerium (R22):
R22/5006
(*v*) Zeitgeschichtlicher Sammlung (ZSg): NSD = ZSg3:
NSD5: Reichstagsfraktion der NSDAP: Nos 1–38
NSD9: Reichsorganisationsleitung der NSDAP: Nos 7, 204, 206
NSD12: Reichspropagandaleiter der NSDAP: Nos 16, 27, 151
NSD13: Reichspressechef der NSDAP: Nos 6–12, 20
NSD38: Thüringen: No. 1
NSD70: Brochüren und Schriftenreihen, Nos 16, 30, 39, 71, 91, 111, 120, 132, 145, 525–8, 533
NSD71: Reden: Nos 193, 194, 195
ZSg1: Partei-und Verbandsdrucksachen: Nos 45, 83, 183, 240
ZSg103: Zeitungsausschnittssammlung Lauterbach: Nos 277, 279, 283, 284, 288, 387, 391, 393, 400–1, 771–832, 1381, 1663, 1665, 1667, 1690, 3128
ZSg2: Allgemeine Drucksachen: Nos 106, 179, 194–6, 226
(*w*) Nachlass Eduard Dingeldey
Nachlass Friedrich Grimm
Nachlass Konstantin Hierl
Nachlass Albert Krebs
Nachlass Karl Passarge
Nachlass Bernhard Schwertfeger
Nachlass Paul Silverberg
Nachlass Gottfried Traub
Nachlass Gottfried Zarnow

2 *Bayerisches Hauptstaatsarchiv: Allgemeines Staatsarchiv:*

(*a*) Staatsministeriums des Innern:
71799, 71800, 73003, 73437/22, 73467, 73480, 73674, 73685, 73689, 73694-99, 73707, 73719–20, 73734
(*b*) Sonderabgabe I:
1745–59, 1761–3, 1765–8, 1770–81, 1786–8, 1790–3, 1797, 1800, 1802, 1807, 1809, 1811, 1814–15, 1817, 1833–4

3 Bayerisches Hauptstaatsarchiv: Staatsarchiv München:

(*a*) Bestand NSDAP: Gauleitung München-Oberbayern:
8, 49, 132, 478, 496, 646
(*b*) Polizeidirektion München:
5430, 6672–93, 6697–6708, 6709–62, 6764–77, 6779–88, 6790–4, 6800–2, 6850
(*c*) Staatsanwaltschaft München I: Akten des Volksgerichts München I:
2576, 3098–3106

4 Bayerisches Hauptstaatsarchiv: Kriegsarchiv:

(*a*) Akten des König. Kriegsministeriums: Offizier-Personal:
OP 49979 (Gregor Strasser)
(*b*) Sammlung Rehse: 3820 (Gregor Strasser)
(*c*) Gruppenkommando 4: Akten des Stabes: Bund 33, 46, 50, 66

5 Bayerisches Hauptstaatsarchiv: Geheimes Staatsarchiv:

(*a*) Bayerisches Staatsministerium des Äussern:
MA 100425–6, 100477, 101235/2, 101235/3, 101238–41, 101247–9, 102136–8, 102141, 102144, 102149, 102151, 102154–6, 102434, 103472–4, 103478, 106670, 106672, 106675, 106677, 106680, 106682
(*b*) Reichsstatthalter Epp:
446, 450–1, 458, 780

6 Berlin Document Center

The personal files of the following were consulted:

Paul Albrecht
Alois Bayer
Herbert Blank
Anton Brandl
Hellmuth Brückner
Ernst Buchrucker
Horst Dressler
J. Erckmann
Gottfried Feder
Wilhelm Frick
Walther Funk
Dr Alexander Glaser
Professor Friedrich Grimm
August Henrichsbauer
Konstantin Hierl
Hans Hinkel
Rudolf Jordan
Herbert Kauert
Karl Kaufmann
Fritz Kiehn (and Sammelliste 59)
Erich Koch
Dr Albert Krebs
Wilhelm Kube
J. F. Lehmann
Hinrich Lohse
Cuno Meyer
Hellmuth von Mücke
Reinhold Muchow
Wilhelm Murr
Martin Mutschmann
Franz Pfeffer von Salomon
Paul Rahl
Fritz Reinhardt
Dr Hans Reupke
Graf Ernst zu Reventlow
Alfred Rosenberg
Dr Erich Rosikat
Carl Röver

Bernhard Rust
Richard Schapke
Walter Schuhmann
Paul Schulz
Jacob Sprenger
Franz Stöhr
Gregor Strasser
Otto Strasser
Gottfried Tarnow
Karl Vielweib
Rudolf Vollmuth
Dr Alexander Voss
Otto Wagener
August Winnig
Elsbeth Zander
Gottfried Zarnow
Franz Zirngibl
Also: Ordnung 402 (Röhm-Putsch)

7 Hauptstaatsarchiv Düsseldorf

RW23: NS-Stellen:
1624: NSDAP Gau Köln-Aachen
4092: NSDAP Gauleitung Westfalen-Nord
NSDAP Gauleitung Ruhr (multi-volumed)

8 Hessisches Hauptstaatsarchiv (Wiesbaden)

Abteilung 483: NSDAP Hessen–Nassau:
244, 254, 285, 291, 581, 597, 885, 1186, 1240, 1247, 1257, 1282, 1746, 2018, 2634, 2657, 2674, 2921, 6753, 6819

9 Hauptstaatsarchiv Stuttgart

E 130II: Akten des Württ. Staatsministeriums, 1813–1943:
Büschel 535–7
E 131: Akten der Pressestelle des Württ. Staatsministeriums, 1919–33:
Büschel 127, 158–71
E 151b: Akten des Innenministeriums, Abteilung II: Recht und Verfassung 1813–1945:
Büschel 72–7
J 150: Flugschriftensammlung 1900–44
Büschel 274–6, 551

10 Institute für Zeitgeschichte (Munich)

(*a*) MA-1300/1: Gregor Strasser, Der Röhmputsch
MA-738: Strasser-Rede, Dortmund
MA-251: Gregor Strasser, Persönlicher Schreiben
MA-697: Denkschrift Strassers betr. NSDAP/andere Bünde 1932
MA-805: Schrift Urban an Strasser, 2.7.32
MA-135: Leipziger Neueste Nachrichten
MA-127: Schrift Werner von Alvensleben an Hitler; Schrift A Heinrichsbauer an Strasser, Sept. 1932
MA-315: Rede Himmlers, July 1944, 'Strasser-Verrat'
MA-736: Reden Strassers
MA-743: Wirtschaftliche Fragen, NSDAP
MA-329: Berger an Reichsführer SS, 3 Dez. 1940
MA-1300/2: Niederschrift Otto Meissner von 20.10.45

MA-393: Otto Strasser; Feder an Hitler, 10.7.30
ED-60/1–4: Wagener – Strasser
ED-60/5: Fall Strasser
ED-60/6: Äusserungen Strassers, 1932
ED-1: Zeugenschrift Liebmann u.a.
ED-118, Band 18: Beurteilung Otto u. Gregor Strasser durch Brüning
ED-118, Band 24: Fall Otto Strasser, A. Raeschke
ED-118, Band 25: Bernhard Strasser über s. Brüder
ED-118, Band 2: Bernhard u. Otto Strasser, Korrespondenz m. Brüning
FA-114: Goebbels – Strasser – Hitler, 1927
F-600/1: Ehrenzeichen der NSDAP für Gregor Strasser, 1934
F86: Diktat Freiherr v. Teichmann betr. 30.6.34
F82: Otto Strasser – Kaufmann, 1927
Z18: Deutsche – Nationale – Zeitung, 1969

(*b*) Zeugenschriften:
ZS 265: Hinrich Lohse
ZS 1862: R. H. Cordemann
ZS 248: Hans Henning von Holzendorf
ZS 177: Franz von Pfeffer
ZS 1723: Hans Zehrer
ZS 1878: Hans Hinkel
ZS 1926: Walther von Etzdorf

11 Staatsarchiv Koblenz

403: Oberpräsidium der Rheinprovinz:
16732–8, 16740-51, 16753, 16759-65, 16798-16802, 16862, 16865-6, 16914–15, 16729
662/3: NSDAP – Kreisleitung Trier-West-Land:
1, 2, 25

12 National Archives Microfilm Collection

FA49: Band 3, NSDAP:
T81, Serial 7: Roll 1
Serial 44: Roll 22
Serial 70: Roll 56
Serial 85: Roll 63
T81, Serial 148: Roll 90
Serial 149: Roll 90
Serial 159: Roll 91
Serial 224: Roll 116
FA49, Band 36, NSDAP:
T81, Serial 176, Roll 159
F49, Band 5, Mischbestand:
T84, Serials 2–17, Rolls 4, 5, 6

Published Sources

1 Contemporary Newspapers and Periodicals

Der Angriff (1927–34)
Berliner Arbeiterzeitung (1926–30)
Berliner Lokal-Anzeiger (1933–4)
Central-Verein-Zeitung (1929–30)
Das Deutsche Tageblatt (1927)

Der Faust (1929–30)
Frankfurter Zeitung (1930–3)
Illustrierter Beobachter (1928–33)
Der Jungdeutsche (1929)
Münchener Post (1930–3)
Nationalsozialistische Briefe (1925–30)
Der Nationale Sozialist (1927–30, and regional editions – extracts)
NS-Jahrbuch (1928–33)
NS-Monatshefte (1930–3)
NS-Partei-Korrespondenz (1932)
Der Reichswart (1931–2)
Die Schwarze Front (1930–2)
Tägliche Rundschau (1932)
Die Tat (1930–3)
Völkischer Beobachter (1921–34)
Völkischer Kurier (1924)
Volkswille (1930–2)
Vorwärts (1930–3)

2 *Secondary Works*

Only a minority of the books, monographs, dissertations, diaries, memoirs, documentary collections and articles quoted in the footnotes to the main text, or indeed of those works consulted in general, are listed here. The following selection comprises only those studies found to be especially pertinent to the subject of this book. Literature published after July 1981 was not used:

Abraham, David, *The Collapse of the Weimar Republic: Political Economy and Crisis* (Princeton, NJ, 1981).
Auerbach, Hellmuth, 'Hitlers politische Lehrjahre und die Münchener Gesellschaft 1919–1923', *Vierteljahrshefte für Zeitgeschichte*, vol. 25 (1977), pp. 1–45.
Ayçoberry, Pierre, *The Nazi Question: An Essay on the Interpretations of National Socialism (1922–1975)* (London, 1981).
Barkai, Avraham, 'Die Wirtschaftsauffassung der NSDAP', *Aus Politik und Zeitgeschichte*, supplement to *Das Parlament*, vol. 25 (1975), pp. 3–16.
Barkai, Avraham, 'Wirtschaftliche Grundanschauungen und Ziele der NSDAP (mit einem unveröffentlichten Dokument aus dem Jahre 1931)', *Jahrbuch des Instituts für Deutsche Geschichte*, vol. VII (1978), pp. 355–85.
Bennecke, Heinrich, *Hitler und die SA* (Munich, 1962).
Berndorff, Hans R., *General zwischen Ost und West. Aus den Geheimnissen der Deutschen Republik* (Hamburg, 1951).
Bessel, Richard, 'The SA in the eastern regions of Germany, 1925–1934', Doctoral dissertation, University of Oxford, 1980.
Bessel, Richard and Feuchtwanger, Edgar J. (eds), *Social Change and Political Development in Weimar Germany* (London, 1981).
Böhnke, Wilfried, *Die NSDAP im Ruhrgebiet 1920–1933* (Bonn–Bad Godesberg, 1974).
Bracher, Karl Dietrich, *Die Auflösung der Weimarer Republik. Eine Studie zum Problem des Machtverfalls in der Demokratie* (Stuttgart, 1957).
Bracher, Karl Dietrich, *The German Dictatorship: The Origins, Structure and Effects of National Socialism* (London, 1973).
Breitman, Richard, *German Socialism and Weimar Democracy* (Chapel Hill, NC, 1981).
Broszat, Martin, *German National Socialism 1919–1945* (Santa Barbara, Calif., 1966).

Brüning, Heinrich, 'Ein Brief', *Deutsche Rundschau*, vol. 70 (July 1947), pp. 1–22.

Brüning, Heinrich, *Briefe und Gespräche 1934–1945*, ed. Claire Nix (Stuttgart, 1974).

Brüning, Heinrich, *Memoiren 1918–1934* (Stuttgart, 1972).

Brüning, Heinrich, *Reden und Aufsätze eines deutschen Staatsmanns*, ed. Wilhelm Vernekohl (Münster, 1968).

Bullock, Alan, *Hitler: A Study in Tyranny* (London, 1965).

Bureau des Reichstags, *Reichstags-Handbuch*, Vols III–VII (1924–32) (Berlin, 1924–32).

Cahill, John J., 'The NSDAP and May Day, 1923: confrontation and aftermath, 1923–1927', doctoral dissertation, University of Cincinnati, 1973.

Carr, William, *Hitler: A Study in Personality and Politics* (London, 1978).

Childers, Thomas, 'The social bases of the National Socialist vote', *Journal of Contemporary History*, vol. 11 (1976), pp. 17–42.

Czichon, Eberhard, Wer verhalf Hitler zur Macht? Zum Anteil der deutschen Industrie an der Zerstörung der Weimarer Republik (Cologne, 1972).

Demant, Ebbo, *Von Schleicher zu Springer. Hans Zehrer als politischer Publizist* (Mainz, 1971).

Diebow, Hans, *Gregor Strasser und der Nationalsozialismus* (Berlin, 1932).

Dixon, Joseph Murdoch, 'Gregor Strasser and the organisation of the Nazi Party, 1925–32', doctoral dissertation, Stanford University, Calif., 1966.

Douglas, Donald M., 'The early Ortsgruppen: the development of National Socialist local groups 1919–1923', doctoral dissertation, University of Kansas, 1968.

Emig, Dieter and Zimmermann, Rüdiger, 'Das Ende einer Legende: Gewerkschaften, Papen und Schleicher: Gefälschte und echte Protokolle', *Internationale Wissenschaftliche Korrespondenz zur Geschichte der deutschen Arbeiterbewegung*, vol. 12 (1976), pp. 19–43.

Faust, Anseln, *Der Nationalsozialistiche Deutsche Studentenbund. Studenten und Nationalsozialismus in der Weimarer Republik* (Düsseldorf, 1973).

Frank, Hans, *Im Angesicht des Galgens* (Munich, 1953).

Fritzsche, Klaus, *Politische Romantik und Gegenrevolution. Fluchtwege in der Krise der bürgerlichen Gesellschaft: Das Beispiel des 'Tat'-Kreises* (Frankfurt, 1976).

Geismaier, Michael (pseud. Otto Strasser), *Gregor Strasser* (Leipzig, 1933).

Gereke, Günther, *Ich war königlich-preussischer Landrat* (East Berlin, 1970).

Gisevius, Hans-Bernd, *Bis zum bitteren Ende. Vom Reichstagsbrand bis zum 20. Juli 1944* (Hamburg, 1947).

Goebbels, Josef, *Das Tagebuch von Joseph Goebbels, 1925–26. Mit weiteren Dokumenten*, ed. Helmut Heiber (Stuttgart, 1961).

Goebbels, Josef, *Vom Kaiserhof zur Reichskanzlei. Eine historische Darstellung in Tagebuchblättern (vom 1. Januar 1932 bis zum 1. Mai 1933)*, 24th edn (Munich, 1938).

Gordon, Harold J. (ed.), *The Hitler Trial before the People's Court in Munich*, 3 vols (Arlington, Va, 1976).

Görlitz, Walter and Quint, Herbert A., *Adolf Hitler. Eine Biographie* (Stuttgart, 1952).

Grotkopp, Wilhelm, *Die Grosse Krise. Lehren aus der Überwindung der Wirtschaftskrise 1929/32* (Düsseldorf, 1954).

Hamel, Iris, *Völkischer Verband und nationale Gewerkschaft. Der Deutschnationale Handlungsgehilfen-Verband 1893–1933* (Frankfurt, 1967).

Hanfstaengl, Ernst, *Hitler: The Missing Years* (London, 1957).

Hayes, Peter, '"A question mark with epaulettes"? Kurt von Schleicher and Weimar politics', *Journal of Modern History*, vol. 52 (1980), pp. 35–65.

Heer, Hannes, *Burgfrieden oder Klassenkampf? Zur Politik der sozialdemokratischen Gewerkschaften 1930–1933* (Neuwied, 1971).

Heiden, Konrad, *Adolf Hitler* (Zurich, 1936).

Heiden, Konrad, *Der Führer, Hitler's Rise to Power* (London, 1967).

Heiden, Konrad, *Geburt des dritten Reiches. Geschichte des Nationalsozialismus bis Herbst 1933* (Zurich, 1934).

Heiden, Konrad, *Geschichte des Nationalsozialismus. Die Karriere einer Idee* (Berlin, 1932).

Heinrichsbauer, August, *Schwerindustrie und Politik* (Essen–Kettwig, 1948).

Hentschel, Volker, *Weimars letzte Monate. Hitler und der Untergang der Republik* (Düsseldorf, 1978).

Hildebrand, Klaus, *Von Reich zum Weltreich. Hitler, NSDAP und die koloniale Frage 1919–1945* (Munich, 1969).

Hitler, Adolf, *Mein Kampf*, ed. D. Watt (London, 1969).

Hoegener, Wilhelm, *Flucht vor Hitler. Erinnerungen an die Kapitulation der ersten deutschen Republik 1933* (Munich, 1977).

Hoegener, Wilhelm, *Der Schwierige Aussenseiter* (Munich, 1959).

Hoegener, Wilhelm, *Die Verratene Republik. Geschichte der deutschen Gegenrevolution* (Munich, 1958).

Horn, Wolfgang, Führerideologie und Parteiorganisation in der NSDAP (1919–1933) (Düsseldorf, 1972).

Hüllbüsch, Ursula, 'Gewerkschaften und Staat. Ein Beitrag zur Geschichte der Gewerkschaften zu Anfang und zu Ende de Weimarer Republik', doctoral dissertation, University of Heidelberg, 1961.

Hüttenberger, Peter, *Die Gauleiter. Studie zum Wandel des Machtgefüges in der NSDAP* (Stuttgart, 1969).

Jäckel, Eberhard and Kuhn, Axel (eds), *Hitler. Sämtliche Aufzeichnungen 1905–1924* (Stuttgart, 1980).

Jacobsen, Hans-Adolf and Jochmann, Werner (eds), *Ausgewählte Dokumente zur Geschichte des Nationalsozialismus 1933–1945* (Bielefeld, 1961).

Jochmann, Werner (ed.), *Nationalsozialismus und Revolution. Ursprung und Geschichte der NSDAP in Hamburg 1922–1933. Dokumente* (Frankfurt, 1963).

Jones, Larry E., 'Between the fronts: the German National Union of Commercial Employees from 1928 to 1933', *Journal of Modern History*, vol. 48 (1976), pp. 462–82.

Jones, Larry E., 'The dissolution of the bourgeois party system in the Weimar Republic', in Bessel and Feuchtwanger (eds), *Social Change*, pp. 268–88.

Jones, Larry E., '"The dying middle": Weimar Germany and the fragmentation of bourgeois politics', *Central European History*, vol. V (1972), pp. 23–54.

Jordan, Rudolf, *Erlebt und Erlitten. Weg eines Gauleiters von München bis Moskau* (Leoni am Starnberger See, 1971).

Kater, Michael H., 'Der NS-Studentenbund von 1926 bis 1928: Randgruppe zwischen Hitler und Strasser', *Vierteljahrshefte für Zeitgeschichte*, vol. 22 (1974), pp. 148–90.

Kater, Michael H., 'Sozialer Wandel in der NSDAP im Zuge der nationalsozialistischen Machtergreifung', in Wolfgang Schieder (ed.), *Faschismus als soziale Bewegung. Deutschland und Italien im Vergleich* (Hamburg, 1976), pp. 25–67.

Kater, Michael H., 'Zum gegenseitigen Verhältnis von SA und SS in der Sozialgeschichte des Nationalsozialismus von 1925 bis 1939', *Vierteljahrschrift für Sozial-und Wirtschaftsgeschichte*, vol. 62 (1975), pp. 339–79.

Kater, Michael, H., 'Zur Soziographie der Frühen NSDAP', *Vierteljahrshefte für Zeitgeschichte*, vol. 19 (1971), pp. 124–59.

Kele, Max H., *Nazis and Workers: National Socialist Appeals to German Labor, 1919–1933* (Chapel Hill, NC, 1972).

Kershaw, Ian, *Der Hitler-Mythos. Volksmeinung und Propaganda im Dritten Reich* (Stuttgart, 1980).

Kissenkoetter, Udo, *Gregor Strasser und die NSDAP* (Stuttgart 1978).

Koktanek, Anton M. (ed.), *Oswald Spengler. Briefe 1913–1936* (Munich, 1963).

Koktanek, Anton M. 'Spenglers Verhältnis zum Nationalsozialismus in Geschichtlicher Entwicklung', *Zeitschrift für Politik*, vol. 13 (1966), pp. 36–55.

Krebs, Albert, *Tendenzen und Gestalten der NSDAP. Erinnerungen an die Frühzeit der Partei* (Stuttgart, 1959).

Kroll, Gerhard, *Von der Weltwirtschaftskrise zur Staatskonjunktur* (Berlin, 1958).

Kühnl, Reinhard, *Die Nationalsozialistische Linke 1925–1930* (Meisenheim, 1966).

Kühnl, Reinhard, 'Zur Programmatik der Nationalsozialistischen Linken: Das Strasser-Programm von 1925/26', *Vierteljahrshefte für Zeitgeschichte*, vol. 14 (1966), pp. 317–33.

Lane, Barbara Miller and Rupp, Leila J. (eds), *Nazi Ideology before 1933: A Documentation* (Austin, Texas, 1978).

Lang, Serge and Schenck, Ernst von (eds), *Porträt eines Menschheitsverbrechers. Nach den hinterlassenen Memoiren des ehemaligen Reichsministers Alfred Rosenberg* (St Gallen, 1947).

Large, David Clay, *The Politics of Law and Order: A History of the Bavarian Einwohnerwehr 1918–1921* (Philadelphia, Pa, 1980).

Ludecke, Kurt G. W., *I Knew Hitler: The Story of a Nazi Who Escaped the Blood Purge* (London, 1938).

Mann, Reinhard (ed.), *Die Nationalsozialisten. Analysen faschistischer Bewegungen* (Stuttgart, 1980).

Marcon, Helmut, *Arbeitsbeschaffungspolitik der Regierungen Papen und Schleicher* (Frankfurt, 1974).

Maser, Werner, *Der Sturm auf die Republik. Frühgeschichte der NSDAP* (Stuttgart, 1973).

Mason, Timothy W., *Sozialpolitik im Dritten Reich. Arbeiterklasse und Volksgemeinschaft* (Opladen, 1977).

Maurer, Ilse and Wengst, Udo (eds), *Politik und Wirtschaft in der Krise, 1930–1932. Quellen zur Ära Brüning*, 2 vols (Düsseldorf, 1980).

Meissner, Otto, *Staatssekretär unter Ebert-Hindenburg-Hitler. Der Schicksalsweg des deutschen Volkes von 1918–1945* (Hamburg, 1950).

Meissner, Otto and Wilde, Harry, *Die Machtergreifung. Ein Bericht über die Technik des Nationalsozialistischen Staatsstreichs* (Stuttgart, 1958).

Merkl, Peter H., *The Making of a Stormtrooper* (Princeton, NJ, 1980).

Merkl, Peter H., *Political Violence under the Swastika: 581 Early Nazis* (Princeton, NJ, 1975).

Mosse, George L., *The Crisis of German Ideology: Intellectual Origins of the Third Reich* (New York, 1964).

Mühlberger, Detlef, 'The rise of National Socialism in Westphalia 1920–1933', doctoral dissertation, University of London, 1975.

Muth, Heinrich, 'Schleicher und die Gewerkschaften 1932. Ein Quellenproblem', *Vierteljahrshefte für Zeitgeschichte*, vol. 29 (1981), pp. 189–215.

Niewyk, Donald L., *The Jews in Weimar Germany* (London, 1980).

Noakes, Jeremy, 'Conflict and development in the NSDAP 1924–1927', *Journal of Contemporary History*, vol. 1, no. 4 (1966), pp. 3–36.

Noakes, Jeremy, *The Nazi Party in Lower Saxony 1921–1933* (London, 1971).

Nyomarkay, Joseph, *Charisma and Factionalism in the Nazi Party* (Minneapolis, Minn, 1967).

Orlow, Dietrich, *The History of the Nazi Party, 1919–1933* (Pittsburgh, Pa, 1969).

Paetel, Karl O., *Versuchung oder Chance? Zur Geschichte des deutschen Nationalbolschewismus* (Göttingen, 1965).

Pridham, Geoffrey, *Hitler's Rise to Power: The Nazi Movement in Bavaria, 1923–33* (London, 1973).

Rhodes, James M., *The Hitler Movement: A Modern Millenarian Revolution* (Stanford, Calif., 1980).

Rosenberg, Alfred, *Letzte Aufzeichnungen. Ideale und Idole der nationalsozialistischen Revolution*, ed. H. Härtle (Göttingen, 1955).

Rosikat, Erich, *Die Lehren der Maiwahlen 1928 für die Partei-völkische Bewegung Deutschlands* (Breslau, 1928).

Schildt, Gerhard, 'Die Arbeitsgemeinschaft Nord-West. Untersuchungen zur Geschichte der NSDAP 1925–26', doctoral dissertation, University of Freiburg, i.B., 1964.

Schmidt, Klaus F., 'Die "Nationalsozialistischen Briefe" (1925-30)', in *Paul Kluke zum 60. Geburtstag* (Frankfurt, 1968), pp. 111–26.

Schneider, Michael, *Das Arbeitsbeschaffungsprogramm des ADGB. Zur gewerkschaftlichen Politik in der Endphase der Weimarer Republik* (Bonn–Bad Godesberg, 1975).

Schüddekopf, Otto-Ernst, *Linke Leute von Rechts. Die nationalrevolutionären Minderheiten und der Kommunismus in der Weimarer Republik* (Stuttgart, 1960).

Schulz, Gerhard, *Aufsteig des Nationalsozialismus. Krise und Revolution in Deutschland* (Berlin, 1975).

Schulz, Gerhard *et al.* (eds), *Staat und NSDAP 1930–1932. Quellen zur Ära Brüning* (Düsseldorf, 1977).

Schulz, Paul, *Meine Erschiessung am 30. Juni 1934* (1948).

Schulz, Paul, *Rettungen und Hilfeleistungen an Verfolgten 1933–1945 durch Oberleutnant a.D. Paul Schulz* (Laichingen, 1967).

Schumann, Hans-Gerd, *Nationalsozialismus und Gewerkschaftsbewegung* (Hanover, 1958).

Schwerin von Krosigk, Lutz Graf, *Memoiren* (Stuttgart, 1977).

Seraphim, Hans-Günther (ed.), *Das Politische Tagebuch Alfred Rosenbergs, 1934/35 und 1939/40* (Munich, 1964).

Skrzypczak, Henryk, 'Fälscher machen Zeitgeschichte. Ein quellenkritischer Beitrag zur Gewerkschaftspolitik in der Ära Papen und Schleicher', *Internationale Wissenschaftliche Korrespondenz zur Geschichte der deutschen Arbeiterbewegung*, vol. 11 (1975), pp. 452–71.

Smith, Bradley F., 'Hitler and the Strasser challenge', thesis, University of California, 1957.

Stachura, Peter D., '"Der Fall Strasser": Gregor Strasser, Hitler and National Socialism 1930–1932', in Stachura, *The Shaping of the Nazi State*, pp. 88–130.

Stachura, Peter D., 'Der kritische Wendepunkt? Die NSDAP und die Reichstagswahlen vom 20. Mai 1928', *Vierteljahrshefte für Zeitgeschichte*, vol. 26 (1978), pp. 66–99.

Stachura, Peter D., *Nazi Youth in the Weimar Republic* (Santa Barbara, Calif., 1975).

Stachura, Peter D., 'The NSDAP and the German working class, 1925–1933', in Isidor Walliman and Michael Dobkowski (eds), *Towards the Holocaust: Fascism and Anti-Semitism in Weimar Germany* (New York, 1982).

Stachura, Peter D., 'The political strategy of the Nazi Party, 1919–1933', *German Studies Review*, vol. III (1980), pp. 261–88.

Stachura, Peter D. (ed.), *The Shaping of the Nazi State* (London, 1978).

Stachura, Peter D., 'Who were the Nazis? A socio-political analysis of the National Socialist *Machtübernahme*', *European Studies Review*, vol. 11 (1981), pp. 293–324.

Stegmann, Dirk, 'Zum Verhältnis von Grossindustrie und Nationalsozialismus 1930–1933. Ein Beitrag zur Geschichte der sog. Machtergreifung', *Archiv für Sozialgeschichte*, vol. XIII (1973), pp. 399–482.

Stephenson, Jill, *The Nazi Organisation of Women* (London, 1981).

Strasser, Father Bernhard, *Gregor und Otto Strasser. Kurze Darstellung ihrer Persönlichkeit und ihres Wollens*, 2nd edn (Munich, 1965).

Strasser, Gregor, *58 Jahre Young-Plan* (Berlin, 1929).

Strasser, Gregor, *Freiheit und Brot. Ausgewählte Reden und Schriften eines Nationalsozialisten*, Teil I, *Idee* (Berlin, 1928).

Strasser, Gregor, *Hammer und Schwert. Ausgewählte Reden und Schiften eines Nationalsozialisten*, Teil II, *Kampf* (Berlin, 1928).

Strasser, Gregor, *Das Hitlerbüchlein. Ein Abriss vom Leben und Wirkens des Führers der nationalsozialistischen Freiheitsbewegung Adolf Hitler* (Berlin, 1928).

Strasser, Gregor, *Kampf um Deutschland. Reden und Aufsätze eines Nationalsozialisten* (Munich, 1932).

Strasser, Gregor (ed.), *Wirtschaftliches Sofortprogramm der NSDAP* (Munich, 1932).

Strasser, Otto, *Aufbau des deutschen Sozialismus* (Leipzig, 1932).

Strasser, Otto, *Die deutsche Bartholomäusnacht* (Zurich, 1935).

Strasser, Otto, *30 Juni: Vorgeschichte, Verlauf, Folgen* (Prague, 1934).

Strasser, Otto, *Exil* (Munich, 1958).

Strasser, Otto, *History in My Time* (London, 1941).
Strasser, Otto, *Hitler und Ich* (Zurich, 1940).
Strasser, Otto, *Mein Kampf. Eine politische Autobiographie* (Frankfurt, 1969).
Strasser, Otto, *Ministersessel oder Revolution? Eine wahrheitsgemässe Darstellung meiner Trennung von der NSDAP* (Berlin, 1930).
Treviranus, Gottfried R., *Das Ende von Weimar. Heinrich Brüning und seine Zeit* (Düsseldorf, 1968).
The Trial of German Major War Criminals. Proceedings of the International Military Tribunal at Nuremberg, 22 parts (London, 1946–51).
Turner, Henry A., *Faschismus und Kapitalismus in Deutschland* (Göttingen, 1972).
Turner, Henry A., 'Hitlers Einstellung zu Wirtschaft und Gesellschaft vor 1933', *Geschichte und Gesellschaft*, vol. 2 (1976), pp. 89–117.
Turner, Henry A. (ed.), *Hitler aus nächster Nähe. Aufzeichnungen eines Vertrauten 1929–1932* (Frankfurt, 1978).
Tyrell, Albrecht, *Führer befiehl . . . Selbstzeugnisse aus der 'Kampfzeit' der NSDAP. Dokumentation und Analyse* (Düsseldorf, 1969).
Tyrell, Albrecht, 'Führergedanke und Gauleiterwechsel. Die Teilung des Gaues Rheinland der NSDAP 1931', *Vierteljahrshefte für Zeitgeschichte*, vol. 23 (1975), pp. 341–74.
Tyrell, Albrecht, 'Gottfried Feder und die NSDAP', in Stachura (ed.), *The Shaping of the Nazi State*, pp. 48–87.
Tyrell, Albrecht, *Vom 'Trommler' zum 'Führer'. Der Wandel von Hitlers Selbstverständnis zwischen 1919 und 1924 und die Entwicklung der NSDAP* (Munich, 1975).
Vogelsang, Thilo, *Reichswehr, Staat und NSDAP. Beiträge zur deutschen Geschichte 1930–1932* (Stuttgart, 1962).
Volkmann, Hans-Erich, 'Das aussenwirtschaftliche Programm der NSDAP 1930–1933', *Archiv für Sozialgeschichte*, vol. XVII (1977), pp. 251–74.
Wegr, Paul (pseud. Peter Strasser), *Das neue Wesen. Betrachtungen und Ausblicke* (Kempten, 1912).
Winkler, Heinrich A., *Mittelstand, Demokratie und Nationalsozialismus. Die Politische Entwicklung von Handwerk und Kleinhandel in der Weimarer Republik* (Cologne, 1972).
Wolffsohn, Michael, *Industrie und Handwerk im Konflikt mit staatlicher Wirtschaftspolitik? Studien zur Politik der Arbeitsbeschaffung in Deutschland 1930–1934* (Berlin, 1977).
Wörtz, Ulrich, 'Programmatik und Führerprinzip. Das Problem des Strasser-Kreises in der NSDAP', doctoral dissertation, University of Erlangen, 1966.

Index